Organize your whole house

Organize your
whole house

Do-it-yourself projects for every room!

From the Editors of **THE FAMILY Handyman**

Reader's Digest

The Reader's Digest Association, Inc.
Pleasantville, New York/Montreal

A READER'S DIGEST BOOK

FOR THE FAMILY HANDYMAN
Editor in Chief: Ken Collier
Project Editor: Mary Flanagan
Administrative Manager: Alice Garrett
Design Director: Sara Koehler
Page Layout: Teresa Marone
Editorial and Production Team: Elisa Bernick, Donna Bierbach, Steven Charbonneau, Roxie Filipkowski, Jeff Gorton, Travis Larson, Brett Martin, Peggy McDermott, Becky Pfluger, Judy Rodriguez, Mary Schwender, Eric Smith, Bob Ungar, Gary Wentz, Marcia Wright Roepke
Photography and Illustrations: Susan Jessen, Bruce Keifer, Mike Krivit, Don Mannes, Ramon Moreno, Shawn Nielsen, Frank Rohrbach III, Eugene Thompson, Bill Zuehlke

FOR READER'S DIGEST
U.S. Project Editor: Kim Casey
Copy Editor: Barbara Booth
Canadian Project Editor: Pamela Johnson
Cover Designer: Nick Anderson
Senior Art Director: George McKeon
Executive Editor, Trade Publishing: Dolores York
Production Manager: Liz Dinda
Associate Publisher, Trade Publishing: Rosanne McManus
President & Publisher, Trade Publishing: Harold Clarke

Library of Congress Cataloging-in-Publication Data:

Organize your whole house.
     p. cm.
  ISBN 978-1-60652-028-4 (hardcover)
  ISBN 978-0-7621-0795-7 (paperback)
1. Built-in furniture. 2. Cabinetwork. 3. Storage in the home. I. Reader's Digest Association.
  TT197.5.B8075 2009
  684.1'6--dc22

2009005170

We are committed to both the quality of our products and the service we provide to our customers. We value your comments, so please feel free to contact us.

The Reader's Digest Association, Inc.
Adult Trade Publishing
Reader's Digest Road
Pleasantville, NY 10570-7000

For more Reader's Digest products and information, visit our website:
www.rd.com
www.thefamilyhandyman.com

Printed in China

1 3 5 7 9 10 8 6 4 2 (hardcover)

3 5 7 9 10 8 6 4 (paperback)

A Note to Our Readers
All do-it-yourself activities involve a degree of risk. Skills, materials, tools, and site conditions vary widely. Although the editors have made every effort to ensure accuracy, the reader remains responsible for the selection and use of tools, materials, and methods. Always obey local codes and laws, follow manufacturer's operating instructions, and observe safety precautions.

p. 90

p. 162

p. 57

p. 144

p. 130

p. 190

Contents

Special Sections

The kitchen is the hardest room to keep organized. Cooking utensils, countertop appliances and groceries quickly fill up storage space, and then end up taking valuable counter space. The following projects offer practical solutions for quick and easy storage, reclaiming space and organizing busy kitchens.

Chapter 1

organize
your
kitchen

7 space-saving tips for small kitchens

1 Single-bowl sink

Photo courtesy of Kohler

During a kitchen remodel, consider installing a single-bowl sink instead of a standard-size double-bowl. Instead of two small bowls, there will be one large one. It'll also allow a smaller sink base and save 6 in. of cabinet and counter space that could be put to better use. The Kohler Alcott (K-6573-5U; less than $1,000) sink (shown) is one example. Team up a 25-in. single-bowl sink in a 30-in. base cabinet with an extra-narrow (18-in.) dishwasher to gain a foot of extra cabinet space.

Photo courtesy of Knape & Vogt

2 Blind-corner cabinet solution

Blind-corner cabinets are cabinets on inside corners that are accessible from only one door. Blind-corner cabinets in kitchens make it hard to reach anything that gets shoved to the back. Most kitchen designers will try to plan space for a lazy Susan base cabinet instead of a blind corner. These have rotating shelves that provide good access to the contents. But homeowners stuck with a blind-corner cabinet and no lazy Susan have a few options worth exploring.

There are a number of ingenious sliding-shelf mechanisms that move the contents within reach, but most, like the Knape & Vogt model BBCT (shown) are rather expensive ($500 to $600). However, a unit by Lee Valley costs about $170. It can be installed in existing blind-corner cabinets that are 35-1/2 to 39-1/2 in. long. Order one online at leevalley.com or call Lee Valley at (800) 871-8158. Order part No. 12K33.10 (door on right side) or 12K33.20 (left).

Half-moon–shaped shelves that swivel and pull out are a less expensive option for blind corners. They only utilize about 60 percent of the space, but provide easy access to the contents. They can be installed in existing blind-corner cabinets.

3 Cabinet-depth refrigerators

Standard-depth refrigerators stick out 6 to 8 in. in front of kitchen cabinets, robbing valuable floor space and crowding passageways. When designing a new kitchen, consider buying a shallow-depth refrigerator. It'll make the kitchen seem much more spacious, and depending on the floor plan, may even gain cabinet space across from the refrigerator. Cabinet-depth refrigerators cost a little more, about $1,500 for the least expensive versions, but the extra cost is easy to justify because it provides extra space.

Recessing a standard-depth refrigerator into the stud wall is another way to increase space (for a gain of about 4 in.). It requires cutting out one or two studs and adding a header over the opening for support. This may also require relocating the outlet if it's located directly behind the refrigerator.

4 Make the most of every inch with rollouts

Base cabinets have tons of room, but it's hard to reach the back. And even then it's hard to see what's back there. Rollout shelves are a great solution. New cabinets are available with rollouts already installed, or they can be easily added to existing cabinets. There are many options. Factory-made units for do-it-yourself installation cost $30 to $400.

Tall, narrow rollouts are perfect for those skinny cabinets that are normally relegated to cookie sheets. These rollouts are great for soda, canned goods or spices. Stock rollout hardware that supports a wide selection of wire baskets is also available.

5 No room for an island? Try a cart instead

Kitchen islands are more popular than ever, but because at least 36 in. all around an island is needed for walking space, they just don't fit in most small kitchens. A rolling kitchen cart offers many of the same benefits of an island and is more versatile. Move it into the center of the kitchen for food prep, or use it as a buffet table when guests arrive. Then just roll it out of the way when it's no longer needed. In new kitchens, leave a spot under the countertop for the cart. Commercially made carts are available with cutting board tops, shelves and hooks on the sides for utensils. The John Boos Cucina Elegante (model No. CUCE50) shown retails for $800, but simpler carts cost as little as $100. Check kitchencarts.com for a sampling of the variety available.

Photo courtesy of John Boos

Photo courtesy of GE

6 Pantry cabinet in a closet

Moving some of the bulkier or seldom-used items out of the kitchen and into a nearby pantry can free up a lot of space. Look around. There may be extra space in a nearby closet or hallway where pantry shelves would fit. A pantry could be as simple as adjustable shelves on wall standards or a more elaborate built-in cabinet. Order closet parts like those shown here online at easyclosets.com.

Photo courtesy of easyclosets.com

7 Add undercabinet lights

Good lighting helps by making the best use of the kitchen space. Dimly lit or shadowy countertops are hard to work at. Adding undercabinet lights is a great way to make the countertops more useful while making a small kitchen feel larger.

It's easy to wire for undercabinet lights with the rest of the wiring during a kitchen remodel. But adding them to an existing kitchen requires a little more ingenuity. Otherwise, fish wires through the basement, crawlspace or attic and pull them through the stud spaces to each light fixture. As a last resort, buy plug-in-type undercabinet lights.

> **tip** Open shelves and glass-front cabinets can help a small kitchen look and feel larger than it really is.

Add-on
kitchen storage

Most kitchens have plenty of storage space—it's just that a good chunk of it is hidden in the hard-to-get-at corners, nooks and crannies of your cabinets. Deep base cabinets and corner cabinets pose particular accessibility problems.

The five projects shown here create more storage space and make existing cabinet space more accessible. Each project is constructed using readily available lumber, plywood, hardware, L-moldings, glue and screws. For speed and accuracy, borrow, buy or rent (about $20 per day) a power miter saw.

Since many cabinet openings differ from the ones shown here in height and width, the how-to steps concentrate on the basic steps and "key measurements" rather than exact dimensions.

Here's what it takes.

tip Some of these projects mount to cabinet doors or face frames. Make sure the cabinets, doors and hinges are in good shape, and don't overload the finished projects with heavy cans and other weighty objects.

1 Door-mounted spice rack p. 14

3 Glide-out and swing-out shelves p. 16

4 Swing-down cookbook rack p. 19

2 Door-mounted lid rack p. 14

5 Roll-out pantry cabinet p. 20

1&2 Door-mounted spice and lid racks

These simple racks will help transform those chaotic gangs of spice bottles and pan lids into orderly regiments. The lid rack uses the same steps as the spice rack, but without the shelves. Each spice rack can hold 20 to 30 bottles, and each lid rack two to six lids, depending on the height and width of your cabinet doors. Before building, measure the spice bottles and lids to determine the spacing of the shelves and dowels. Here are other key measurements and clearances to keep an eye on:

Existing shelf depth. If the existing cabinet shelves are full depth, narrow them by about 2 in. to accommodate each door-mounted rack. Shelves that are permanently affixed in grooves in the cabinet sides will need to be cut in place with a jigsaw. Adjustable shelves can be removed, cut along the back side with a circular saw or table saw, then replaced. Move brackets or add holes to remount narrowed shelves, if needed.

Spice rack depth and positioning. Make certain the new rack won't hit the cabinet frame when the door swings. Fitting the rack between the two 2-in.-wide vertical stiles (Photo 1) gives

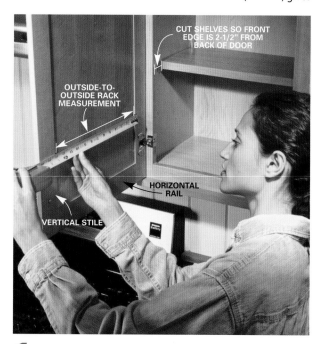

1 Measure the distance between the two vertical stiles and the two horizontal rails to determine the outside dimensions of your spice rack. Cut existing shelves back 2-1/2 in. so they don't interfere with the rack when the door is closed.

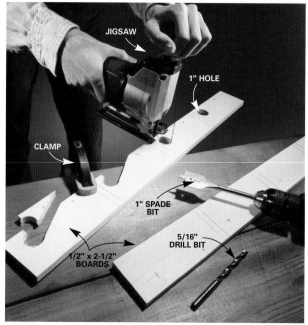

2 Transfer the dimensions from Figure A onto 1/2 x 2-1/2-in. side boards. Cut out the sides of the spice rack. Drill 1-in. holes to create the circular shape, then finish the cutout with a jigsaw. Drill 5/16-in. holes for the dowels. Sand the edges and surfaces smooth.

adequate room. If the doors are solid wood or laminate, hold in place a scrap of wood the same depth as the spice rack (2-1/2 in. is the depth used here) and swing the door. Move it away from the door edge until it no longer makes contact with the cabinet frame, then mark the door. This will determine the overall width of the spice rack.

The woods used here for both the spice and lid racks are soft pine and basswood. If using a harder wood, like maple or oak, position the pieces, then predrill holes through the side pieces and into the shelf ends. This will prevent splitting and make nailing easier. Install the shelves one at a time. Always nail on a flat, solid surface.

tip Use high-gloss polyurethane for natural wood, high-gloss enamel for painted wood. These finishes are more "scrubbable."

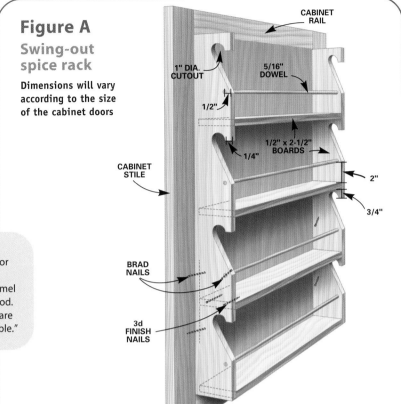

Figure A
Swing-out spice rack

Dimensions will vary according to the size of the cabinet doors

CABINET RAIL

1" DIA. CUTOUT

5/16" DOWEL

1/2"

1/4"

1/2" x 2-1/2" BOARDS

2"

3/4"

CABINET STILE

BRAD NAILS

3d FINISH NAILS

1/2" x 2-1/2" SHELVES

3/4" BRAD

5/16" DOWELS

3 Glue and nail the shelves in place one at a time, using 3d finish nails. Then use 3/4-in. brads to pin the dowels in place. Sink all nailheads using a nail set. Apply polyurethane or other finish to match the cabinets.

1/16" DRILL BIT

CLAMP

4 Clamp the finished rack to the door, then drill angled pilot holes through the rack and into the door every 8 in. Secure with brad nails (remove the door for this step if a more solid surface is needed for hammering). Use carpenter's glue for a more permanent installation.

3 Blind corner glide-out and swing-out shelves

Blind-corner cabinets—those with a blank face that allows another cabinet to butt into them—may be great for aging wine, but they're darn near impossible to see and reach into. This pair of accessories puts an end to this hidden wasteland. The hinged shelf swings out of the way, and the gliding shelf slides forward to access food items stored in the back. Use the same hardware and techniques for making base cabinets more accessible too.

The key measurements and clearances:

Glide-out shelf dimensions. Only make the unit as long as the door opening is wide (or else it can't fit inside!). Make the unit about 1/2 in. narrower than the inside width of the cabinet.

tip Test-fit the shelf units in the cabinet as they're built.

HINGED SWING-OUT SHELF

GLIDE-OUT SHELF

Build the glide-out shelf

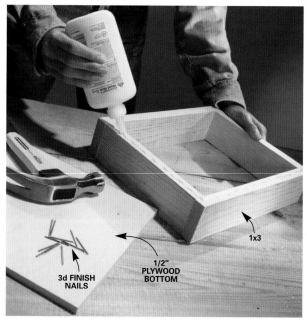

1x3

3d FINISH NAILS

1/2" PLYWOOD BOTTOM

1 Glue and nail the 1x3s together using 4d finish nails, then secure the plywood bottom with 3d finish nails.

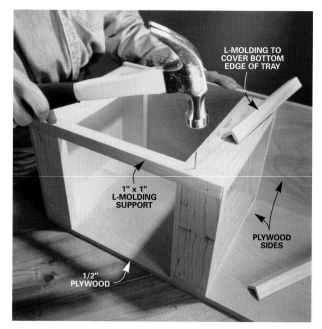

L-MOLDING TO COVER BOTTOM EDGE OF TRAY

1" x 1" L-MOLDING SUPPORT

PLYWOOD SIDES

1/2" PLYWOOD

2 Cut out the two plywood sides, then glue and nail the corners. Connect the trays to the two plywood sides using 1-in. drywall screws, then cut and nail L-molding to support the front corner. Cut and install L-moldings to support and cover the exposed plywood edges of the upper tray. Install 3/4-in. screen molding to cover the plywood edges of the bottom tray.

Figure B
Glide-out and swing-out shelves

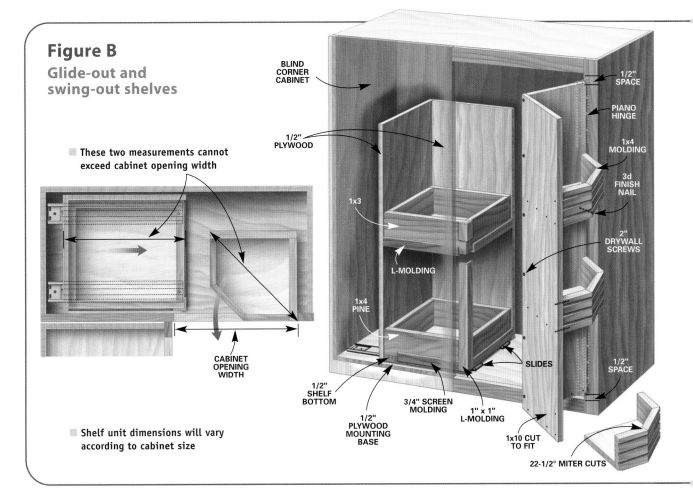

■ These two measurements cannot exceed cabinet opening width

■ Shelf unit dimensions will vary according to cabinet size

BLIND CORNER CABINET

1/2" PLYWOOD

1x3

L-MOLDING

1x4 PINE

1/2" SHELF BOTTOM

1/2" PLYWOOD MOUNTING BASE

3/4" SCREEN MOLDING

1" x 1" L-MOLDING

SLIDES

1x10 CUT TO FIT

22-1/2° MITER CUTS

1/2" SPACE

PIANO HINGE

1x4 MOLDING

3d FINISH NAIL

2" DRYWALL SCREWS

1/2" SPACE

CABINET OPENING WIDTH

METAL SLIDES

PLYWOOD MOUNTING BASE

COMPLETED TRAY UNIT

3 Cut the mounting base plywood slightly smaller than the other tray bottoms, then secure the two slides parallel to each other about 1 in. from each edge. Slip this mounting base into the opening, extend the slides, then screw them to the cabinet bottom at the rear of the cabinet. Install the slides parallel to the cabinet sides, so the base slides back and forth.

SECURE UNIT TO MOUNTING BASE WITH 3/4" DRYWALL SCREW

4 Screw the tray unit to the mounting base using 3/4-in. screws. After installing the first screw, slide the unit forward and back, then adjust it until it runs parallel to the cabinet sides and install three more screws.

Build the swing-out shelf

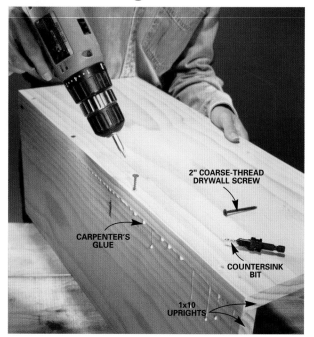

2" COARSE-THREAD DRYWALL SCREW

CARPENTER'S GLUE

COUNTERSINK BIT

1x10 UPRIGHTS

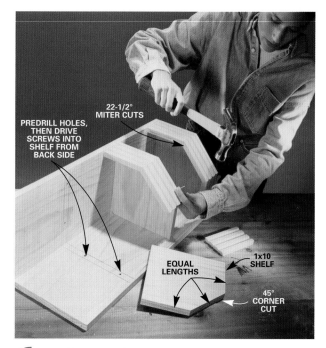

22-1/2° MITER CUTS

PREDRILL HOLES, THEN DRIVE SCREWS INTO SHELF FROM BACK SIDE

EQUAL LENGTHS

1x10 SHELF

45° CORNER CUT

5 Cut the 1x10 swing-out uprights to length and width (one should be 3/4 in. narrower than the other). Use a countersink bit to predrill holes along one edge, then glue and screw the two edges together. The diagonal measurement (see Figure B) should be less than the cabinet opening.

tip Beg, borrow or rent a compressor, finish nailer and brad gun, if possible, to work faster, eliminate hammer marks and split the wood less often than you would hand-nailing.

Swing-out tray dimensions. The corner-to-corner or diagonal measurement of the unit (Figure B) can't exceed the width of the door opening (or else that won't fit either!). Make the unit about 1 in. shorter than the opening height so it has room to swing freely when installed.

Piano hinges and bottom slides are available from Rockler Woodworking and Hardware, (800) 279-4441. rockler.com. The front moldings (No. 673) are manufactured by House of Fara

tip Use a damp sponge to wipe up glue drips immediately. It'll save hours of sanding down the line.

(800-334-1732; houseoffara.com). House of Fara products are available at Menards, The Home Depot and Lowe's stores. Call the company to help find a dealer.

6 Assemble the shelf unit. First mark the shelf positions on the uprights and predrill holes from the front side. Create the three shelves by cutting a 1x10 to length and width, then cutting the corner at 45 degrees. Hold the shelves in place and drive drywall screws through these holes from the back side into the shelves. Cut the 22-1/2-degree angles on the front moldings and secure them with 3d finish nails. Use any type of wide decorative molding that's at least 1/2 x 3 in.

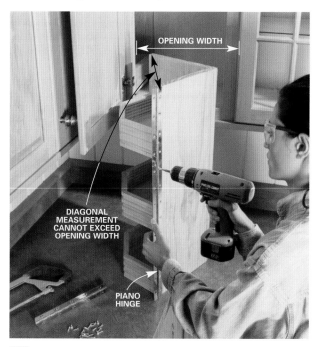

OPENING WIDTH

DIAGONAL MEASUREMENT CANNOT EXCEED OPENING WIDTH

PIANO HINGE

7 Screw the piano hinge to the front edge of the swing-out unit, then to the edge of the cabinet face frame. Make certain the swing-out has 1/2 in. of clearance top and bottom.

4 Swing-down cookbook rack

When counter space is at a minimum and counter mess at a maximum, this swing-down rack will keep cookbooks up and out of the fray. The special spring-loaded brackets swing cookbooks down when needed, then out of the way when finished.

The cookbook platform tucks under a single cabinet. If desired, make the platform larger to hold larger books, then mount it beneath two cabinets. With a little creativity, this same hardware can create a swing-down knife rack or spice rack too.

Fold-down brackets are available from Organize-It, (800) 210-7712, organizeit.com and Kitchen-Organizers (The Hardware Hut), (800) 708-6649, kitchen-organizers.com.

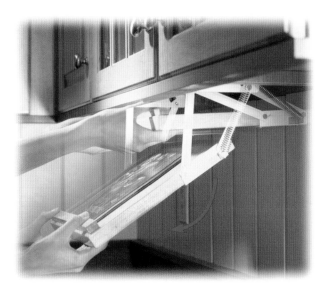

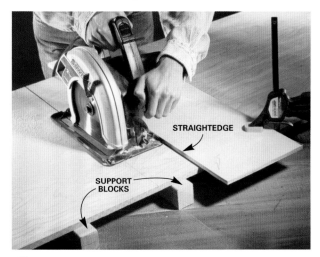

1 Cut the 1/2-in.-thick plywood base to size. To get straight cuts, measure from the edge of the circular saw base to the edge of the blade, then clamp a straight board to the plywood that distance from the cutting line to serve as a guide. Cut with the plywood's "good" side down.

STRAIGHTEDGE

SUPPORT BLOCKS

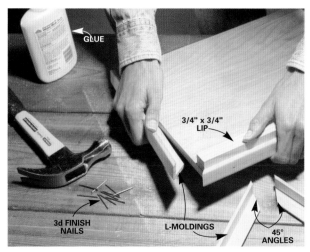

GLUE

3/4" x 3/4" LIP

3d FINISH NAILS

L-MOLDINGS

45° ANGLES

2 Glue and nail the 3/4 x 3/4-in. lip to the front of the base, then "picture frame" the plywood with L-moldings. For an exact measurement, cut one end at 45 degrees on a miter saw, hold it in position and mark the other end. Put a "reminder mark" on the board to help remember which direction to cut the angle. Secure the pieces with carpenter's glue and 3d nails.

Figure C
Swing-down cookbook rack

MACHINE BOLT WITH WASHER AND LOCK NUT

PLYWOOD

3/4" x 3/4" LIP

SWING-DOWN HINGES

3d FINISH NAIL

1" x 1" L-MOLDINGS

Overall dimensions can vary according to space available

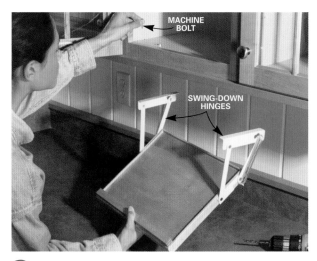

MACHINE BOLT

SWING-DOWN HINGES

3 Mount the hinges to the base using wood screws. Hold the assembled unit in position under the cabinet, then mark the holes for the brackets (a two-person job). Drill the holes, then secure the brackets to the cabinet using short machine screws, washers and nuts.

5 Roll-out pantry cabinet

Most cabinet manufacturers now include rollout shelves in their base cabinets. But this project will one-up those shelves with an entire rollout pantry.

The hardware consists of two heavy-duty bottom-mounted slides and one center-mounted top slide that together can support 130 lbs. The bottom tray is 3-1/2 in. tall and the upper ones are 2-1/2 in. tall. Include only two trays if the pantry will be storing cereal boxes and other tall packages.

Since this project converts the door from swinging to rolling mode, remove the door and hinges. Also remove the existing handle and reinstall it centered on the door. If the hardware mounts from the back side, install it before attaching the door (Photo 6, p. 21).

The key measurements and clearances:

Rollout unit measurements. The plywood front and back panels should be about 1/8 in. shorter than the distance between the installed top and bottom glides (Photos 1 and 2). The width of the unit should be 1/2 in. narrower than the cabinet opening. The depth of the unit should be 1/2 in. less than the depth of the cabinet (not including the face frame).

Accuride Pantry slides (No. 91968) are available from Rockler Woodworking and Hardware, (800) 279-4441, rockler.com.

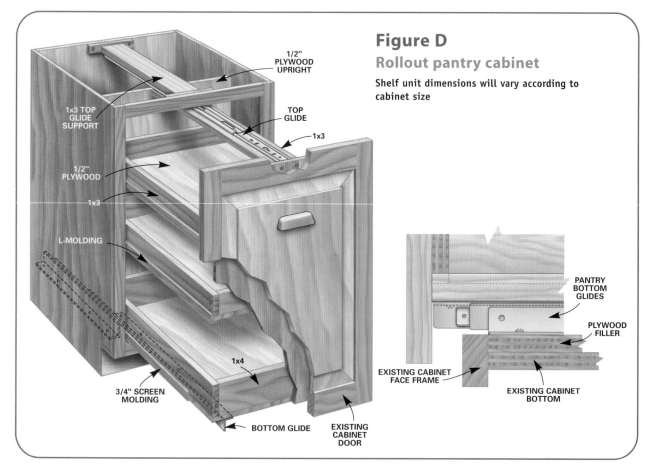

Figure D
Rollout pantry cabinet

Shelf unit dimensions will vary according to cabinet size

1/2" PLYWOOD UPRIGHT

TOP GLIDE

1x3

1x3 TOP GLIDE SUPPORT

1/2" PLYWOOD

1x3

L-MOLDING

1x4

3/4" SCREEN MOLDING

BOTTOM GLIDE

EXISTING CABINET DOOR

PANTRY BOTTOM GLIDES

PLYWOOD FILLER

EXISTING CABINET FACE FRAME

EXISTING CABINET BOTTOM

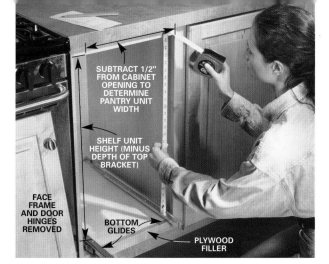

1 Measure the cabinet face frame opening, then subtract the height of the top and bottom glides. Calculate the depth, width and height of the unit. Install the bottom glides to run parallel to the cabinet sides. If necessary, use plywood to raise the cabinet bottom even with the bottom lip of the face frame.

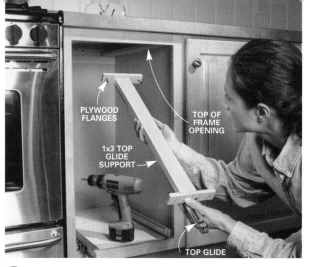

2 Install the top glide support and top glide so the support is level and flush to the top of the frame opening. Screw plywood flanges to each end of the 1x3 support beforehand to make it simpler to secure it to the front and back of the cabinet.

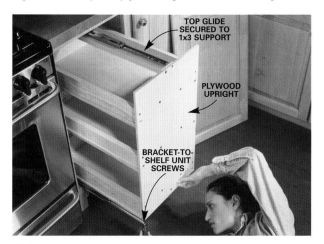

3 Assemble the pantry trays using 1x4s, 1x3s, 6d nails and carpenter's glue. Use the plywood bottoms to "square up" the trays before nailing them on. L-moldings support and cover the plywood edges of the upper two trays; 3/4-in. screen molding covers the exposed plywood edges of the bottom tray.

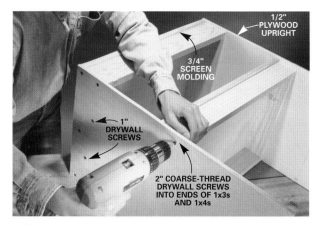

4 Secure the trays to the 1/2-in. plywood uprights using glue and drywall screws. Arrange the spacing of the trays to meet your needs.

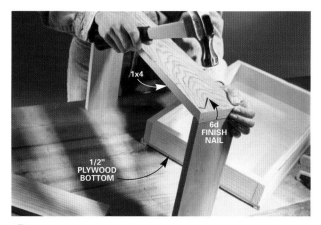

5 Screw the tray assembly to the bottom runners, making sure it's centered in the opening and running parallel to the cabinet sides. The extended portion of the top slide is secured to a 1x3 screwed between the two plywood uprights. Loosen this 1x3, then adjust the height so the top glide runs flat and smooth.

6 Clamp the cabinet door to the front of the pantry assembly; center it and make the height even with adjacent doors. Predrill eight holes through the plywood upright and drive screws into the back of the cabinet door. After installing two screws, close the door to check its alignment with the adjacent doors. Make adjustments, then install the remaining screws. Use short screws so they don't penetrate the front of the cabinet door.

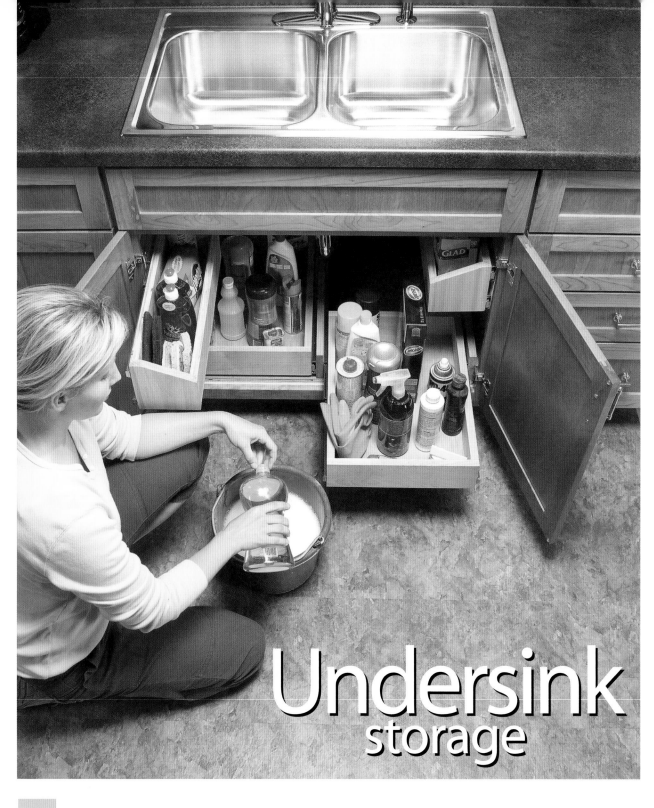

Undersink
storage

hese two types of rollout trays, which ride on smooth-action ball-bearing drawer glides, will get everything under the sink out in the open.

This project isn't difficult. In fact, there aren't even any miter joints. All the parts are glued together and then nailed or screwed. The building products are readily available at home centers or hardware stores for as little as $75.

Simple carpentry tools and some careful measuring are all that's needed, although a table saw will help zero in on more exact measurements, especially for the lower tray bases where accuracy is important for the ball-bearing drawer glides. The nail gun shown in the photos is also optional, but it makes assembly a lot faster and less tedious. It shoots thin 18-gauge nails.

Adapt the project dimensions to fit a particular sink space. For example, a bulky garbage disposer may not allow both upper slide-out trays. In that case, just make one tray instead. If plumbing comes up through the floor of the sink cabinet, shorten the lower trays to fit in front of the plumbing. In any case, add as many parts of this project as space permits to organize this black hole once and for all.

Getting the right stuff

At a home center or lumberyard, look for hardwood plywood. Buy 2 x 4-ft. pieces instead of a whole sheet, if possible. The hardwood plywood has two good sides and is smoother and flatter than exterior-grade softwood plywood. It costs more too.

In the hardware department, look for ball-bearing side-mount drawer glides. The pairs of the brand shown here are exactly the same—there's no specific right or left, which makes things easier if parts get misplaced. The project shown has 20-in.-long side-mount glides to fit the 20-in.-long trays. This gives some wiggle room in the back and a bit of extra space to get the pieces into place. If plumbing comes up through the bottom of the cabinet, shorten the trays and buy shorter drawer glides if needed.

Then follow the photos for the step-by-step measuring and assembly instructions. Here are a few specifics to consider:

- If the opening between the open doors is narrower than the opening between the sides of the frame, use the shorter dimension when making the base.

1 Measure the width of the kitchen base cabinet inside the frame. Cut the base (A) 1/4 in. narrower than the opening.

2 Find the center of the base (A) and mark it for the center partition. Cut the 20-in.-long partitions (B) from 1x4 stock.

Materials list

(This list applies to the rollout trays shown; quantities may vary.)

Item	Qty.
3/4" x 4' x 8' hardwood plywood	1
1x4 x16' maple	1
1/2" x 2' x 2' hardwood plywood	1
1x6 x 2' maple	1
20" ball-bearing drawer glides	4 prs.
Woodworker's glue	1 pt.
Construction adhesive	1 pt.
6d finish nails, small box	1
1-5/8" wood screws, small box	1

Figure A
Sink cabinet tray detail

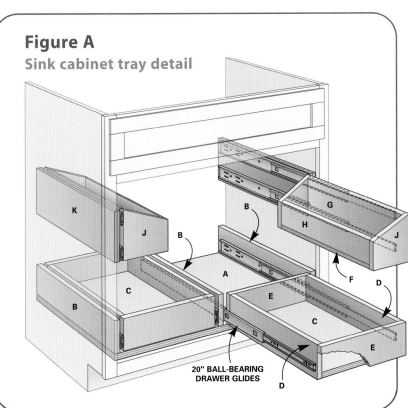

20" BALL-BEARING DRAWER GLIDES

Cutting list

(This list applies to the rollout trays shown; dimensions may vary.)

Key	Pcs.	Size & description
A	1	3/4" x 32-3/4" x 20" plywood base
B	3	3/4" x 3-1/2" x 20" base partitions
C	2	3/4" x 12-3/4" x 18-1/2" plywood tray bottom
D	4	3/4" x 3-1/2" x 18-1/2" tray sides
E	4	3/4" x 3-1/2" x 14-1/4" tray fronts and backs
F	2	1/2" x 5-1/2" x 18-1/2" upper tray bottoms
G	2	3/4" x 5" x 18-1/2" upper tray (high side)
H	2	3/4" x 3" x 18-1/2" upper tray (low side)
J	4	3/4" x 5-1/2" x 5-1/2" upper tray front and back
K	4	1/2" x 5-1/2" x 20" side cleats (double layer)

- If there's a center stile or partition between the doors, make two separate bases for each side and a tray for each to get them to fit.
- Make sure the base and the tray parts are cut square and accurately so the trays slide smoothly.

A word about drawer glides

The ball-bearing glides are designed to mount on the sides of the trays (Photos 6 and 7). The glides require exactly 1/2 in. of space between the partition and drawer on each side to work properly, so make sure the trays are exactly 1 in. narrower than the distance between the partitions. If the trays are too wide, they'll bind and be tough to

RELEASE LEVER

BALL-BEARING DRAWER GLIDE

open. If that happens, take them apart and recut the tray bottom. If the trays are too narrow, the glides will not engage. Fixing this is a bit easier. Just shim behind the glides with thin washers.

Watch for protruding hinges and other obstructions when mounting the lower or upper trays. Adjust the height or placement of the trays to accommodate them.

Seal the trays with polyurethane

Spills or leaks are inevitable under the sink, so it's best to seal the wood. Once the project is finished, remove the trays and glides, sand them with 150-grit sandpaper and brush on two coats of polyurethane. Let the trays dry thoroughly, then look through all that stuff stored under the sink. Toss out the old and combine duplicate products—and enjoy the reclaimed and now easily accessible space.

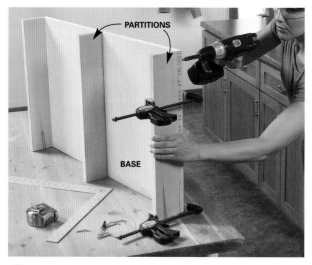

3 Clamp the partitions to the base, drill pilot holes, and glue and screw them to the base with No. 8 x 2-in. screws.

PARTITIONS
BASE

4 Measure the exact distance between the partitions. Make the outer dimension of the tray 1 in. narrower than this measurement to allow for the glides.

CENTER PARTITION
B
A
B

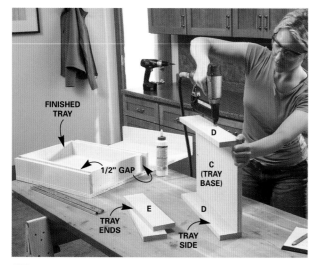

5 Cut the parts for the trays and glue and nail them together. Cut the bases perfectly square to keep the trays square.

FINISHED TRAY
1/2" GAP
D
C (TRAY BASE)
E
D
TRAY ENDS
TRAY SIDE

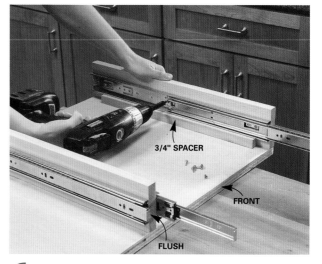

6 Set the drawer glides on 3/4-in. spacers, holding them flush with the front. Open them to expose the mounting holes and screw them to the partitions.

3/4" SPACER
FRONT
FLUSH

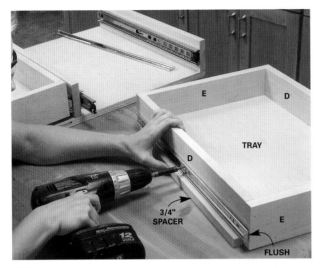

7 Remove the inner sections of the glides and screw them to the sides of the trays. Reassemble the glides and make sure they glide smoothly.

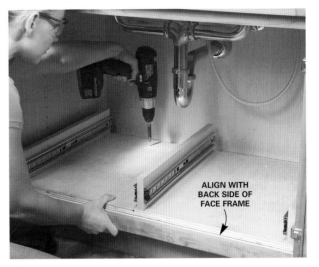

ALIGN WITH BACK SIDE OF FACE FRAME

8 Insert the base assembly into the floor of the cabinet. Align the front of the base flush with the back side of the face frame. Screw the base to the floor of the cabinet.

FINISHED UPPER TRAY

9 Cut the parts for the upper trays, drill pilot holes, and glue and screw them together. Cut two thicknesses of plywood and glue them together to make the 1-in.-thick side cleats (K).

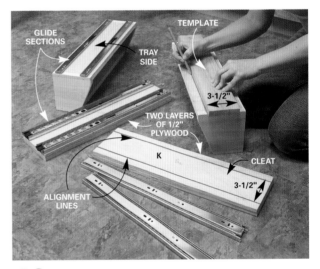

GLIDE SECTIONS

TEMPLATE

TRAY SIDE

3-1/2"

TWO LAYERS OF 1/2" PLYWOOD

K

CLEAT

3-1/2"

ALIGNMENT LINES

10 Cut a 3-1/2-in.-wide template, center it on the cleats and the tall side of each tray and trace the edges. Center the mounting holes of the glides on these lines and screw them to the cleats (outer sections) and tray sides (inner sections).

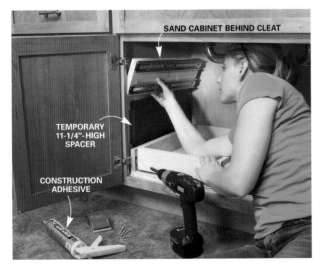

SAND CABINET BEHIND CLEAT

TEMPORARY 11-1/4"-HIGH SPACER

CONSTRUCTION ADHESIVE

11 Sand the side of the cabinet to increase the adhesion, then glue and screw the cleats to the sides of the cabinet. Cut a plywood spacer to hold the cleat even.

12 Slide the upper trays into position and test the fit. Seal the trays with two coats of polyurethane to make cleaning easier.

9 ways to

BEFORE

Cooking caddy for quick clear-off

The best place for salt, cooking oils and favorite spices is next to the stove for everyday use. But they don't have to take up valuable counter space full time. Place them all in a caddy that can be instantly stowed in a cabinet after cooking. Caddies are available in various shapes, sizes and prices ($8 and up) at any store that sells kitchenware.

clear the clutter

Off-the-counter microwave

Microwave ovens are the biggest space hogs on most countertops. With a few models, manufacturers offer optional mounting kits for mounting the microwave under cabinets. To find a cabinet-mountable microwave and mounting hardware (an additional $35), type "under cabinet microwave" into an online search engine. To raise your old microwave, consider the sturdy brackets shown here (leevalley.com, 800-871-8158, item No. 00K79.01). But first measure its height and the height of the space above the countertop; with a larger microwave, the space under it may be too small to be useful.

BRACKET KIT

Undercabinet storage racks

Pull-down racks provide instant access to kitchen essentials without the clutter of countertop spice racks or knife holders. When the cooking is done, the rack swings up against the underside of the cabinet. The acrylic knife rack shown here costs about $70. Or buy a pair of hinges only (about $33 plus shipping) and make a wooden rack to hold knives, spices or other small items that take up counter space. Go to wwhardware.com (800-383-0130) and search for items FEPDH (hinges only), KVUCKR (knife rack shown above) or KVUCCB (cookbook rack).

Expand the counter with a kitchen cart

A rolling kitchen cart is the next best thing to adding cabinets and countertop space. The top provides extra work space when preparing that big Thanksgiving dinner. And the shelves below hold items that would otherwise consume countertop space. To use a cart for food preparation, choose one with a tough top like butcher block, stainless steel or plastic laminate. Some cart tops are glossy finished wood—beautiful, but not very durable. Carts come in a variety of wood finishes, so there's a good chance one will match the existing cabinets. Or choose an eclectic look with a shiny metal or painted cart. Kitchen carts cost $100 and up. For a huge selection, shop online; a good place to start is kitchencarts.com, (800) 667-8721.

Concealed message center

Don't let shopping lists, phone messages and to-do notes clutter up counter space. Mount a dry-erase board and a plastic bin on the inside of a cabinet door with double-sided foam mounting tape. The bin will protrude into the cabinet, so be sure to position it where it won't collide with shelves or the stuff inside. Get the board, bin and tape at a discount or office supply store for about $15 altogether.

Tidy file center

Countertops are a landing pad for paper—mail, news clippings and other assorted notes. Get that mess off the counter with folders and a file holder. The one shown here ($8 at an office supply store) mounts with screws or double-sided foam tape. If there's not a suitable vertical surface, get a file holder that sits on the countertop. It will take up less space (and look neater) than a stack of loose papers.

Decorative backsplash rack

Backsplash racks offer easy access and stylish storage. Most versions take just a few minutes to install. Type "backsplash rack" into any online search engine to find a range of styles. They're available in a range of prices (up to $60 per foot!). The stainless steel rails shown here cost about $3 per foot, and add-on shelves and bins range from $6 to $20 plus shipping (www.ikea.com). Backsplash racks have a few disadvantages, though. The kitchen utensils have to look good, since they're on display. And if the rack is later removed, the screw holes remain in the backsplash; not a big problem with drywall, but ugly and unfixable in tile.

Undercabinet entertainment center

Replace that countertop TV with an undercabinet model. On most models, the screen folds up and out of the way when not in use. Basic models (less than $200) include a radio, and pricier versions play CDs or DVDs too. The Sony TV/CD player shown here costs about $260. Find undercabinet TVs at electronics stores. To compare more than a dozen models online, go to amazon.com and search for "under cabinet TV." For about $700, buy an undercabinet TV system that includes a camera, to monitor the front door or the backyard from the kitchen (nutoneintercom.com). Undercabinet TVs are easy to mount—all that's needed is a drill and a screwdriver. But running cable or antenna wire to the TV probably won't be so easy.

Tucked-away coffeemaker

For serious coffee drinkers, stowing the coffeemaker inside a cabinet just doesn't make sense. Here's a solution: An undercabinet coffeemaker ($60) is always available and doesn't take up valuable counter space. To find a retailer, go to blackanddeckerappliances.com.

Kitchen cabinet rollouts

Base cabinets have the least convenient storage space in the entire kitchen. Rollouts solve that problem. They make organizing and accessing cabinet contents back-friendly and frustration-free.

This section shows how to retrofit nearly any base cabinet with rollouts that'll work as well as or better than any factory-built units.

The project will go faster with a table and a miter saw to cut out all the pieces. A circular saw and cutting guide will work too; it'll just take a little longer. Building a pair of rollouts takes about half a day, and costs about $20 per shelf.

What wood products to buy

The rollout drawers are entirely made of 1/2-in. Baltic birch plywood. Baltic birch is favored by cabinetmakers because it's "void free," meaning that the thin veneers of the plywood core are solid wood. Therefore, sanded edges will look smooth and attractive. If local home centers don't stock Baltic birch, find it at any hardwood specialty store (look under "Hardwood Suppliers" in the yellow pages to find a source). Baltic birch may only come in 5 x 5-ft. sheets, so don't expect to fit it in a minivan. But home centers often carry smaller pieces. Baltic birch plywood may not even be labeled as such at the home center. But it's easy to recognize by comparing it with other hardwood plywood in the racks. Baltic birch will have more and thinner laminations in the plywood core.

The sides of the rollout drawers can be made from any 1x4 solid wood that matches the cabinets, and then finished to match (use plywood for the bases). But if 3/4-in. material is used for the sides, subtract 3 in. from the opening to size the rollout (not 2-1/2 in., as described in Photo 2). (See "Building rollouts in cabinets with center dividers," p. 35, for an example.)

The drawer carriers (Figure A) are made from pine 1x4s for the sides (Photo 7) and 1/4-in. MDF (medium density fiberboard) for the carrier bottom (Photo 9). The MDF keeps the drawer base spaced properly when being shimmed and attached to the cabinet sides. It can be removed and reused for other carriers after installation. If MDF isn't available, substitute any other 1/4-in. hardboard or plywood.

Side-mounted slides are the best choice among drawer slide options. Their ball-bearing mechanisms and precise fit make for smooth-operating drawers that hold 90 lbs. or more. This project uses 22-in. full-extension KV brand side-mount drawer slides that have a 90-lb. weight rating. That means they'll be sturdy enough even for a drawer full of canned goods. Full-extension slides allow the rollout to extend completely past the cabinet front for easy access to all the contents. Expect to pay about $6 to $15 per set of slides at any home center or well-stocked hardware store.

Measure carefully before building

Nearly all standard base cabinets are 23-1/4 in. deep from the inside of the face frame (Photo 1) to the back of the cabinet. So in most cases, 22-in.-long rollout drawer and carrier sides will clear with room to spare. Check the cabinets to make sure that 22-in. rollouts will work. If the cabinets are shallower, subtract whatever is necessary when building the rollouts and their carriers (see Figure A).

Then measure the cabinet width. The drawer has to clear the narrowest part of the opening (Photo 1). When taking this measurement, include hinges that protrude into the opening, the edge of the door attached to the hinges, and even the doors that won't open completely because they hit nearby appliances or other cabinets. Plan on making the drawer front and rear parts 2-1/2 in. shorter than the opening (Figure A).

FACE FRAME

1 Open the cabinet doors to their widest point and measure the narrowest part of the cabinet opening (usually at the hinges).

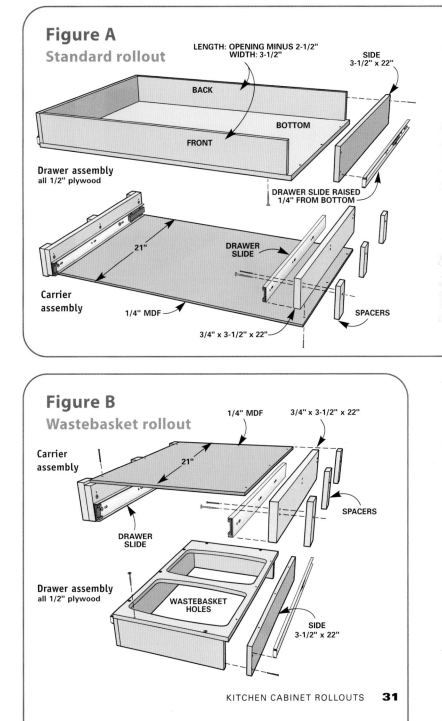

Figure A
Standard rollout

LENGTH: OPENING MINUS 2-1/2"
WIDTH: 3-1/2"

SIDE 3-1/2" x 22"

BACK

BOTTOM

FRONT

Drawer assembly all 1/2" plywood

DRAWER SLIDE RAISED 1/4" FROM BOTTOM

21"

DRAWER SLIDE

Carrier assembly

1/4" MDF

SPACERS

3/4" x 3-1/2" x 22"

Figure B
Wastebasket rollout

1/4" MDF

3/4" x 3-1/2" x 22"

Carrier assembly

21"

SPACERS

DRAWER SLIDE

Drawer assembly all 1/2" plywood

WASTEBASKET HOLES

SIDE 3-1/2" x 22"

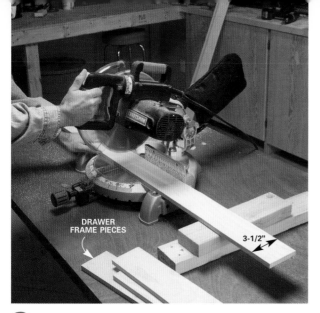

2 Rip 1/2-in. plywood down to 3-1/2 in. wide and cut two 22-in. lengths (drawer sides) and two more to the measured width minus 2-1/2 in. (drawer front and back; Figure A).

3 Clamp or screw two straight 12-in. 2x4s to the corner of a flat surface to use as an assembly jig. Use a carpenter's square to ensure squareness. Leave a 2-in. gap at the corner.

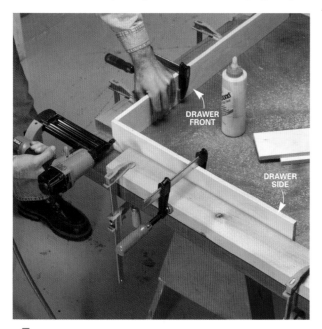

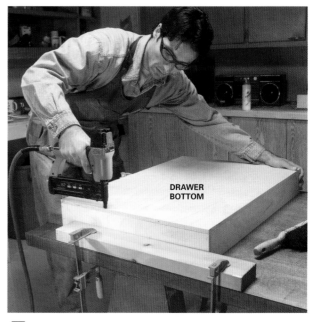

4 Spread woodworking glue on the ends and clamp a drawer side and front in place, then pin the corner together with three 1-1/4-in. brads. Repeat for the other three corners.

5 Cut a 1/2-in. plywood bottom to size. Apply a thin bead of glue to the bottom edges, and nail one edge of the plywood flush with a side, spacing nails every 4 in. Then push the frame against the jig to square it and nail the other three edges.

This project shows drawers with 3-1/2-in.-high sides, but they can be customized. Plan on higher sides for lightweight plastic storage containers or other tall or tippy items, and lower sides for stable, heavier items like small appliances.

Drawer slides aren't as confusing as they seem

Drawer slides are sold in pairs and each of the pairs has two parts. The "drawer part" attaches to the rollout while the "cabinet part" attaches to the carrier. To separate them for mounting, slide them out to full length and then push, pull or depress a plastic release to separate the two parts. The release button position and shape vary among manufacturers. The cabinet part, which always encloses the drawer part, is the larger of the two, and the mounting screw hole locations will be shown in the directions. (Screws are included with the drawer slides.) The oversized holes allow for some adjustment. When mounting the slides, make sure to hold them flush with the front of the rollout drawer and carrier sides (Photos 6 and 7). The front of the drawer part usually has a bent metal stop that faces the front of the drawer.

Assembling parts and finishing the rollouts

It's important to build the rollout drawers perfectly square for them to operate properly. Photos 3 and 4 show a simple squaring jig that can clamp to a corner of any workbench to help. Use the

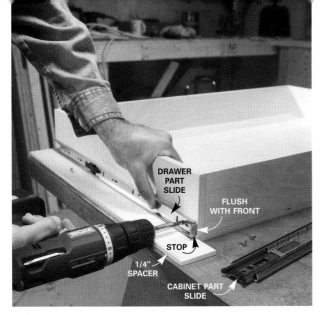

6 Separate the drawer slides and space the drawer part 1/4 in. up from the bottom. Hold it flush to the front and screw it to the rollout side.

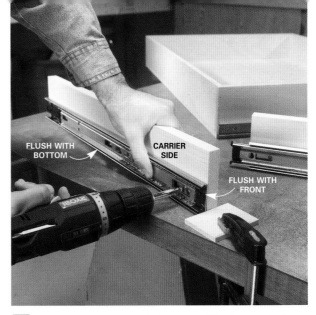

7 Mount the carrier part of the drawer slide flush with the bottom and front of the carrier sides.

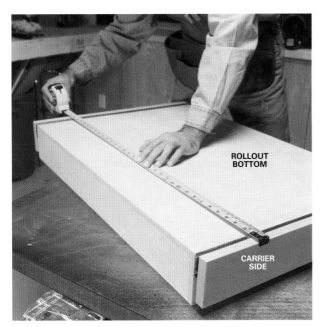

8 Slide the drawer and carrier sides together and measure the carrier width. Cut 1/4-in. MDF to that width and 1 in. less than the carrier depth (usually 21 in.).

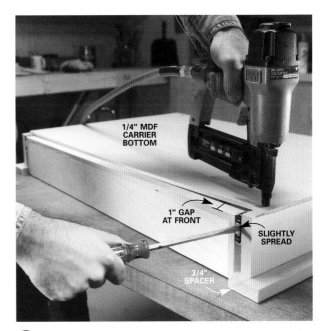

9 Rest the carrier assembly on 3/4-in.-thick spacers, pull the carrier sides slightly away from the drawer, then nail on the carrier bottom (no glue).

jig to nail the frame together, but even more important, to hold the frame square when nailing on the bottom panel. If it hangs over the sides even a little, the drawer slides won't work smoothly.

Use 1-1/4-in. brads for all of the assembly. Glue the drawer parts together, but not the bottom of the carrier. It only serves as a temporary spacer for mounting. (After mounting the carrier and drawer, remove the carrier if it catches items on underlying drawers.) To finish the rollout for a richer look and easier cleaning, sand the edges with 120-grit paper and apply a couple of coats of water-based polyurethane before mounting the slides.

To figure the spacer thickness, rest the lower carrier on the bottom of the shelf, push it against one side of the cabinet and measure the gap on the other (Photo 10). Rip spacers to half that measurement and cut six of them to 3-1/2 in. long. Slip the spacers between both sides of the carrier to check the fit. They should slide in snugly but not tightly. Recut new spacers if needed. In out-of-square cabinets, custom-cut spacers may be needed for each of the three pairs of spacers, so check each of the three spacer positions. It's easiest to tack the spacers to the rollouts to hold them in place before predrilling 1/8-in. holes and running the screws through the rollout frames and spacers and into the cabinet sides (Photo 11, p. 34).

Slip the rollout into its carrier and check for smooth operation. By following this process, it should work perfectly. If it binds, it's probably because the spacers are too wide or narrow. Pull out

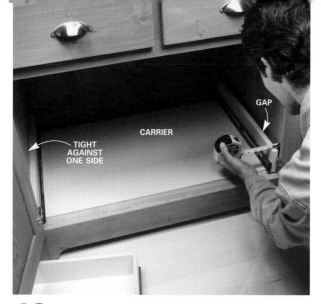

10 Remove the drawer, tip the carrier into the cabinet and push the carrier against one side. Measure the gap and rip six 3-1/2-in.-long spacers to half of the thickness.

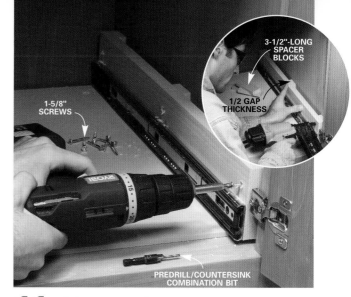

11 Nail the spacers to the center and each end of the carrier sides (not into the cabinet; see inset photo). Then predrill and screw the carrier sides to the cabinet in the center of each shim. Slide the drawer back into place.

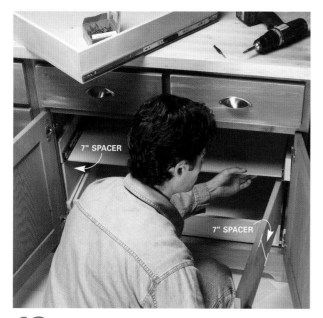

12 Cut plywood spacers to temporarily support the upper rollout and set them onto the carrier below. Rest the second carrier on the spacers and install it as shown in Photo 11.

13 Build an upside-down version of the carrier and rollouts for the wastebasket drawer (Figure B). Center and trace around the rim of the wastebasket(s). Use a compass to mark the opening 1/2 in. smaller.

the carrier, remove the spacers and start the spacer process all over again.

The best way to level and fasten the upper rollout is to support it on temporary plywood spacers (Photo 12). The pieces of plywood shown are 7 in. high, but the exact height can vary. To store tall boxes of cereal on the bottom rollout and shorter items on the top, space the top rollout higher. Build and install three or more rollouts in one cabinet for mega storage of short items like cans, cutlery or beverages. (Those now-obsolete shelves being replaced with rollouts are good stock to use for the spacers.) Again, pin the spacers in place with a brad or two to hold them while predrilling and screwing the carriers to the cabinet sides. Be sure to select screw lengths that won't pene-

trate exposed cabinet sides! In most cases, 1-5/8-in. screws are the best choice. Strive for 1/2-in. penetration into the cabinet sides. Countersink the heads as far as necessary to get the proper penetration.

Building wastebasket rollouts

Wastebasket rollouts are just upside-down versions of standard rollouts. That is, the carrier is mounted on the top rather than the bottom of the rollout and the slides are positioned at the bottom edge of the carrier sides. That lets the wastebasket lip clear the MDF. Follow Figure B on p. 31 for the details.

This wastebasket rollout is built inside an 18-in.-wide cabinet, so two plastic containers fit back to back. For 15-in. cabinets, size

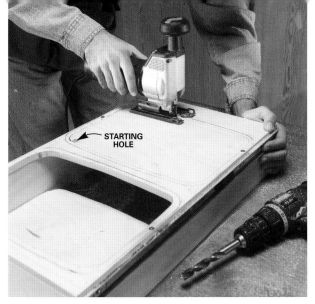

14 Drill 1/2-in. starting holes and cut the openings with a jigsaw.

15 Mount the wastebasket carrier and drawer as shown in Photos 10 and 11.

may be limited to one container mounted sideways. Buy containers ahead of time to fit the opening.

Some wastebasket rollouts require knocking the MDF free from the carriers after mounting so the wastebasket lips will clear. That's OK; it won't affect operation.

It may not always work to center rollout assemblies in all openings with equal spacers on each side. That's especially true with narrow single cabinets that only have one pair of hinges. Cheat the wastebasket assembly away from the hinge side an additional 1/2 in. or so, if needed. Again, it's best to test things before permanent mounting. But if a mistake is made, unscrew the assembly, adjust the shims and remount everything.

Building rollouts in cabinets with center dividers

Many two-door cabinets have a center divider (photo above), which calls for a slightly different strategy. The rollouts will need to be narrower versions on each side of the divider. (Check to be sure they won't be so narrow that they're impractical.) The key is to install a 3/4-in. plywood, particleboard or MDF panel between the center divider and the cabinet back to support the carriers.

Cut the panel to fit loosely between the divider and the cabinet back and high enough to support the top rollout position. Center the panel on the back side and middle of the divider and screw it into place with 1-in. angle brackets (they're completely out of sight). Use a carpenter's square to position the panel perfectly centered and vertical on the cabinet back and anchor it there, again using angle brackets. Measure, build and install the rollouts as shown on the previous pages.

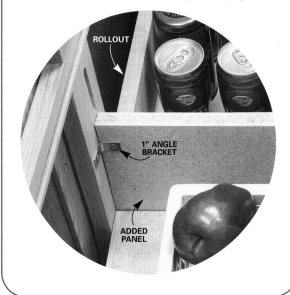

Above-cabinet
shelving

This project only requires basic carpentry tools and skills. Even the miter joints can be cut with a simple handsaw miter box. An 18-gauge finish nailer will make the job go faster; otherwise, predrill and hand-nail. Don't worry about trying to match the cabinet's finish or wood type. The shelf will look great if painted to match another accent color in the room. Adding shelves to about 8 ft. of upper cabinets costs about $40.

Get what you need at the lumberyard

The best material for the main shelf is 3/4-in. plywood (Photo 4, p. 38). Get a finished grade that is smooth and easy to sand. The cleats under the shelf (Photo 2) are fillers to elevate the shelf just enough so the crown molding fits under the shelf and yet comfortably clears the doors below. Carefully cut cleats with a circular saw and an edge guide, or simply use a table saw. Besides the 2-1/4-in. crown molding, trim is needed to cover the edge of the plywood (Photo 6, p. 38) for a finished look. Use

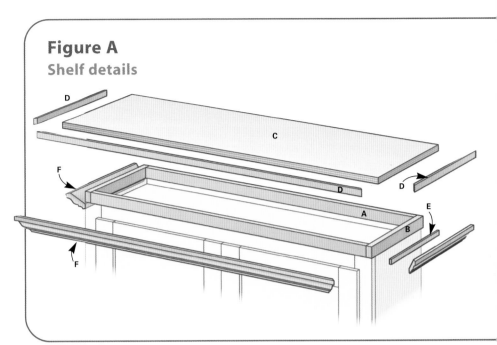

Figure A
Shelf details

✳ Cutting list

Key	Description
A	3/4" x 1-1/4" board cut 1-1/2" shorter than the cabinet face width
B	3/4" x 1-1/4" board cut the same as cabinet depth
C	3/4" plywood cut 3" longer than the cabinet face width and 1-1/2" deeper than the cabinet depth
D	1/4" x 3/4" molding cut and mitered to cover exposed plywood
E	Filler piece to fill void between the face frame and the wall
F	2-1/4" crown molding cut and mitered to fit over cabinet face and under shelf

1 Measure the tops of your cabinets to determine your materials list. Also check the distance above the cabinet doors to determine the support cleat height for the shelf.

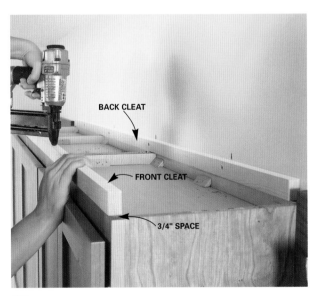

BACK CLEAT

FRONT CLEAT

3/4" SPACE

2 Nail cleats to the tops of the cabinets to elevate the shelf. Leave 3/4 in. of space on each side for the side cleats. The side cleats will overhang on the cabinet side (see Photo 3).

"screen" molding or "parting stop" available at home centers, or just rip a strip from a wider board to 1/4 in. or thicker.

Follow the photos for details about sizing and fitting the shelf pieces.

Paint your molding to match

Finish up by filling the nail holes and sanding the wood with 150-grit sandpaper. Prime the wood and then select a satin or gloss paint finish that'll be easy to wipe clean. Because

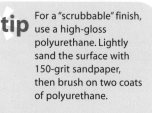

tip For a "scrubbable" finish, use a high-gloss polyurethane. Lightly sand the surface with 150-grit sandpaper, then brush on two coats of polyurethane.

it's difficult to get an exact cabinet color match for natural wood cabinets, simply pick a color that will accent the kitchen countertops or cabinets.

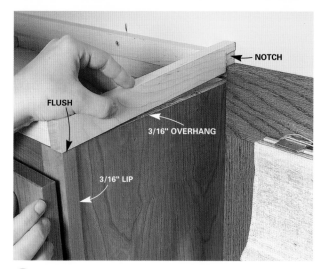

3 Fit the side cleats so there's a consistent overhang on the edge. Notch the cleat to fit behind the window molding, if needed.

NOTCH

FLUSH

3/16" OVERHANG

3/16" LIP

3/4" PLYWOOD TOP

CONSISTENT OVERHANG

4 Measure and cut the top from 3/4-in. plywood, overhanging 1-1/2 in. on the front and each side.

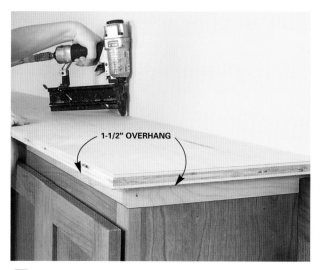

1-1/2" OVERHANG

5 Nail the top to the cleats with 2-in. finish nails. Make sure the overhang is even on each side.

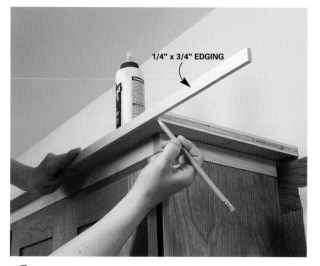

1/4" x 3/4" EDGING

6 Glue and nail the 3/4-in.-wide edge molding to the exposed plywood edges. Miter the corners for a more finished appearance.

BOTTOM SIDE OF CROWN MOLDING

7 Position the molding upside down in the miter box to support both the top and the bottom of the molding. Check the direction of the angle twice before cutting.

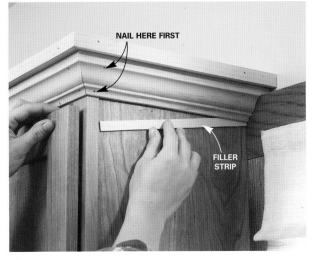

8 Nail the crown molding to the face of the cabinet and up into the shelf at an angle. The molding will completely cover the cuts.

9 Fit the side pieces of crown molding and slip a 3/16-in.-thick filler strip under the front edge to hide the gap created by the face frame overhang.

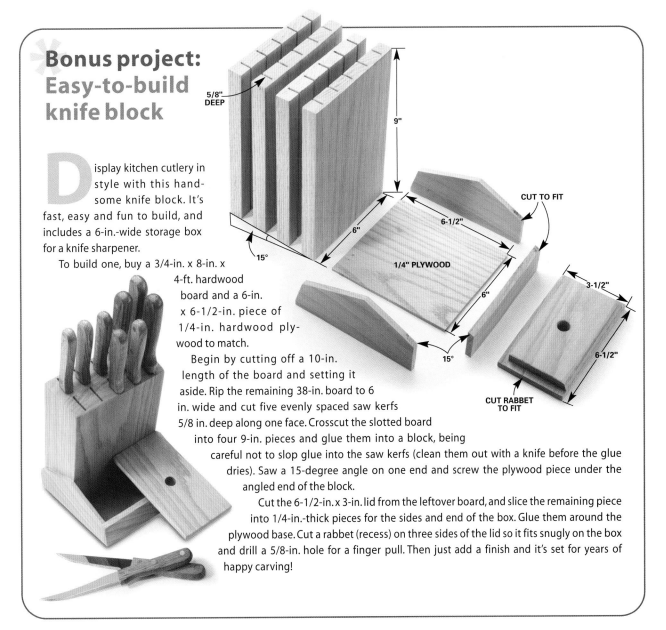

✳ Bonus project:
Easy-to-build knife block

Display kitchen cutlery in style with this handsome knife block. It's fast, easy and fun to build, and includes a 6-in.-wide storage box for a knife sharpener.

To build one, buy a 3/4-in. x 8-in. x 4-ft. hardwood board and a 6-in. x 6-1/2-in. piece of 1/4-in. hardwood plywood to match.

Begin by cutting off a 10-in. length of the board and setting it aside. Rip the remaining 38-in. board to 6 in. wide and cut five evenly spaced saw kerfs 5/8 in. deep along one face. Crosscut the slotted board into four 9-in. pieces and glue them into a block, being careful not to slop glue into the saw kerfs (clean them out with a knife before the glue dries). Saw a 15-degree angle on one end and screw the plywood piece under the angled end of the block.

Cut the 6-1/2-in. x 3-in. lid from the leftover board, and slice the remaining piece into 1/4-in.-thick pieces for the sides and end of the box. Glue them around the plywood base. Cut a rabbet (recess) on three sides of the lid so it fits snugly on the box and drill a 5/8-in. hole for a finger pull. Then just add a finish and it's set for years of happy carving!

Open
kitchen shelves

Converting a few wall cabinets to open shelving is a great way to create display space for dishes or to keep cookbooks and cooking supplies within easy reach. Anyone handy with a paint brush can complete this project in a leisurely weekend. Don't forget to order the glass shelves about a week before they're needed.

This project requires a screwdriver, hammer and tape measure as well as basic painting equipment like a paint brush, putty knife, masking tape, and sandpaper or sanding sponge. Use a drill with a 9/32-in. bit to drill holes for the metal sleeves (Photo 3).

Some cabinets are easy to convert by simply removing the doors and ordering glass shelves. Others may require a little carpentry work, like removing a fixed shelf. Take a close look inside the cabinet to see whether there are hidden challenges. If it looks good, remove the doors and carefully measure for shelves. Measure from one side of the cabinet to the other and from front to back. Deduct 1/8 in. from these measurements to arrive at the glass size. Look in the yellow pages under "Glass" to find a company that will cut the glass and polish all of the edges. The six 1/4-in.-thick glass shelves in this kitchen cost $60. Ask the glass salesperson what thickness is needed for strength and safety. Longer spans require thicker glass.

While waiting for the glass to arrive, paint the cabinet interiors. Choose a color that matches or complements a floor or wall color. Preparation is the key to a long-lasting, perfectly smooth paint job. Photos 1 and 2 show the painting steps. If painting over Melamine or another hard, shiny surface, make sure to thoroughly roughen the surface with 80-grit sandpaper and prime with shellac before brushing or spraying on the coats of paint.

Photo 3 shows the hardware used to support the glass shelves. If there aren't holes for the shelf pins, use a tape measure and square to mark the hole locations and bore 9/32-in. holes to accept the metal reinforcing sleeves. The shelf pins, sleeves and round rubber pads are available from Rockler Woodworking and Hardware. Call (800) 279-4441 or visit rockler.com.

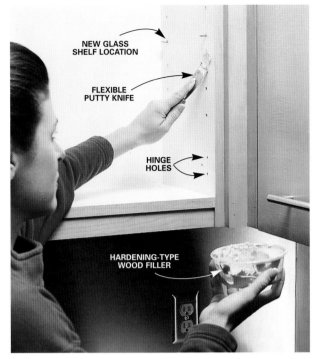

1 Remove the cabinet doors and hinges. Fill all extra shelf bracket or hinge holes with a hardening-type wood filler. Allow this to harden, sand it smooth, and apply a coat of lightweight surfacing compound to fill low spots left after the wood filler shrinks. Let the second coat dry. Then sand the entire cabinet interior with 80-grit paper to provide a "rough" surface for the paint to grab.

2 Paint the cabinet interior. Use masking tape to protect unpainted areas. Prime the interior with white pigmented shellac (BIN is one brand) to keep the filler from showing through and to provide a binder for the final coats of paint. Sand the primer lightly with a fine sanding sponge after it dries. Remove the dust with a vacuum cleaner and brush on the final coats of latex or oil paint.

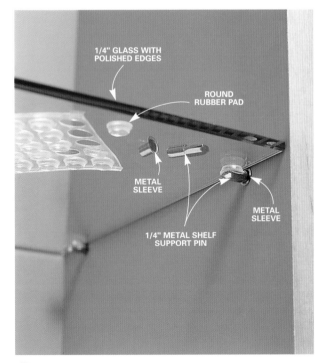

3 Support glass shelves with metal shelf pins inserted into holes drilled in the cabinet sides. To prevent the pins from enlarging the holes, drill 9/32-in. holes and tap in metal sleeves. Then insert the metal shelf support pins in the sleeves and apply a self-adhesive round rubber pad to each pin to keep the glass shelves from sliding off.

Bonus project:
Thyme saver spice rack

An hour is all it takes to make this nifty rack that slips neatly into the drawer. Use leftover scraps of 1/4-in. and 1/2-in. plywood laying around the shop.

Family message center

This simple organizing cabinet has an erasable calendar for busy schedules and immediate messages; plenty of cork for photos, invitations, coupons and permission slips; a pull-down door with a notepad for short messages and shopping lists; and storage for a good supply of pens, postage stamps, tissues and other items that usually clutter nearby tabletops. It also has hooks for keys and shallow bins for magazines, mail, dog leashes, address books and homework (completed, no doubt!).

This cabinet is designed to slip back into the wall between empty stud spaces, so people won't bump it as they go by and knock stuff off the board. And the closed doors keep most of the clutter out of sight.

The message center fits inside a standard interior wall, which is usually constructed of 2x4s spaced 16 in. on center, with 14-1/2 in. of space between studs. Exterior walls won't work because they have insulation in them. Some interior walls won't work either, if they have heating ducts, pipes and wiring running through them. This project can be easily adapted to any size and as many open cavities as desired. The basic concept is simple—just cut a hole in the drywall, insert a wooden box, and add trim to it. The materials cost $90, including hinges.

Detective work comes first

Before cutting into the wall, try to get an idea of what's concealed inside it. Find stud locations with a stud finder or by tapping on the wall and listening for variations in tone. Be aware that blank walls can conceal a wide variety of framing—especially in older houses. **Note:** Locating studs in old plaster walls may require a more sensitive, higher-priced stud finder.

After locating studs, check both sides of the wall and the rooms above and below for heat registers, plumbing and electrical fixtures. If potential obstructions are visible on adjacent floors, use an outside wall for a reference point to estimate if it'll obstruct the cabinet. Even if the location looks clear, cut small holes in both cavities and double-check for obstructions. Cutting the hole with a utility knife is difficult, but it's safer than using a saw because it keeps the cuts shallow and away from any electrical wires (Photo 1, p. 44). If obstructions are present, don't despair. Half of the message center is only 3/4 in. deep (not including trim). It may fit over the obstructions without any problem. Another option is to make the box shallower, or extend

wires around the boxes by rewiring, but consult an electrician or electrical inspector first.

Cut the openings

Draw plumb lines at stud locations, then mark the rough opening height (34 in. from the floor to the bottom and 83 in. to the top). Adjust this height above the floor, if necessary, so the message center lines up with nearby door or window trim (Photo 2, p. 44).

Check the studs for plumb (Photo 3, p. 44) and adjust the box dimensions as needed to fit cleanly between them. It's generally best to leave the center stud in place.

Build the boxes

The message center spans two stud cavities, with a deep side for shelves and miscellaneous storage and a shallow side for a cork message board and calendar. To maximize space, the sides of the deep box are made from 1/2-in. birch plywood and the sides of the shallow message board from 1/2-in. x 3/4-in. pine. Nailing trim to a 1/2-in. edge is finicky work, so use a brad nailer or predrill the nail holes.

Cut the backs and side pieces from a 4 x 4-ft. sheet of 1/2-in. birch plywood using a table saw or a circular

Shopping list

One 4' x 4' x 1/2" birch plywood (A, B, C)
One 2' x 4' x 3/4" birch plywood (K, L)
Two 1/2" x 3/4" x 8' pine (A1, B1, J)
One 3/4" x 3/4" x 4' pine (D)
One 1x4 x 6' pine (E)
One 1x3 x 4' pine; two 1x3 x 8' pine (F, G)
One 1x2 x 6' (H)
1" brads
1-1/2" brads
2-1/2" finish nails
Wood glue

Figure A Message center details

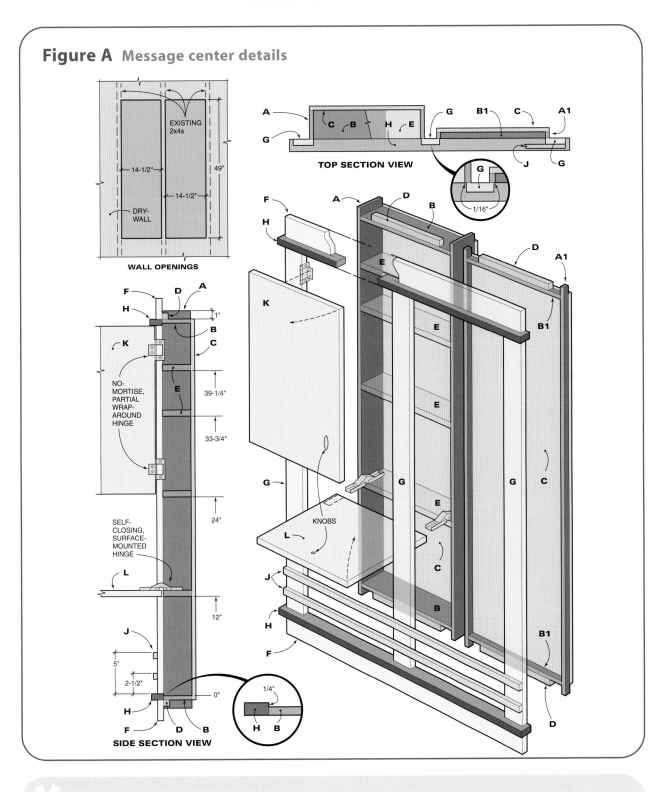

WALL OPENINGS

14-1/2" 14-1/2" 49"

EXISTING 2x4s

DRY-WALL

TOP SECTION VIEW

A G C B H E G B1 C A1 J G

G 1/16"

SIDE SECTION VIEW

F D A H B C K E 39-1/4" 33-3/4" 24" L 12" J 5" 2-1/2" 0" H F D B 1"

NO-MORTISE, PARTIAL WRAP-AROUND HINGE

SELF-CLOSING, SURFACE-MOUNTED HINGE

1/4" H B

F H A E B D A1 B1 K E E G E C G C L KNOBS J B B1 H F D

✳ Cutting list

Key	Pcs.	Size & description
A	2	3-1/2" x 47-7/8" x 1/2" birch plywood (sides for deep box)
B	2	3-1/2" x 13-1/4" x 1/2" birch plywood (top and bottom for deep box)
A1	2	1/2" x 3/4" x 47-7/8" pine (sides for shallow box)
B1	2	1/2" x 3/4" x 13-1/4" pine (top and bottom for shallow box)
C	2	14-1/4" x 45-7/8" x 1/2" birch plywood (backs for both boxes)
D	4	3/4" x 3/4" x 10" pine (nailers for top and bottom trim F)

Key	Pcs.	Size & description
E	4	3/4" x 3-1/2" x 13-1/4" pine (shelves)
F	2	3/4" x 2-1/2" x 34-1/8" pine (top and bottom trim)
G	3	3/4" x 2-1/2" x 44-3/8" pine (center and side trim)
H	2	3/4" x 1-1/2" x 35-1/8" pine (top and bottom sill)
J	2	1/2" x 3/4" x 34-1/8" pine (bottom crossbars)
K	1	3/4" x 13-1/8" x 20-1/8" birch plywood (upper door)
L	1	3/4" x 13-1/8" x 12-1/4" birch plywood (lower door)

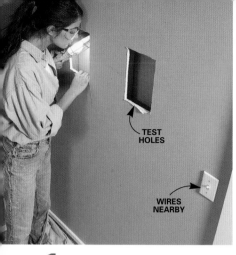

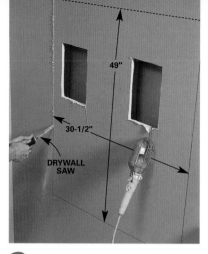

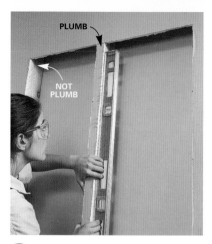

1 Find nearby studs with a stud finder, then cut a small opening with a utility knife in each stud cavity and check for obstructions. Save the cutouts in case you have to repair the wall.

2 Cut the opening to the desired height and size of the message center, following the studs with the drywall saw. Smooth ragged edges with a rasp or knife.

3 Check the studs for plumb, and adjust the width and spacing of the boxes as needed to allow them to slip in easily.

saw with an edge guide. If using a circular saw, cut from the back side to avoid chipping the birch veneer. If possible, gang-cut pieces that are the same length (Photo 4). Use 1/2-in. plywood for the back for rigidity and to give solid support for the corkboard and any other items that will be mounted.

Cut the long sides of the boxes 47-7/8 in. (A, A1, in Figure A, p. 43), and nail the top and bottom pieces (B, B1) 1 in. in from the end to create nailer legs for the top and bottom trim pieces (F); see Photo 5. Glue and nail the back (C) down onto the box, aligning the edges and squaring the box as you nail (Photo 5). Tack down the back with 1-in. brad nails; longer nails might angle and break through the plywood sides. Use a damp cloth to wipe off any glue that oozes to the inside.

Install shelves

Nail the shelves (E) into place before joining the two boxes (Photo 6). Gang-cut the shelves from 1x4 pine, then slide them into position and hold them tight against square blocks of wood clamped to the sides. Mark the center of the shelf on the outside of the box frame to ensure accurate nailing (Photo 6). Use four 1-1/2-in. brads on each side and then flip the box over, connect the nailing lines from each side across the back, and shoot a few brads in through the plywood back for extra strength and rigidity.

Join the boxes with the trim

Line the two boxes up with each other, then glue and nail the center trim (G) to join the sides, leaving a 1/16-in. reveal on each side. Center the center trim lengthwise to leave it about 1/4 in. short of each end. When attaching the top and bottom sills (H), this will give a 1/4-in. lip to help keep papers and odds and ends from sliding out the bottom (Photo 8). Remove the spacer blocks after nailing the center trim.

Glue and nail the sills (H) at the top and bottom edges of the boxes (Photo 8). Center them on the center trim. They'll overlap the side trim by about 1/2 in. Then glue and nail the side trim (G)

flush with the edges of the boxes. Nail the sills to the side trim as well with 1-1/2-in. brads. Cut the nailers (D) and nail them to the tops and bottoms of the boxes to support the top and bottom trim (Photo 8). Finally, glue and nail on the slats (J); see Photo 9 and Figure A.

Take a break and let the glue set up. Then sand out all the rough edges.

Set the message center into the wall

The message center should slide right into the opening cut in the wall and cover all the rough edges as well (Photo 10). Level it and adjust the height before nailing it to the studs through the trim with 2-1/2-in. finish nails.

Install a door (K) on the upper part of the deep box, and a small, drop-down writing surface (L) below it. Special hinges hold the drop-down door at 90 degrees without supports (Photo 11). These doors are both inset, so they have to be aligned with each other and evenly spaced in relation to the trim. This can take some time and patience. At first, install the hinges with only one screw in the adjustable slot, then lock them into place with additional screws after all adjustments are complete.

Fill and sand all nail holes, then paint the message center. Finally, install knobs on the doors and put the message center to use.

UPPER DOOR HINGE

LOWER DOOR HINGE

Shown here is a no-mortise, partial wrap-around hinge for the upper doors (item No. 49393; $8 per pair) and a self-closing surface-mounted hinge with a 90-degree stop for the drop-down desk (item No. 66639; $9 per pair). Both are available from Rockler Woodworking, (800) 279-4441 or rockler.com.

4 Cut out all the pieces, following the dimensions in the Cutting list (p. 43). Clamp and gang-cut matching parts when possible.

5 Glue and nail the sides, top and bottom first, then glue and nail on the 1/2-in. plywood back (C) to square each box. Wipe off excess glue with a damp rag.

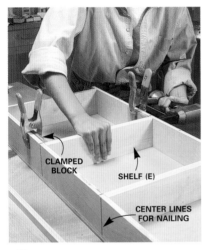

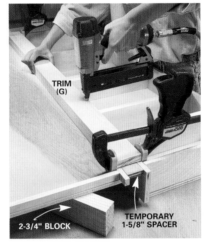

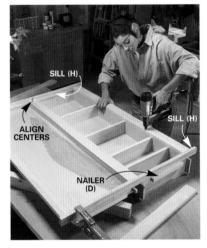

6 Cut and nail the shelves into the deep box. Clamp square blocks to the sides to hold the shelf at a right angle while you nail it.

7 Prop the shallow box even with the deeper one, space them with a 1-5/8-in. block and clamp them. Nail on the center trim (G).

8 Center the top and bottom sills (H) and glue and nail them to the center trim. Glue and nail the side trim (G) to the sides and to the sills. Glue and nail 3/4-in. x 3/4-in. blocks to the top and bottom for nailers (D).

9 Nail on the top and bottom trim (F). Position and clamp the two 1/2-in. x 3/4-in. crossbars (J). Nail with 1-in. brads.

10 Set the completed message center in the opening and level it. Then nail through the trim into the studs to secure it.

11 Screw hinges to the doors and align them in the openings. Inset doors can be fussy to adjust— use just one screw per hinge until you complete the alignment.

Space is always at a premium in bathrooms and laundry rooms. There's never enough storage room, let alone places to display knickknacks and liven up the area. This chapter offers creative solutions for adding storage space and shelving in hidden and unused areas.

Chapter 2

organize
your
bathroom
& laundry
room

Three bathroom storage projects

Bathrooms never have enough storage or shelf space. There's hardly enough room to display knickknacks, let alone store unsightly items like extra toilet paper, blow dryers, curling irons, plus cans, soaps and bottles. Once the vanity is filled, there's really no more storage in a small bathroom.

Three solutions:

1. Upsize existing storage space by replacing that tiny medicine cabinet or mirror with a larger, surface-mounted cabinet.
2. Utilize existing space by adding glass shelving to the unused space over the toilet.
3. Steal space from an adjoining room or closet by insetting kitchen pantry cabinets (or tall utility cabinets) into the wall.

Installing a new medicine cabinet and shelving is easy and fast. Each project takes less than an hour. For these simple projects, a screw gun and a 2-ft. level are all that's needed. This project features a foolproof way to solidly support the cabinets, regardless of the type of wall behind them.

The flush-mounted pantry cabinets are more challenging because they require cutting into the wall and stealing space from a neighboring room or closet. But don't worry. The following step-by-step photos show the cutting and fitting. A drywall saw, a few 8-ft. 2x4s (Photo 3, p. 53) and a table and miter saw for trimming out the pantry cabinets are needed to complete the project. It takes one day to install the cabinets, but allow another day for walling in the cabinet backs in the room or closet behind the bathroom.

BEFORE

2
Glass shelves
p. 51

1
Bigger medicine cabinet
p. 50

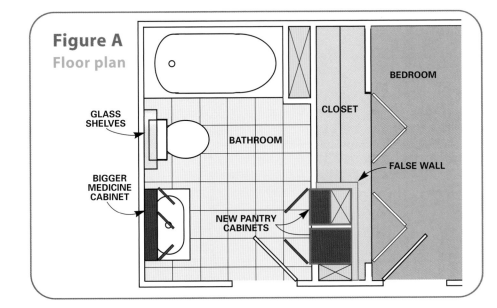

Figure A
Floor plan

GLASS SHELVES

BIGGER MEDICINE CABINET

BATHROOM

NEW PANTRY CABINETS

CLOSET

FALSE WALL

BEDROOM

Bonus: The larger mirror on the medicine cabinet will make your bathroom feel larger.

3
Built-in pantry cabinets p. 52

Buying the cabinets

A wide variety of medicine cabinets and shelves is available at home centers and kitchen and bath specialty stores. When sizing a medicine cabinet, measure the space available behind the sink, both height and width. Keep a few inches away from existing light fixtures (unless the plan calls to move them). Buy a cabinet that fits within those dimensions.

When sizing the larger kitchen pantry cabinet(s) to recess into the wall, look for 7-ft.-tall, 15-in.-wide cabinets to fit between the wall studs. If they're not in stock, special-order them. Special-ordering allows a wider style selection. Expect to pay a minimum of $200 for a bare-bones, 7-ft. tall pantry cabinet, or up to $1,500 for an upscale cherry unit with fluted glass doors.

For storing linens, towels or larger items, go with 24-in.-deep cabinets, but if the closet they project into is less than 24 in. deep, go with the 12-in. units or cut down the 24-in. ones. When ordering pantry cabinets, also order three matching, prefinished 8-ft. long, 1/4-in. x 2-in. mullion strips for trim around the outside (Photo 12, p. 54). Also order an 8-ft. long, 3/4-in. x 2-in. filler strip to join the cabinets in the center (Photos 9 and 10, p. 54). If buying unfinished cabinets, get unfinished boards of the same wood type in the millwork area at the store.

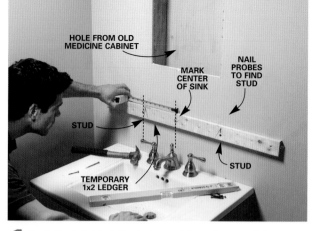

1 Mark the height of the bottom of the cabinet and draw a line with a 2-ft. level. Find the studs by probing with a nail and mark the stud positions above the level line. Screw a temporary 1x2 ledger board through the drywall into the studs. Mark the center of the sink on the ledger, and then measure over from the center mark to the left and right studs.

1 Bigger medicine cabinet

Surface-mounting a large medicine cabinet is simply a matter of centering it, leveling it and screwing it to the wall studs.

An old cabinet may be surface-mounted or recessed into the wall cavity between the framing. Remove a recessed unit simply by opening the door, backing out the screws in the side of the cabinet and pulling it out of the recess. Cut around it with a utility knife if it's caulked or painted in around the edges. Have a helper support surface-mounted cabinets then back out the screws; or if working alone, hold the cabinet by screwing a temporary 1x2 support ledger under the cabinet as shown in Photo 1. Move or replace the lighting beside or above the old cabinet, if needed.

Hold the new medicine cabinet against the wall and adjust it up and down to find the perfect height, then mark the bottom and set the cabinet aside. Use the mark to draw a level line for positioning the 1x2 ledger (Photo 1). Then follow Photos 2 and 3 for installation details.

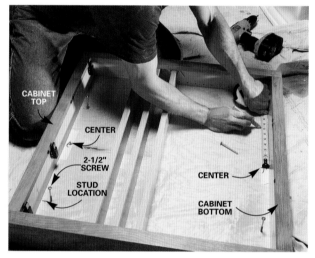

2 Mark the center of the cabinet at the top and bottom and transfer the center-to-stud locations inside the cabinet. Start 2-1/2-in. screws at those marks.

3 Set the cabinet on the ledger and line up the center of the cabinet with the center mark on the ledger. Drive the screws into the studs, then remove the ledger. Fill the screw holes with spackling compound and touch up the paint.

2 Glass shelves

Most bathrooms have one space for additional storage, and that's over the toilet. Open glass shelving is a great way to display decorative bathroom bottles or knickknacks. There are zillions of glass shelving systems on the market. Follow the directions that come with the system for the installation details, but read on for help anchoring them to the wall because studs probably aren't exactly where they're needed. Use masking tape to avoid marking the walls.

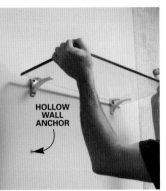

HOLLOW WALL ANCHOR

BRACKET LOCATIONS

CENTER LINE

1 Apply a strip of 2-in.-wide masking tape above the center of the toilet and on both sides where the shelf brackets will be mounted. Draw a center line with a level and mark the shelf heights on the center tape. Transfer the heights to the bracket tape with a 2-ft. level. Measure from the center line to mark the exact left and right locations for the brackets.

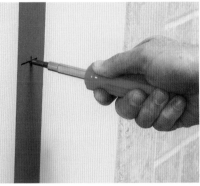

2 Indent the drywall at the marks with a Phillips head screwdriver and then remove the tape.

3 Drive hollow wall anchors through the drywall.

90-LB.–RATED WALL ANCHOR

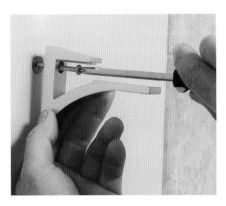

4 Screw the brackets to the wall using the screws included with the anchors.

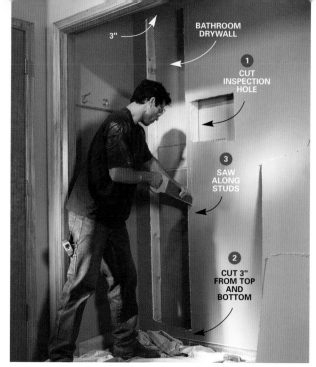

3 Built-in pantry cabinets

Most small bathrooms have all of the plumbing on one wall and the door usually swings against a blank wall. Often, there's a closet on the other side of the blank wall to steal space from. If there's not a closet, it's possible to take 1 or 2 ft. of floor space from the other room, but that requires going to the trouble of framing, drywalling, taping, painting and trimming a false wall to conceal the unsightly cabinet backs.

Instead, add one or two cabinets to a wall using the method shown here. To add more, it's better to reframe the entire wall. A full 14-1/2-in.-wide stud space is needed for each cabinet in the blank wall (that space will be expanded to 15-1/2 in. wide). It's easiest to go into the bathroom and find the studs with a stud finder to see how many 14-1/2-in. stud spaces are available.

When a bathroom backs against a closet, there are rarely electrical cables inside the wall. This project shows cutting an inspection hole to check for cables or other obstructions (Photo 1). Reroute an electrical cable if there is one.

If there's carpeting, unhook it from the tack strips and pull it and the padding back a couple of feet. Cut them both around the

tip Sometimes a stud will bow in the center. If it bows toward the opening, push it into position and hold it there by running drywall screws through the drywall into the stud.

cabinets (or false wall), then staple down the padding and push the carpet onto new tack strips when the project is finished. Chop off the tack strip in front of the wall openings with a chisel and reuse it at the back of the cabinets.

Crib up the cabinets with overlapping 2x4s to establish the cabinet height (Photos 3 and 4). At a minimum, keep the bottom of the face frame 2-1/2 in. above the bathroom base trim. This eliminates any trim or tile-

1 Remove the closet rod and shelf from the closet behind the bathroom wall. Cut a rough inspection hole, then check for electrical cables by peering down into the stud spaces with a flashlight. Cut horizontally between the studs 2 to 3 in. from the ceiling and the baseboard. Then cut out drywall using the studs as a guide.

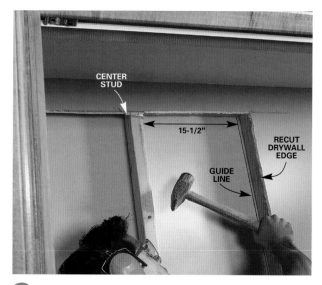

2 Draw a line along the studs on the back side of the drywall, and then use a 2-lb. maul to pound the side studs over until each opening is 15-1/2 in. wide. Use the line as a guide to tell when the stud has moved about 1 in. Pound mostly at the very top and bottom of the stud to slide it along the plates. Smaller taps between the top and bottom will loosen the grip of drywall screws or nails. Toe-screw the studs to the plates with 3-in. screws and cut off the overhanging drywall edge.

work to hassle with inside the bathroom. If using shorter cabinets, adjust the height for convenience and the best appearance.

Finishing around the cabinet backs is optional if they're in a closet. Build a separate wall (Photo 13, p. 54) or put drywall directly against the cabinet backs if desired. Lay drywall against the cabinets; don't use screws or nails because they'll penetrate the

24" CABINET CAVITY

12" CABINET CAVITY

CRIBBING

CABINET DEPTH MINUS 5"

EVEN WITH CABINET BACK

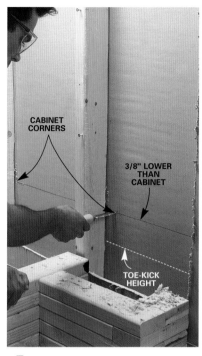

CABINET CORNERS

3/8" LOWER THAN CABINET

TOE-KICK HEIGHT

3 Subtract 5 in. from the depth of the cabinets and draw lines on the floor to mark the cabinet backs. Use the lines to position the bottom row of 2x4 cribbing. Center the middle 2x4 over the center stud so it supports both cabinets. Position the outside 2x4s even with the side studs. Overlap the rows at the corners and nail them together with 10d nails.

4 Draw level lines on the back side of the bathroom drywall to mark the top and bottom of the cabinet face. (Base the layout on the cabinet face frame. The recessed toe-kick does not protrude into the bathroom.) Poke a drywall saw through the drywall to mark the corners of each cabinet.

5 Use the corner cuts from inside the bathroom to redraw the top and bottom cuts, adding 1/4 in. to the top and bottom for wiggle room. Cut out the bathroom drywall from the bathroom side. Remove the thin strip of drywall that covers the center stud (Photo 6).

DRYWALL STRIP REMOVED

1x2 STOP BLOCK

1/2" BLOCK

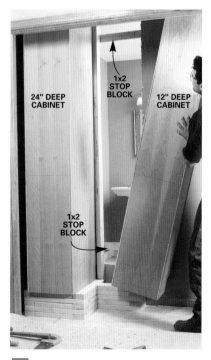

24" DEEP CABINET

1x2 STOP BLOCK

12" DEEP CABINET

1x2 STOP BLOCK

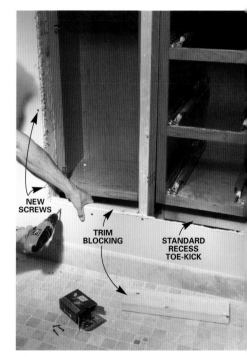

NEW SCREWS

TRIM BLOCKING

STANDARD RECESS TOE-KICK

6 Tack four 1/2-in.-thick spacer blocks about 6 in. in from the top and bottom edges of the opening, then screw 1x2 stop blocks across both bays with 3-in. screws.

7 Remove the doors, drawers and shelving from the cabinets and slip them into the stud spaces to make sure they'll fit.

8 Screw the bathroom-side drywall into the shifted studs. Push back the cabinets a few inches and screw 2x4 blocking to the drywall at the top and bottom for trim backing.

9 Rip the 3/4-in. filler strip to 1-3/4 in. wide and cut it the exact length of the cabinet face frames. Slip the filler into the opening, then place it between the cabinets. Pull the cabinets against the stop blocks.

10 Clamp the filler strip flush with the face of the cabinet frames and with the top and bottom. Shim under the cabinet bases to get the tops and bottoms aligned, if needed. Then drill pilot, clearance and screwhead countersink holes and screw both cabinets to the filler strip with 2-1/2-in. screws spaced about every 12 in.

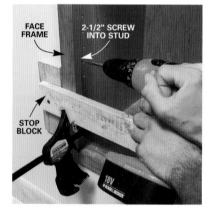

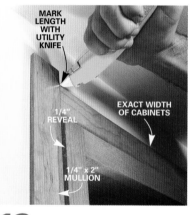

11 Hold the face frames tight against the stop blocks with clamps and screw the cabinets to the studs with 2-1/2-in. screws spaced about every 12 in. Be careful not to overtighten the screws and pull them through the cabinet sides.

12 Cut the 1/4-in.-thick x 2-in.-wide mullion strips the exact width of the top and bottom of the cabinets and nail them on with 1-1/2-in. brad nails. Then mark the side trim for length and cut and nail it to the side studs.

13 Frame 2x4 stud walls directly behind the cabinets. Nail the bottom plates into the subflooring and the top plates into the ceiling framing with 10d nails. Use construction adhesive to glue any plates and studs that join surfaces that don't have underlying framing. Hang and tape the drywall and corner bead, then paint.

tip Check the existing doorstop to make sure the knob doesn't hit the new cabinets. If a standard stop isn't adequate, use hinge- or floor-mounted stops.

cabinet backs. Instead, glue the drywall to the cabinet backs with construction adhesive and use paper-flanged corner beads that you tape on instead of nail. To minimize taping, stand the drywall sheets upright to eliminate seams to tape. Cut the drywall to fit tightly into existing drywall at walls and the ceiling, and caulk those seams with paintable caulk.

Buyer's Guide

MEDICINE AND UTILITY CABINETS: Dura Supreme Designer Series. Door style: Homestead door. Wood: Cherry. Finish: Harvest Cherry. (888) 711-3872. durasupreme.com

EZ-TOGGLE DRYWALL ANCHORS: Find them at any home center or hardware store. Smith Fastener Co., (323) 587-0382. smithfast.com

Add a behind-the-door medicine cabinet

The biggest challenge in installing a recessed cabinet is finding unobstructed stud cavities in an open wall. The wall behind the door is usually open, but make sure that pipes, ducts and wiring don't get in the way. To choose the location for the cabinet, begin by finding the studs with a stud finder. Hold the cabinet to the wall at the best height and mark the cabinet near one side of a stud. Find the exact location of that stud by sawing through the drywall until the blade is stopped. Use the cuts to define one cabinet side, and draw the cabinet outline on the wall.

Cut out the drywall and then cut off the exposed stud (Photo 2). Add the framing, then screw the cabinet to the framing (Photo 5). Add trim around the edges if necessary to conceal the rough drywall edges.

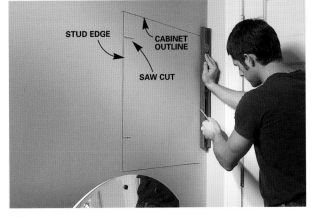

STUD EDGE · CABINET OUTLINE · SAW CUT

1 Outline the inset medicine chest to fall against a stud on one side and cut out the opening with a drywall saw.

2 Cut the intermediate stud flush with the drywall on the back side. Push it sideways to release the drywall screws on the back side and remove the stud.

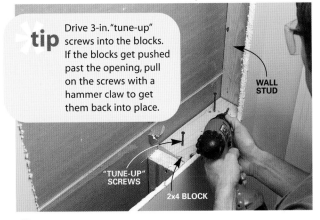

tip Drive 3-in. "tune-up" screws into the blocks. If the blocks get pushed past the opening, pull on the screws with a hammer claw to get them back into place.

WALL STUD · "TUNE-UP" SCREWS · 2x4 BLOCK

3 Screw blocking to adjacent studs at the top and bottom of the opening. Predrill when toe-screwing.

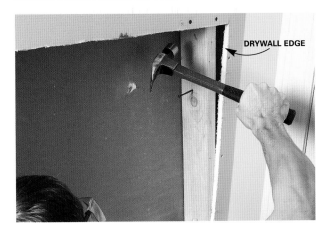

DRYWALL EDGE

4 Cut and tap in vertical backing flush with the drywall edge, then toe-screw it to the blocking.

2" SCREW

5 Slip the cabinet into the opening and anchor it with pairs of 2-in. screws. Add trim if needed.

Clutter-free
laundry room

> **tip** You can buy a sink-mounted soap dispenser in the kitchen section at home centers. Expect to pay about $12 to $25.

Soap dispenser

Get rid of that gross bar of soap that sits on the back-splash of the sink. Buy a soap dispenser at a home center and mount it to the acrylic tub. It requires a drill, a 1-1/4-in. hole saw and liquid hand soap. Keep in mind that any liquid soap can be put in the dispenser.

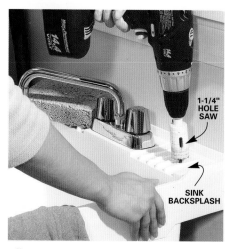

1-1/4"
HOLE
SAW

SINK
BACKSPLASH

1 Drill through the backsplash of the acrylic laundry tub with a hole saw. Measure precisely so there will be clearance for the soap bottle below. Choose a hole saw just a bit larger than the threaded base of the pump.

BASE

HOLE

RETAINING
NUT

2 Insert the threaded pump base into the hole and tighten the retaining nut to the underside of the backsplash. Fill the soap bottle with liquid soap and thread it onto the base of the pump.

Closet rod and shelf

> **tip** Get these great-looking Lido Rail chrome brackets and rod at home centers or buy them online. One source is aubuchonhardware.com.

This project saves hours of ironing and organizing. Hang up shirts and jackets as soon as they're out of the dryer—no more wrinkled shirts at the bottom of the basket. This project also gives an out-of-the-way upper shelf to store all sorts of odds and ends.

Just go to a local home center and get standard closet rod brackets, a closet rod and a precut 12-in.-deep melamine shelf (all for about $25). Also pick up some drywall anchors, or for concrete, some plastic anchors and a corresponding masonry bit. Follow the instructions in Photos 1 and 2.

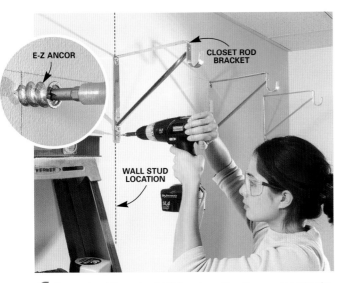

E-Z ANCOR

CLOSET ROD BRACKET

WALL STUD LOCATION

1 Draw a level line about 78 in. above the floor and locate the studs behind the drywall. Fasten at least two of the closet rod brackets into wall studs (4 ft. apart) and then center the middle bracket with two 2-in.-long screws into wall anchors (inset).

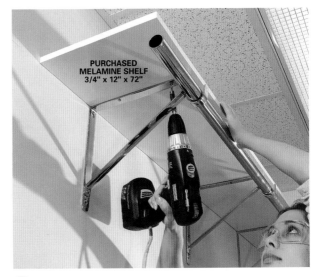

PURCHASED MELAMINE SHELF 3/4" x 12" x 72"

2 Fasten your 12-in.-deep melamine shelf onto the tops of the brackets with 1/2-in. screws. Next, insert your closet rod, drill 1/8-in. holes into the rod, and secure it to the brackets with No. 6 x 1/2-in. sheet metal screws.

tip Looking for a basic towel bar like this one? Find one at any hardware store. Expect to pay about $8.

Towel bar

Get those messy rags out of the sink and onto a towel bar so they can actually dry. Shop for an easy-mounting towel bar that can be shortened if needed. Pick one up at the hardware store or home center that has easy mounting holes right on the face of the mounting plate and a removable bar. Cut the bar to size with a hacksaw so it will fit nicely on the side of the sink. Also buy stainless steel mounting bolts, washers and acorn nuts to mount the bar. This project uses 7/8-in. No. 8-24 bolts.

ACORN NUTS

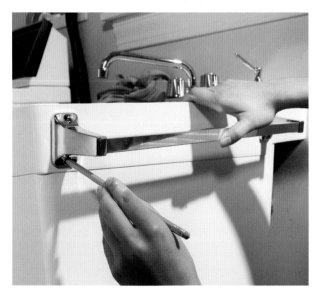

1 Mark the location of the towel bar on the thick rim near the top of the sink. Shorten the bar first by pulling the bar from the ends and trimming it to about 16 in., if needed.

ACRYLIC LAUNDRY TUB

2 Drill clearance holes at your marks and fasten the towel bar ends to the sink with bolts, washers and acorn nuts.

Undersink shelf

Tired of moving all that stuff under the sink to mop the floor? Just buy a melamine closet shelf ($5) from a home center and a length of suspended-ceiling wall angle (sorry, it only comes in 10-ft. lengths, but it's cheap and can be cut for transport). Also pick up four 1/2-in. No. 8-24 bolts, washers and nuts. Follow Photos 1 – 3.

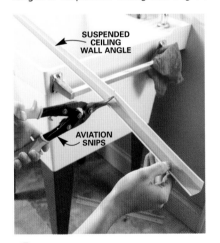

1 Using aviation snips, cut two lengths of suspended ceiling angle to support the undersink shelf.

2 Clamp pieces of ceiling angle or aluminum angle to your sink legs (about 11 in. from the floor) and drill through with a 3/16-in. bit. Insert 1/2-in.-long No. 8-24 bolts from the inside and thread on acorn nuts to cover sharp bolt edges.

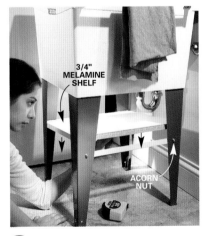

3 Cut a shelf from the 3/4-in. melamine board and drop it onto the angle braces. Notch the shelf if the sink trap is in the way. Paint the raw edges of the board to protect them from moisture.

tip Buy an easy-to-clean melamine wall cabinet from a local home center—no painting required. Expect to pay about $100.

CABINET POSITION

DRYER VENT

BACK SIDE

6" DIA. SEMICIRCLE

2" FROM BACK SIDE

BACK SIDE OF CABINET

All-purpose wall cabinet

Turn that wall space above the washer and dryer into a valuable dust-free storage space by adding a utility wall cabinet. This project shows a 54-in. wide, 24-in.-high and 12-in.-deep cabinet that's available at home centers. It's prefinished inside and out, so it'll be easy to clean.

Chances are, a dryer vent or some other obstruction exists right where the new cabinet goes. To solve this problem, simply cut away the back and insert a 4-in. galvanized duct as a liner to give the cabinet a 1-in. clearance from the dryer vent, preventing heat from building up inside the cabinet. With the liner in place, the vent is isolated behind the cabinet, keeping everything inside cool and clean. Follow the step-by-step how-to in Photos 1 – 5.

1 Draw a 6-in.-diameter circle 2 in. in from the back edge of the cabinet to correspond with the location of the dryer vent. Flip the cabinet upside down and draw the same circle to correspond with the top.

2 Cut slots 6 in. apart on the back side of the cabinet that align with the edges of the semicircles. Set the circular saw for a 2-in. depth of cut. Once the back is cut, use a jigsaw to cut along the circles at the top and bottom of the cabinet.

CIRCULAR SAW SET 2" DEEP

JIGSAW

FRAMING SQUARE

3"   3"

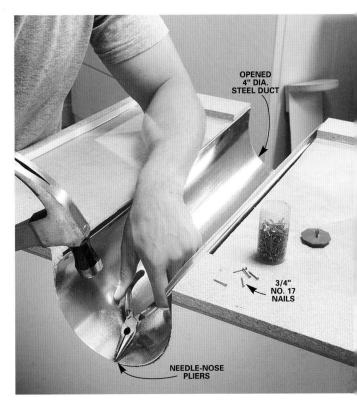

3 Nail a 4-in. steel vent pipe to the cabinet to act as a liner for the dryer vent. Use 3/4-in.-long, No. 17 wire nails. This liner will prevent heat buildup inside the cabinet and allow the contents of the cabinet to stay cool.

OPENED 4" DIA. STEEL DUCT

3/4" NO. 17 NAILS

NEEDLE-NOSE PLIERS

4 Level and screw a temporary 1x4 cleat to the wall studs with 2-1/2-in. drywall screws. The cabinet will rest on the cleat and a partner will be able to slide the cabinet left or right to align it. Once the cabinet is in place, screw it to the studs with the cabinet screws provided.

3" SCREW INTO STUD

1x4 CLEAT

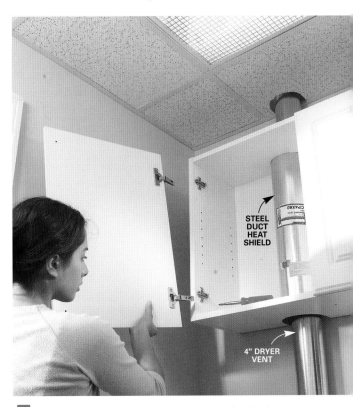

5 Reattach the cabinet doors and drill holes for the door pulls. Cut the shelves for the cabinet with a jigsaw to fit around the new heat shield.

STEEL DUCT HEAT SHIELD

4" DRYER VENT

Fold-away folding table

This 2 x 5-ft. table is a handy option for any laundry room. Located right across from the washer and dryer, it's the perfect place for sorting colors before washing and folding the clothes as soon as they're dry. This project uses heavy-duty brackets that'll hold more than 100 lbs. and neatly fold the top down (preventing future clutter).

Buy the countertop (and end cap) at a home center or salvage one from a friend who's getting new countertops. Also buy three 8-ft. pine boards—a 1x2, a 1x3 and a 1x4—as well as some wood screws. Buy 1-1/4-in. and 2-1/2-in. wood screws for mounting the wall cleats and the countertop stiffeners. Follow Photos 1 – 6 for clear step-by-step instructions.

> **tip** You'll need to order the clever fold-away brackets for this project. Get them from Rockler Hardware, (800) 279-4441, rockler.com, part No. 29819 ($25).

UNDERSIDE OF COUNTERTOP BLANK

1 Buy a 6-ft. plastic laminate countertop blank from a home center. Measure in 1-1/2 in. from the back side, and draw a straight line. Cut this section away with a circular saw equipped with a sharp blade. Trim the countertop to length, cutting from the back side. Longer tables will sag without an additional bracket. Space the brackets no farther than 32 in. apart.

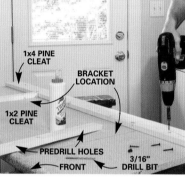

1x4 PINE CLEAT
BRACKET LOCATION
1x2 PINE CLEAT
PREDRILL HOLES
FRONT
3/16" DRILL BIT

2 Glue and screw 3/4-in.-thick pine supports to the underside of the countertop. Use a 1x4 along the back and 1x2s at the bracket locations. The supports will stiffen the countertop and provide better backing for the bracket screws.

LEVEL LINE
FOLD-AWAY BRACKET
1x3 PINE STRIP

3 Draw a level line 1-1/2 in. below the finished height of the laundry table. This one is 33 in. high including the thickness of the top. Screw 1x3 pine strips to the wall into the studs behind. For concrete walls, predrill holes for anchors and then screw the steel laundry table brackets to the strips and wall with 2-1/2-in. screws.

LEAVE 1/8" GAP AT END WALL
BRACES IN LOCKED POSITION

4 Set the top onto the brackets and screw them into the pine cleats (use 1-1/4-in. screws) under the table. Remember to keep about 1/8-in. clearance between the wall and the end for wiggle room when you lift and close the table. This will keep the wall from scarring each time the tabletop is lifted and closed.

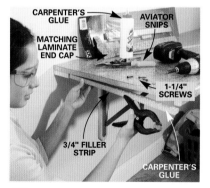

CARPENTER'S GLUE
AVIATOR SNIPS
MATCHING LAMINATE END CAP
1-1/4" SCREWS
3/4" FILLER STRIP
CARPENTER'S GLUE

5 Glue and screw the 3/4-in.-thick filler strips to the exposed bottom edge of the counter. Align the filler strip so it's flush with the edge of the top.

6 Trim the laminate end cap with an aviator snips to fit the size of the end panel. Set the iron on medium heat and slide it across the whole end panel until the glue bonds. Ease any sharp edges with a smooth-cutting metal file.

Bathroom innovations

Clutter-free bath and shower

Organizing bathroom clutter is a high priority in most houses. Sterling has found a way to maximize space in the bathtub and shower. The "Stor-ganize" bypass door system has a built-in vertical storage column with up to six removable shelves (for easy cleaning) that store up to 15 bottles, plus accessories and bath toys. Two removable hooks handle washcloths, mesh sponges and scrub brushes. It sure beats rusty shower caddies and suction cup wall brackets.

Mount the integrated storage column on the left- or right-hand side of the bypass door. The door systems are available for bathtubs and showers. They're sold at Sterling distributors (find them on the Web site) and many home centers.

Sterling, (888) 783-7546. sterlingplumbing.com

Double the space on towel bars

Convenience Concepts' Double-Up Towel Bar fits (without fasteners) over an existing towel bar to hold twice the number of towels—but without taking up twice the wall space. Put nice decorative towels on the mounted towel bar (where they won't get used), then place everyday towels on the double-up bar for drying hands.

Two sizes are available, 18 in. and 24 in. They cost $4.50 and $5, respectively, plus shipping. The bars are available in white or chrome. To buy them, call the manufacturer.

Convenience Concepts, (847) 931-9902.

EXISTING TOWEL BAR

DOUBLE-UP TOWEL BAR

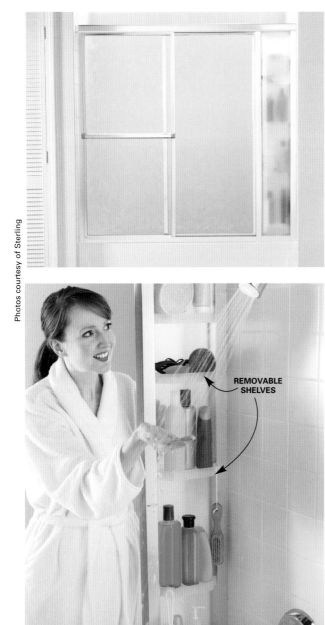

REMOVABLE SHELVES

Photos courtesy of Sterling

Hang it
straight, level & solid

Hang pictures straight and level

The first challenge in hanging a picture is deciding exactly where to put it. Most experts recommend hanging a picture with its center about 60 in. from the floor, or its bottom edge 6 to 8 in. above a piece of furniture. Use these heights as a starting point. Then adjust the position of the picture, and mark the top center with the corner of a sticky note. Use the technique shown in Photos 2 – 6 to complete the job.

A group of pictures is trickier. First cut out paper patterns and arrange them on the wall with low-adhesive masking tape. The temporary red line from a laser level is helpful for aligning a series of photos level with one another (Photo 1). The laser level is ideal because it gives a perfectly straight line without having to mark up the walls. A standard carpenter's level will also work.

When the grouping looks pleasing, mark the top center of each pattern with the corner of a sticky note (Photo 1). Use the bottom corner of each sticky note as a reference point for locating the picture hangers.

Then position the picture hangers (Photos 2 – 4). Use two hangers for each picture for extra support and to help keep the picture from tipping. Choose picture hangers that are rated to support the weight of the art. The best bet is to use professional hangers like the one shown at right. They work fine in drywall. These are available at home centers or from most picture-framing shops. OOK is one popular brand. Plaster may not support pictures as well as drywall does. To hang heavier art on plaster walls, use picture hangers with double or triple nails.

PRO-STYLE PICTURE HOOK

Photos 2 and 3 show how to measure the space between the hangers and the distance from the top of the picture frame. The distance between hangers isn't critical. Just use fingers to space several inches from the outside edges of the picture frame. Transfer these measurements to the wall (Photo 4). An inexpensive level with inches marked along the edge is a great picture-hanging tool (Photo 4). Otherwise, just stick masking tape to the edge of a level and transfer measurements to the tape (Photo 2, p. 66). Then line up the *bottom* of the hooks with the marks and drive the picture-hanger nails through the angled guides on the hooks (Photo 5).

1 Project a level line and tape exact-size paper patterns on the wall. Mark the top center of each pattern with the corner of a sticky note.

Labels: LASER LEVEL, CENTER MARK, PAPER PATTERN

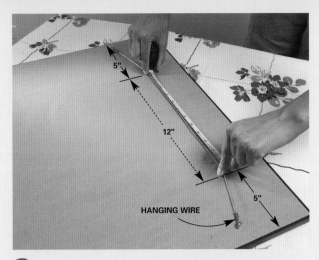

2 Stretch the hanger wire with two fingers spaced equally distant from the edges of the picture frame. Keep the wire parallel to the top of the frame. Measure the distance between your fingertips.

Labels: 5", 12", 5", HANGING WIRE

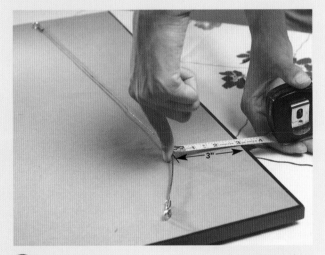

3 Leave one finger in place and measure from the wire to the top. Use this dimension and the dimension from Photo 2 to position the picture hangers.

Label: 3"

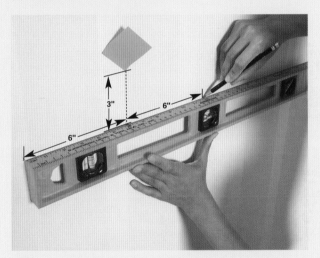

4 Find the hanger positions by measuring down from the sticky note and to each side from center. Keep the hangers level.

Labels: 3", 6", 6"

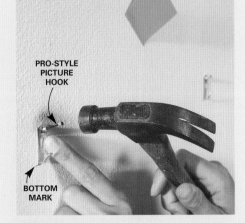

5 Align the bottom edge of a picture hook with the mark and drive a nail through the hook's guide.

Labels: PRO-STYLE PICTURE HOOK, BOTTOM MARK

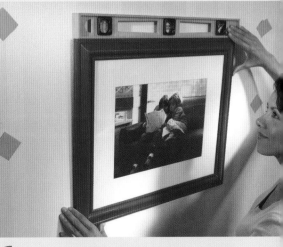

6 Slip the wire over both hooks. Slide the picture sideways across the wires until it's level. Use the same process to hang the remaining pictures.

tip

Before hanging the picture, stick a pair of clear rubber bumpers on the back lower corners of the frame to protect the wall and help keep the picture level. They're available with the picture hanging supplies or in the cabinet hardware department (they're called "picture frame bumpers").

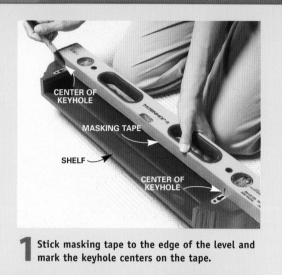

1 Stick masking tape to the edge of the level and mark the keyhole centers on the tape.

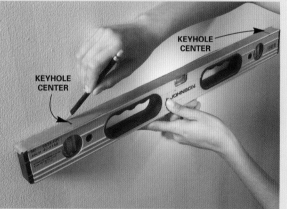

2 Place the level against the wall at the desired shelf height. Adjust it to level it and mark the wall at the two keyhole locations.

Align keyhole-slot shelves

Many light-duty shelves have keyholes in the back. The keyholes slide over protruding screws for support. The trick is to precisely place the screws so they align with the keyholes.

Photos 1 – 5 shows a foolproof method that doesn't require any measuring or math. Photo 2 shows a trick for transferring the keyhole locations to the wall. If the mounting screw locations don't land over studs, use wall anchors to support the shelf. This project shows using a slick toggle-type anchor that holds 60 to 100 lbs. and is easy to install. This brand, Snaptoggle, is available at most home centers (find them online at www.toggler.com). Make sure the screw heads supplied with the anchor fit the keyhole slot before installing the anchor. Otherwise go to a smaller size anchor.

Drill holes for the anchors at each mark and mount the anchors in the wall. Let the screws protrude enough for the keyholes to slide over them. Test-fit the shelf by aligning the keyholes with the screws and sliding it down. If the shelf won't slide on or is too loose, remove the shelf and adjust the screws until you get a snug fit.

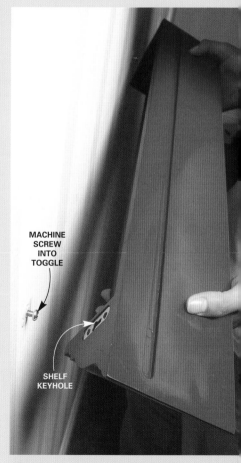

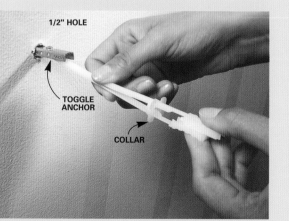

3 Drill a hole into the drywall at each mark and slip the toggle through the hole. Push in the plastic collar tight to the drywall.

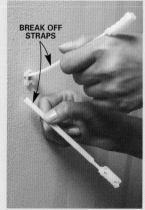

4 Then break off the straps flush with the collar.

5 Drive the included machine screw into the toggle, letting it protrude about 3/16 in. Test-fit the shelf.

Hang a quilt without damaging it

One good way to display a quilt is to hang it on a wall. But don't just tack it up by the corners or it'll stretch out of shape. Instead, use this method for hanging quilts or other decorative textiles because it distributes the weight evenly for smooth hanging and minimal stress to the fabric. The hand stitching (Photo 1) used in this method doesn't damage the quilt because it only goes through the backing, and it's easy to remove.

Measure the top edge of the quilt and purchase the same lengths of 1-1/2-in.-wide sew-on hook-and-loop fastener strip and 2-1/2-in.-wide cotton or synthetic webbing. The hook-and-loop strip is available at a fabric store and the webbing at an upholsterer's shop. The project requires a length of 1-1/2-in.-wide pine or poplar, a staple gun and several 2-1/2-in. wood screws.

Photos 1 – 3 show how to prepare and hang the quilt. If the quilt pattern allows, it's best to rotate the quilt 180 degrees every month or so. This relieves stress on the fabric and helps prevent uneven fading. To be able to rotate the quilt, sew another strip of hook-and-loop along the opposite edge.

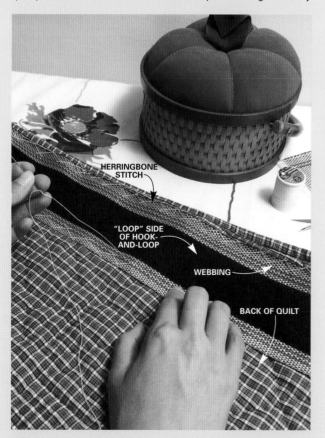

HERRINGBONE STITCH

"LOOP" SIDE OF HOOK-AND-LOOP

WEBBING

BACK OF QUILT

1 Sew the loop side of the hook-and-loop to the webbing. Then stitch the webbing to the back of the quilt using a herringbone stitch as shown.

STUD LOCATION

HOOK SIDE OF HOOK-AND-LOOP

1/4" STAPLE

2-1/2" SCREW

3/4" x 1-1/2" WOOD STRIP

2 Staple the hook side of the hook-and-loop to the wood strip. Determine the best position, and level the wood strip and screw it to the studs.

3 Hang the quilt by smoothing the hook-and-loop tape that's sewn on the back of the quilt along the tape stapled to the wood strip.

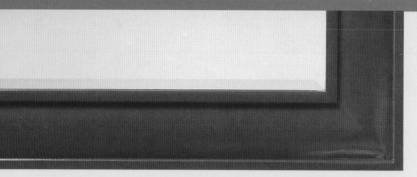

Hang heavy mirrors with confidence

Take extra precautions when hanging a heavy mirror. If the mirror has a hanging wire on the back, remove it and instead screw D-rings to the frame (Photo 1). (Mirrors without frames should be hung with special mirror hangers.) Locate the D-rings an equal distance from the top of the frame, about one-third of the total height down. Then measure the exact distance between the centers of the D-rings (Photo 1). The trick is to hook the tape measure on one edge of a D-ring, and measure to the same edge of the second D-ring. Record this measurement. Then measure down to the top of the D-rings (Photo 2).

Photo 3 shows how to transfer the measurements to the wall. But first hold the mirror up to the wall and choose the best position. Start with the center of the mirror at about 60 in. from the floor. When it's in position, mark the top center with a sticky note.

Some picture hangers are rated to support heavy mirrors, but it's safer to install strong hollow-wall anchors instead, like the screw-in type anchor shown at left. It's rated to support 40 lbs. Weigh the mirror and choose the appropriate type of anchor. Use toggle-type anchors (Photo 3, p. 62) for heavier mirrors. Measure from the reference point to position the anchors (Photo 3, p. 65). Make starter holes with an awl or Phillips screwdriver. If the awl hits a stud, simply drive a screw. Photo 5 shows how to hang the mirror. If the top doesn't end up level, wrap a few turns of electrical tape around the D-ring on the low side to raise that side slightly.

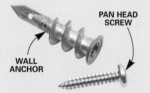

WALL ANCHOR
PAN HEAD SCREW

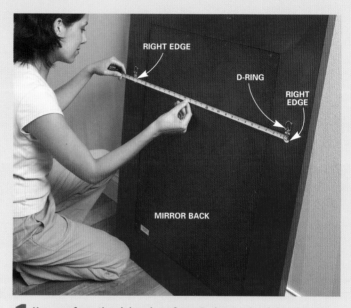

RIGHT EDGE
D-RING
RIGHT EDGE
MIRROR BACK

1 Measure from the right edge of one D-ring to the right edge of the second D-ring to find the exact distance between the centers of the hanging D-rings.

TOP EDGE OF MIRROR
TOP OF D-RING

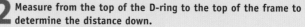

2 Measure from the top of the D-ring to the top of the frame to determine the distance down.

Hanging tips for difficult wall surfaces

It's usually not hard to hang things on drywall. It's easy to drive nails, and studs are simple to locate. Other types of walls present unique challenges. Plaster is harder than drywall and can crumble. But the pros say as long as professional picture hangers are used (like the ones shown here, which have sharper nails and built-in angle guides), and the hangers are a little larger than required, the project will turn out fine. In brick or stone, drive a thin nail into the space between the mortar and the brick or stone. In brick, stone and concrete, avoid making large holes because they're virtually impossible to hide if the picture is moved. A good method for brick, stone or concrete walls is to drill a hole that's slightly smaller than the threaded part of a drywall screw. Use a masonry bit in a hammer drill and drill the hole at a slight downward angle. Then thread the screw into the hole, leaving about 1/4 in. sticking out for use as a hanger.

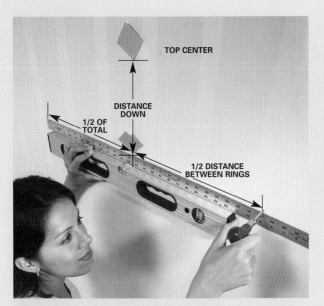

3 Use a level and a ruler to plumb down the correct distance. Mark the spot with the corner of a sticky note. Then use the level and ruler to find the exact hanger positions.

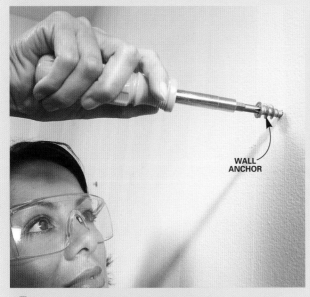

4 Make a starter hole in the drywall at each hook location. Then, drive a wall anchor into each hole.

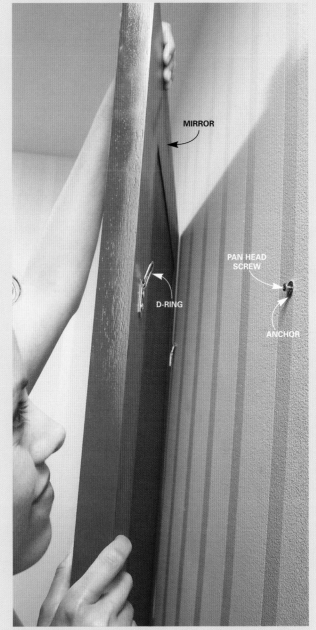

5 Screw a pan head screw into the anchor. Leave the screw sticking out about 1/4 in. Hook the D-rings onto the protruding screws.

Hang anything
quickly and easily

H ere are five hollow wall anchors that cover a range of weight requirements from lightweight knickknack shelves all the way up to heavy-duty utility shelf brackets. Of course, it's always best to anchor into solid wood, but for those situations where it just isn't possible, these five anchors will provide superior holding power with the least amount of hassle.

Pictures and mirrors

S pecial plastic anchors are available for hanging heavy mirrors and pictures, but they leave a sizable hole to repair if relocating the object. The best choice is to do what the pros do. Choose a picture hanger based on the weight of the picture or mirror. The triple nail version shown here holds up to 100 lbs., more than enough for even the heaviest mirrors. Or, just use a pair of them spaced about a foot apart for an extra margin of safety. Using picture hangers in pairs like this also prevents the picture or mirror from tipping if it slides on the hanging wire. This type of hanger is available in most full-service hardware stores and home centers or at picture framing shops. They range in price from about 29¢ to $2 for the triple nail version shown here (the OOK 100-lb. picture hanger; see the Buyer's Guide on p. 74).

100-LB.
CAPACITY
PICTURE
HANGER

1 Slide the small nails (included) through the angled hole and tap them into the wall with a hammer. To remove the hanger, grab the end of the nail with a pliers and twist it out.

Light-duty shelving

Most lightweight shelves like the one shown come with expanding plastic anchors, but don't rely on them. Instead, use these self-drilling, screw-in type anchors. They're rated to hold about 30 to 50 lbs. each (depending on the size) and take only seconds to install. These anchors (metal or plastic versions) work great for hanging small shelves and other decorative items that aren't subject to much use and don't have to support a lot of weight. On a ceiling, don't use these anchors to hang anything heavier than a smoke detector.

The anchors can be screwed in by hand with a No. 2 Phillips screwdriver, but a drill with a No. 2 driver bit works better. Slow the drill to a crawl as soon as the large threads engage in the drywall. Then carefully turn the fastener until the face is almost flush. Overtightening will damage the drywall and compromise the holding power. These same precautions apply to the screw. Turn it in slowly and stop as soon as the screw is snug to the object. Overtightening will strip the threads. If the anchor loosens and spins, back it out and replace it with a toggle-type anchor in the same hole. The Buildex E-Z Ancor self-drilling drywall anchors work great (see the Buyer's Guide on p. 74).

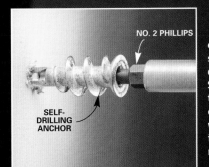

NO. 2 PHILLIPS

SELF-DRILLING ANCHOR

1 Center the anchor point on the mark and spin it in with a drill or by hand. Slow down when the large threads engage, and stop when the anchor is snug and nearly flush.

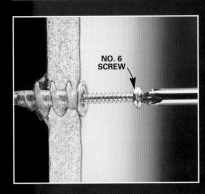

NO. 6 SCREW

2 Slowly drive a No. 6 screw into the anchor. For shelves like this with keyhole mounting, leave enough space behind the screwhead for the metal keyhole to slip over.

Heavy shelves

It's best to locate a stud or other framing member to mount shelf brackets that support heavy weight. But if mounting a shelf bracket on drywall, use these Toggler anchors. They're easier to use and stronger than standard wing-type toggle bolts. Plus, they allow removing the machine screw without losing the toggle inside the wall, which allows mounting items that may occasionally need to be taken down and reinstalled.

The only drawbacks to Toggler bolts are that they're a little harder to find and slightly more expensive than standard "molly" bolts. The Hilti brand Toggler bolts at a local home center ($8 for a package of 10) work great. If the local hardware store or home center doesn't carry them, see the Buyer's Guide on p. 74 for online and mail order sources. The photos below show how to install Toggler bolts.

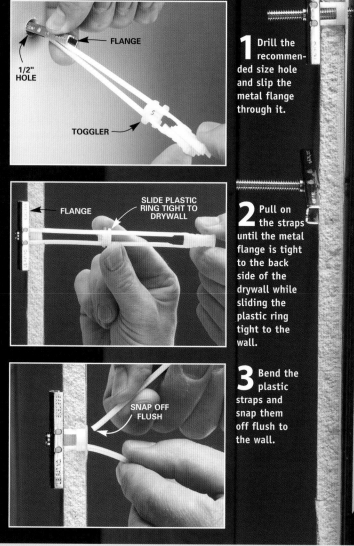

FLANGE

1/2" HOLE

TOGGLER

1 Drill the recommended size hole and slip the metal flange through it.

FLANGE

SLIDE PLASTIC RING TIGHT TO DRYWALL

2 Pull on the straps until the metal flange is tight to the back side of the drywall while sliding the plastic ring tight to the wall.

SNAP OFF FLUSH

3 Bend the plastic straps and snap them off flush to the wall.

Medium-duty shelves and racks

Most shelf brackets and standards have several mounting holes, so the combined strength of many fasteners will support them. But they require an anchor that won't pull out of the wall when tightening the screw. Plastic toggles meet both of these requirements. They're rated to support about 30 to 50 lbs. each and are designed to prevent pullout by hooking the backside of the drywall.

Drill a hole for these anchors. Hold the shelf standard at the right height and use a level to align it vertically (plumb). Mark the hole locations with a sharp pencil. Drill the recommended hole size (3/8 in. for these 5/8-in. Kwik-Tog anchors) at each mark. Then install the anchors as shown in the photos. Some types of plastic toggles require you to "pop" them out after sliding them into the hole. Take care not to overtighten the screws or the plastic will strip and the screw won't hold. See the Buyer's Guide for more information on the Hilti Kwik-Tog anchor.

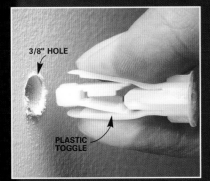

3/8" HOLE

PLASTIC TOGGLE

1 Drill a hole sized to the anchor. Then fold the anchor's wings flat and push it through the hole.

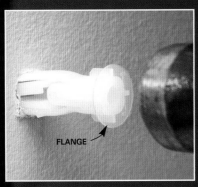

FLANGE

2 Tap the anchor gently until the flange rests against the wall.

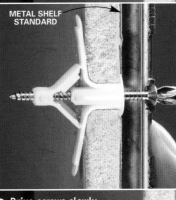

METAL SHELF STANDARD

3 Drive screws slowly through the standard into the anchors. Stop as soon as the screw is snug to the standard and the standard is snug to the wall.

Curtain rod brackets, towel bars and coat hooks

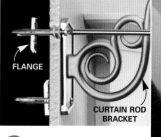

Curtain rod brackets dangling from loose anchors or towel bars pulled out of the wall are all too common. That's because the plastic anchors usually provided just aren't up to the task. Buy some of these slick, self-drilling metal toggles instead. At about $1 each, they're not cheap. But they're easy to install and hold like crazy. Simply screw them in at the desired locations (Photo1). Then while tightening the mounting screw, the metal flange flips out and is drawn tight to the back side of the drywall. The object can be removed for painting, and the anchor will remain in the wall, ready for reuse.

The only drawback to these anchors is that they require using the screw provided or one with the same type of thread. This may mean abandoning the decorative screws included with the hardware. The screwheads may need to be spray-painted to match, or a decorative screw with the same threads may need to be located.

Install these toggles just like their smaller cousins (see photos on p. 71). But make sure to probe the wall first to determine if there's room for the metal flange to flip open. The E-Z Toggle shown here has arrows on the face to show the alignment of the flange when it opens. This is handy if there are two toggles close together. It keeps the flanges from clashing and prevents the flange from hitting a stud that's close to the edge of the toggle. Turn the E-Z Toggle in or out slightly to adjust the orientation of the metal flange. See Buyer's Guide below for more information on Buildex E-Z Toggle self-drilling drywall toggle bolts.

E-Z TOGGLE

FLANGE

NO. 2 PHILLIPS DRIVER

1 Mark the mounting holes and drive an E-Z Toggle in at each mark. Slow down as soon as the threads engage in the drywall. Slowly tighten the toggle until it's snug and nearly flush.

FLANGE

CURTAIN ROD BRACKET

2 Slide the screw through the bracket and thread it into the anchor. Tighten the screw to draw the metal flange against the back of the drywall.

4 tips for choosing anchors

1. Before shopping for anchors, probe to determine the thickness of the covering, the depth of the cavity and any obstructions. Drill a 1/8-in. hole through the drywall or plaster at the anchor locations. Bend a 1-in. long, 90-degree hook on the end of a coat hanger and slide it through the hole. Twirl it to feel for obstructions. Push it all the way in and make a mark flush to the wall with a marker or tape. Now pull it tight to the back side of the wall covering and make a second mark. Remove the wire and measure from the bend to your marks to determine the thickness of the wall covering and the depth of the cavity.
2. Check the anchor package to see what type and thickness of wall the anchors work in. Some plastic toggles have a grip range of

3/8 in. to 1/2 in. and won't work on plaster walls that are 3/4 in. thick. Most anchors are available in a number of sizes with different "grip ranges."
3. Some anchors come with sheet metal screws, but a similar size wood screw or drywall screw can usually be substituted. Metal toggles, on the other hand, only accept screws that match their threads. If screws are provided with the anchors, check the package for the "maximum fixture thickness." If using the decorative screws that are included with the item being installed, look for an anchor that will work with those screws.
4. Make sure there's room in the wall. Choose the anchor carefully if mounting to exterior basement walls, walls in manufac-

tured homes or other unusual wall types. Metal toggles require a certain amount of depth and space for the toggle to flip open. They can't be used in thin walls or walls with rigid foam insulation.

Buyer's Guide

The anchors are available in home centers and full-service hardware stores, or contact the manufacturer listed below for a retailer.

Hilti: (800) 879-8000, hilti.com. Kwik-Tog plastic toggles, Toggler brand toggle bolts and other Hilti brand drywall anchors.

Impex Systems Group Inc.: (800) 933-0163, ooks.com. OOK picture hanger.

ITW Buildex: (800) 284-5339, 1itwbuildex.com. E-Z Toggle self-drilling toggle bolts and E-Z Ancor self-drilling drywall anchors.

Photo positioning tip 1

To hang a picture frame right where you want it, make a guide for your nail. Tape over the head of a thumbtack or stick the head on double-faced tape right under the picture's mounting bracket. Hold the picture in place and push on the frame until the tack's point pricks the wall. Now you have a tiny mark to show you where to place your hanging nail.

POSITION
AND PUSH

Photo positioning tip 2

Here's a nifty way to mark nail hole positions on walls when you're hanging that new picture. Glue two pushpins top to top with a cyano-acrylate glue (such as Super Glue). Find the center of the picture along the upper back edge of the frame and press in one of the pins. Now just hold the picture up, maneuver it to the best spot, and press in to mark for the nail. This tip works best when you're hanging pictures with hardware screwed on the back of the frame, but if you're putting up wire-hung pictures, just measure the distance from the top of the wire to the pushpin hole and move the nail down that distance.

GLUE TOP TO TOP

Perfect keyhole template

When you're installing a wall hanging that has keyhole slots on the back, create a template to help you position the wall screws. Lay a piece of paper over the slots and do a pencil rubbing à la Sherlock Holmes. Level and tape the guide to the wall. Mark the top of the keyholes with a nail and your screws will be in perfect position.

Easy picture hanging

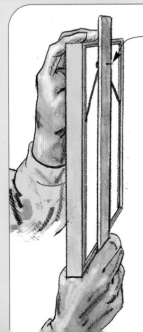

BRAD

Sometimes slack in the picture wire makes it hard to figure out exactly where to put the nail when you're hanging a picture. Here's an easy solution. Put a brad through a stick, hang your picture on the brad, hold it where you want it, then push in on the stick to mark the wall.

Soda-tab picture hanger

The photo says it all! These hangers work great for pictures and even small shelves, and you can't beat the price!

The key to keeping bedrooms and closets organized is having enough space for all of your clothes—and making them easy to find when you're ready to wear them. This chapter features projects that will increase your storage space and utilize every inch of your closets.

Chapter 3

organize
your
bedroom
& closets

His and hers
closet organizer

Annoyed by an overstuffed closet packed so tightly that favorite shirts and shoes get lost? Where the closet rod bends under the weight of all of "his" and "her" clothing?

If so, this simple closet organizing system is a great solution. It utilizes the closet space much more efficiently by dividing the closet into zones that give slacks, dresses, shirts, shoes and other items their own home. As a result, clothing is better organized. It also prevents "closet creep," where "her" clothing tends to infringe on "his" zone (or vice versa!). Overall, this

project doubles the useful space of a traditional single pole and shelf closet.

This section shows how to build this simple organizer, step-by-step, and how to customize it to fit closets of different sizes.

Don't buy it—build it!

While it's tempting to buy a prefabricated organizer, it's surprisingly expensive after tallying up the cost of all the pieces. The materials for this organizer cost only $150. It uses 1-1/2 sheets of oak veneer plywood, plus several types of stan-

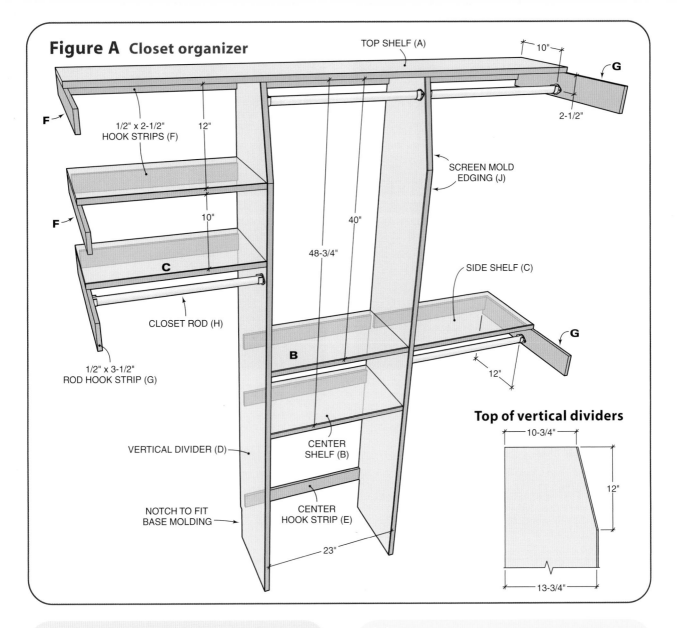

Figure A Closet organizer

TOP SHELF (A)

10"

G

F

1/2" x 2-1/2"
HOOK STRIPS (F)

12"

2-1/2"

SCREEN MOLD
EDGING (J)

F

10"

40"

C

48-3/4"

SIDE SHELF (C)

CLOSET ROD (H)

G

1/2" x 3-1/2"
ROD HOOK STRIP (G)

B

12"

VERTICAL DIVIDER (D)

CENTER
SHELF (B)

Top of vertical dividers

10-3/4"

12"

NOTCH TO FIT
BASE MOLDING

CENTER
HOOK STRIP (E)

23"

13-3/4"

Materials list

Item	Qty.	Item	Qty.
3/4" x 4' x 8' sheets of oak plywood	1-1/2	1/4" x 3/4" x 8' screen molding	4
1/2" x 2-1/2" hook strip	24'	1-1/16" closet rod	8'
1/2" x 3-1/2" hook strip	9'	Pairs of rod holders	4
		6d finishing nails	1 lb.

Cutting list

Key	Qty.	Size & description
A	1	3/4" x 10-3/4" x closet length, plywood (top shelf)
B	2	3/4" x 13-1/2" x 23" plywood (center shelves)
C	3	3/4" x 13-1/2" x measured length plywood (side shelves)
D	2	3/4" x 13-3/4" x 82" plywood (vertical dividers)
E	4	1/2" x 2-1/2" x 23" (center hook strips)
F	7	1/2" x 2-1/2" x measured lengths (hook strips)
G	3	1/2" x 3-1/2" x closet depth (hook strips for rods)
H	4	1-1/16" x measured lengths (closet rods)
J		1/4" x 3/4" x measured lengths (screen molding)

dard oak trim available at most home centers and lumberyards. (See the Materials list above.) Keep in mind that other wood species may not have matching trim, and may need to be custom-cut from solid boards on a table saw. If painting the organizer, use less expensive plywood and trim to cut expenses by about one-third.

Begin by measuring the width of the closet. This system works best in a 6-ft. closet. If the closet only measures 5 ft., consider using a single vertical divider, rather than the two shown in Figure A, above.

1 Measure the closet dimensions and cut the plywood vertical dividers and shelves to size (Figure A, p. 79). Use a guide to make crosscuts perfectly square.

2 Measure the baseboard height and thickness and cut notches with a jigsaw on the vertical dividers to fit over it.

Assemble the center unit

After referring to the Cutting list and the closet dimensions, rip the plywood into two 13-3/4-in. pieces for the vertical dividers. If planning to rip plywood with a circular saw, be sure to use a straightedge to get perfectly straight cuts. This project uses hook strips to attach the center unit and shelves to the closet walls, as well as for spacing the uprights (Figure A, p. 79). To save a bit of cash, rip these strips from the leftover plywood (and enjoy the gratification that comes from using the entire sheet). Cut the plywood to length using a factory plywood edge as a guide (Photo 1). Always check for accuracy by just nicking the plywood with the blade to make sure the blade hits the mark. Fully support the project with 2x4s so the cutoff doesn't fall and splinter. Also, for smoother cuts, use a sharp blade with at least 40 teeth.

> **tip** To make perfect crosscuts on plywood, score the pencil line with a utility knife. This gives a finer cut with less splintering of the veneer.

Cutting out the baseboard in the closet or even trimming the back side of the dividers to fit the profile of the baseboard isn't necessary. The back of the organizer will be mostly out of sight, so square notches will do (Photo 2).

Trim the tops of the dividers back to 10-3/4 in. to make it easier to slide stuff onto the top shelf (unless it's an extra-deep closet). This cut is angled to be flush with the top shelf (Figure A).

Apply the screen molding to hide the raw plywood edges on the dividers and shelves. Cut a 7-degree angle on the molding with a circular saw, jigsaw or miter saw to get a perfect fit on the dividers. Cut this angle first and when it's a nice fit, cut the other ends to length. Another option is to apply edge veneer (iron-on) or any other 3/4-in. wood strips to cover the edges.

Now sand all the parts to prepare them for finishing. A random orbital sander (starting at about $50) with 120-grit sandpaper will make quick work of this, but a few squares of sandpaper and a wood block will also do the trick. After sanding, wipe the surface of the wood with a clean cloth to remove dust.

It's easiest to apply the finish before assembly. This project shows a warm fruitwood-tone Danish Finishing Oil. This type of finish brings out the natural grain of the wood, looks velvety smooth, and is easy to renew when scratched or scuffed. Use a small cloth to rub a generous amount of oil into the surface until the plywood and hook strips have an even sheen, and allow it to dry overnight.

After the finish oil dries, assemble the center unit. Lightly mark the vertical dividers where the interior shelves and hook strips will be positioned and drill 1/8-in. pilot holes to simplify the nailing. Then spread a thin bead of glue onto the shelf ends and clamp the unit together. Use four 6d finish nails to pin the shelves securely (Photo 4), then countersink the nail heads with a nail set. Nails and glue are strong enough for holding garments and other light items, but to support extra-heavy loads, put a cleat under the shelf to bear the weight.

Position one of the center unit's interior hook strips at the very top of the dividers and one above the bottom notches, and one under each shelf. The strips will shore up the unit and keep the plywood from bowing when it's installed.

In the closet

If there's a thin carpet and pad in the closet, place the center unit directly on top of it. However, if there's a plush rug with a soft padding, stability is a concern. After determining the exact placement of the unit (by centering the unit on the midpoint of the closet; Photo 5), mark and cut out two 3/4-in.-wide slots in the

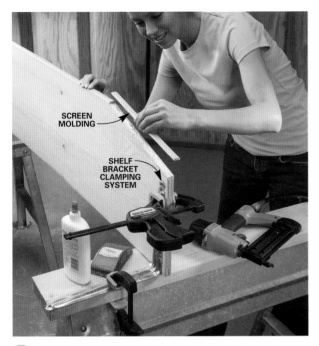

SCREEN MOLDING

SHELF BRACKET CLAMPING SYSTEM

3 Smooth the cut plywood edges with 80-grit sandpaper and a block, then glue and tack 3/4-in. screen molding onto the edges that will show. Apply a stain or finish and let it dry.

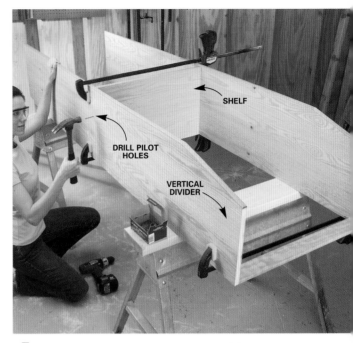

SHELF

DRILL PILOT HOLES

VERTICAL DIVIDER

4 Lay out the intermediate shelf positions with a square, spread glue on the shelf edges and nail the shelf to the dividers with 6d finish nails. Nail the 1/2-in. hook strips to the dividers as well.

CENTER OF UNIT

CENTER OF CLOSET

WALL STUD

5 Set the center unit in the closet, level it with shims, predrill and tack the hook strips to the wall studs with 6d finish nails.

HOOK STRIPS

6 Level the hook strips with the top of the dividers, then predrill and nail them to the studs. Continue the strip around the closet sides.

carpet and pad so the dividers rest on the solid floor below.

Find the studs using a stud finder and mark them with masking tape. Also measure and mark the center of the wall on tape. This avoids marking up the walls. Set the unit in its position against the wall. Level

and shim as necessary (Photo 5).

Predrill the hook strips with a 1/8-in. bit, then nail the unit to the studs. Level and nail on the remaining hook strips (Photo 6), starting with wider hook strips along the side walls to accommodate the hanging rod hardware (Figure A and Photo 8, p. 82).

tip When gluing and nailing the screen molding (Photo 3), have a damp cloth handy to promptly wipe away any glue ooze.

TOP SHELF

ROD HOLDER

ROD HOLDER

WIDE HOOK STRIP

7 Trim the top shelf ends to fit the side walls, drop the shelf into place, and nail it to the tops of the vertical dividers and to the hook strip with 6d nails.

8 Sand the cut edge of the side shelves to prepare them for glue. Determine the exact shelf placement and drill pilot holes. Spread glue on the shelf end and secure it with 6d nails.

tip Reduce bowing by storing plywood sheets flat rather than leaning them up on an edge.

The inside walls of the closet will never be perfectly square because of the mudding and taping of the drywall corners. Measure the closet width and cut the shelf to the widest dimension, then tilt the shelf into position. At the corners, mark a trim line along each end to achieve a snug fit (Photo 7).

Getting the top shelf over the central unit and onto the hook strips may take some finagling. Once the shelf rests squarely, drill pilot holes and nail it into the tops of the dividers and the hook strips (Photo 7).

Clothes rods and hardware

To avoid working around shelves, install all the closet rod hardware before putting in the side shelves.

The hardware for the closet rods should be positioned about 1-1/2 to 2 in. down from the shelf above and about 10 to 12 in. from the back wall. In this closet, the top rods hang 10 in. from the back, which is good for pants, and the bottom rods, for shirts and blouses, at 12 in. To make the top rod 12 in. out, make the top shelf 12 in. wide and trim less off the top of the vertical dividers.

Installing side shelves

To best secure the side shelves, sand the cut edge that will be in contact with the center unit with 100-grit paper. This will break up any finishing oil and provide a cleaner surface for the glue.

Lay out the remaining shelves on their side wall hook strips and use a level to determine their exact position on the center unit.

Mark and drill the pilot holes through the center unit, then lift out the shelf and apply a thin bead of glue. To prevent smearing, put the center unit side in first while tipping up the wall side of the shelf. Keep a cloth handy to wipe up the inevitable glue smudges.

Nail the shelves in place and start filling up the closet!

Buyer's Guide

The shoe cabinets shown on the doors are available for $15 at IKEA stores. For help locating the nearest IKEA store, visit ikea.com.

The drawers and clothes hampers shown are available at Storables locations. Look for similar items at other organization stores and discount stores.

Protect prime space

Bedroom closet space is valuable real estate, and the only way to protect it is to store off-season or rare-occasion clothing elsewhere. Place those clothes in garment bags, plastic bins or a freestanding wardrobe to free up your closet.

Many mid-century homes have closets on the main level that are 4-1/2 ft. deep or better, and they're perfect candidates for off-season storage. Deep closets can fit double rods mounted parallel to each other in the front and back. It's an ideal setup for tightly stashing off-season outfits. Add a rolling bin on the closet floor to store accessories, beachwear or ski gloves in Ziploc Big Bags. This keeps the bedroom closet clear and active gear at hand.

Wood closet
storage system

It's surprisingly easy and economical to squeeze more storage out of limited space. Discover how to remodel a standard 8-ft.-long, 30-in.-deep closet, a size that's found in millions of homes. Here's how to maximize that space.

Cabinet module: The 2-ft.-wide, 23-in.-deep, 78-in.-tall cabinet module is designed to provide extra drawer and shelving space. The unit is mounted 6 in. above the floor for easy cleaning. The mounting height also makes installation easier because it eliminates removing and reinstalling carpeting or baseboards.

Clothes rods: Rod capacity is maximized because the rods are double-stacked at one end of the closet for shorter clothes like shirts and skirts. The single rod at the other end of the closet is for slacks and dresses.

Shoe shelves: A two-tier shoe shelf tames shoe scatter. Including the space under the shelves, there's 9 luxurious feet of shoe storage—enough for even those beat-up, knockabout shoes.

Custom-build the closet system

It's easy to upgrade the typical single rod and shelf found in standard closets for more efficient "closetry." Home centers offer several lines of mix-and-match

Figure A Closet assembly

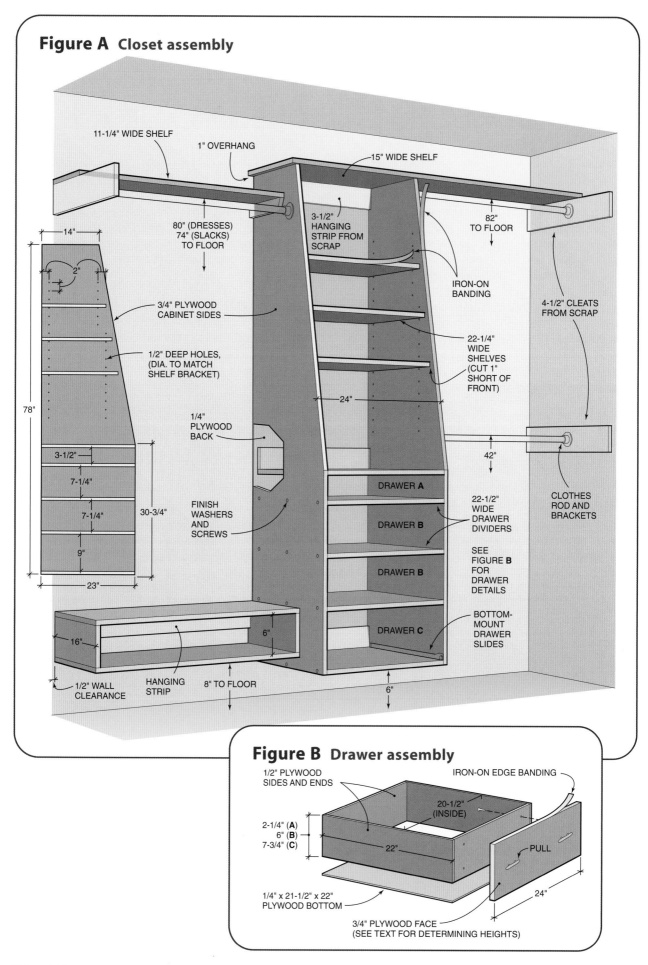

11-1/4" WIDE SHELF

1" OVERHANG

15" WIDE SHELF

3-1/2" HANGING STRIP FROM SCRAP

82" TO FLOOR

IRON-ON BANDING

4-1/2" CLEATS FROM SCRAP

80" (DRESSES) 74" (SLACKS) TO FLOOR

3/4" PLYWOOD CABINET SIDES

14"

2"

1/2" DEEP HOLES, (DIA. TO MATCH SHELF BRACKET)

22-1/4" WIDE SHELVES (CUT 1" SHORT OF FRONT)

24"

78"

1/4" PLYWOOD BACK

3-1/2"

7-1/4"

7-1/4"

30-3/4"

9"

42"

CLOTHES ROD AND BRACKETS

FINISH WASHERS AND SCREWS

DRAWER **A**

DRAWER **B**

22-1/2" WIDE DRAWER DIVIDERS

SEE FIGURE **B** FOR DRAWER DETAILS

DRAWER **B**

23"

16"

6"

DRAWER **C**

BOTTOM-MOUNT DRAWER SLIDES

1/2" WALL CLEARANCE

HANGING STRIP

8" TO FLOOR

6"

Figure B Drawer assembly

1/2" PLYWOOD SIDES AND ENDS

IRON-ON EDGE BANDING

20-1/2" (INSIDE)

2-1/4" (**A**)
6" (**B**)
7-3/4" (**C**)

22"

PULL

1/4" x 21-1/2" x 22" PLYWOOD BOTTOM

24"

3/4" PLYWOOD FACE (SEE TEXT FOR DETERMINING HEIGHTS)

1 Cut the sides to length and width using a ripping jig. Rip the drawer dividers to width only. Cut the angles on the front edge of each cabinet side.

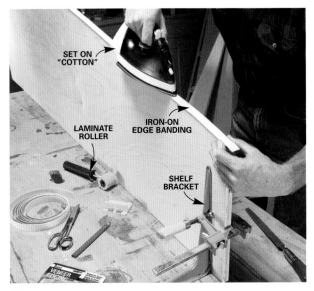

2 Clean off any sawdust on the edges and then iron the edge banding onto the outside edges of the sides and the two lengths of drawer divider stock.

closet cabinets and organizers to design and install a custom closet system. Those systems look inexpensive—but the parts add up quick! A similar-size melamine cabinet module alone will cost about $300. This system offers a more handsome, lower-cost alternative—a custom-built, personalized closet system. For that same $300, this project offers a closet full of cabinetry that's so good-looking the closet doors can stay open.

This project doesn't call for any fancy woodworking joints. All the parts are end-cut and simply screwed together. While that makes for easy construction, it means using plywood-core, veneered plywood (any type of wood) because it'll hold screws and has a smooth, even surface ready for finishing. If using particleboard-core sheets, plan on joining parts with biscuits, dowels or another fastening system. All of the materials shown in this project are found at any well-stocked home center. See the list below right.

Required tools include a good circular saw, a screw gun, a carpenter's square and two 30-in. bar clamps. The project also requires a clothes iron to apply the edge banding (Photo 2). But there are a few other optional tools that will be useful. While it is possible to hand-nail the parts together, a brad nailer (Photo 8) will speed up construction. (Since brad nailers cost under $100, this project is a good excuse to buy one.) Also pick up an edge-banding trimmer for quick, accurate edge trimming (less than $10; Photo 3, p. 86).

Building the cabinet box

Start the project by cutting the cabinet box sides (Photo 1) and two 23-in.-wide lengths for the drawer dividers; see Photos 1 and 5. Consult Figure A for all of the cutting dimensions. Before cutting the drawer dividers to length, edge-band one edge. That way the exposed edges will be finished before they're cut to length (Photo 5, p.86).

Before assembling the cabinet, drill the holes for the adjustable shelving. Use a pegboard jig for consistent hole spacing (Photo 4, p. 86). Because the sides taper, shift over a row or two of holes to keep the narrower top shelf brackets within a few inches of the front. Try to keep the front and rear holes about 2 in. from the edge. Buy a drill bit that matches the shaft on the shelving brackets being used. It's best to use a "brad point" drill bit to keep from splintering the veneer. Either use a depth stop or mark the drill bit with a piece of tape to keep from drilling through the plywood.

Begin assembling the cabinet on its back by attaching a spacer strip at the top and then screwing the bottom drawer divider into place (Photo 6, p. 86). Predrill with a 1/8-in. bit and drive 2-in.-long No. 8 oval head screws with finish washers (left). Then stand the cabinet and, using spacer blocks ripped from scraps, position and hold the drawer dividers in place while screwing them to the sides. Keeping the dividers tight to the spacers as they're screwed into place is important for the drawers to work properly.

NO. 8 FINISH WASHER

2" NO. 8 OVAL HEAD SCREW

Materials list

Item	Qty.	Item	Qty.
3/4" plywood	3 sheets	Closet rod end brackets	3 sets
1/2" plywood (buy a 4x4 sheet if it's available)	1 sheet	No. 8 finish washers	50
1/4" plywood	1 sheet	No. 8 2" oval head screws	40
Iron-on edge banding	3 rolls	No. 8 3" oval head screws	12
Construction adhesive	1 tube	22" "Liberty" bottom-mount drawer slides	4 sets
Woodworking glue		Drawer pulls	4 (or 8)
8' chrome closet rod	1	Shelf brackets	12
6' chrome closet rod	1		

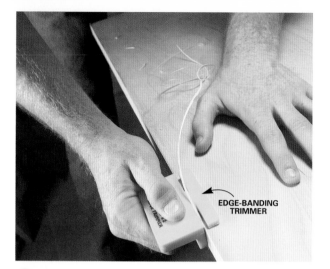

3 Trim the overhanging edges of the edge banding with a trimming tool, then file and sand the edges smooth and flush with the edge.

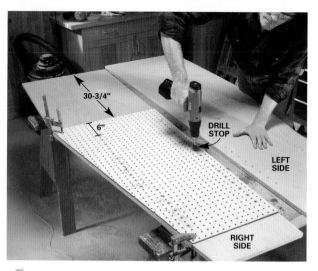

30-3/4"

6"

DRILL STOP

LEFT SIDE

RIGHT SIDE

4 Mark the shelf bracket hole locations on pegboard and use it as a drilling template. Flip the pegboard to drill the other side.

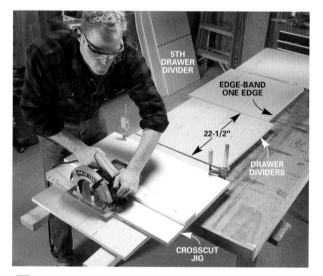

5TH DRAWER DIVIDER

EDGE-BAND ONE EDGE

22-1/2"

DRAWER DIVIDERS

CROSSCUT JIG

5 Cut the five edge-banded drawer dividers to length with the crosscutting jig, four from one length and one from the other.

SCRAP

22-1/2"

BOTTOM DRAWER DIVIDER

6 Screw a scrap to the top of the cabinet, spacing the sides 22-1/2 in. apart, then clamp the bottom drawer divider between the sides. Predrill and fasten.

Edge-banding basics

It only takes a couple of attempts at iron-on edge banding to achieve proficiency. Don't worry about making a mistake; run the iron over it again and the heat-sensitive glue will release so the piece can be adjusted and ironed back on again. Cut each strip of banding about 1 in. extra long with sharp scissors. Leave about 1/2 in. or more of banding overhanging the starting corner because it tends

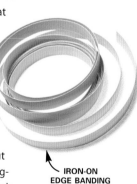

IRON-ON EDGE BANDING

to creep when ironed. Move the iron along (set on "cotton") at about 1 in. per second all the way to the other end. Guide the banding, making sure the banding edges hang over each side of the plywood. Before it cools, push a block or roller over it to embed the banding. Then let the banding cool for 30 seconds or so and check for voids. Re-iron and embed any loose spots.

Cut the ends as close to the plywood as possible with scissors and then run the edge-band trimmer down both sides to trim off the overhang. Make multiple passes to get all of the spots flush. The trimmer works best trimming with the grain. Sometimes that means reversing direction in the middle of trimming. Use a file held at a 45-degree angle to remove oozed-out glue and banding that's still a little proud, then sand all the joints smooth with a sanding block and 100-grit paper.

Save a lot of time by edge-banding all the parts after ripping them to width and before cutting them to length. Then there won't be so many individual parts to edge-band, or those pesky short drawer front ends to deal with. Pay attention to the simple little clamping tip shown in Photo 2. Screw a shelf bracket down and clamp the wood to it. That'll hold the pieces steady for edge banding.

Drawer construction

The prospect of building drawers makes many do-it-yourselfers nervous, but don't worry—it's not all that hard. The key is to build

7 Stand the cabinet upright and rip spacer blocks from scrap to space and support the other drawer dividers as they're screwed into place.

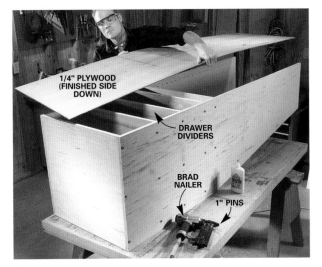

8 Glue and pin the cabinet back to the sides and dividers to square the cabinet. Then glue and pin the hanging strips to the back and sides.

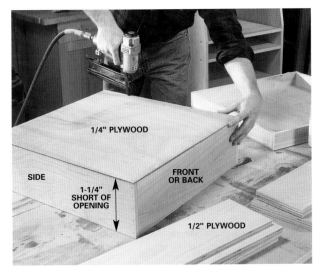

9 Glue and pin the drawer sides together with 1-in. brads. Before the glue sets, square each drawer by gluing and pinning the bottom in place.

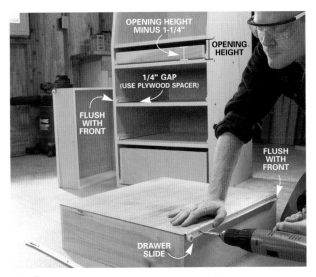

10 Screw the drawer slides into the cabinet and bottom edges of the drawer boxes. Slide each drawer into place to check the fit.

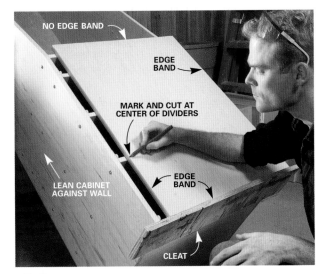

11 Set the drawer front panel (edge-banded on three sides) on a temporary cleat screwed to the cabinet bottom. Mark and cut the lowest drawer front. Edge-band the raw edges.

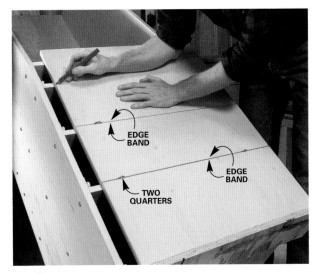

12 Space each panel two quarter (the coin!) thicknesses apart, then measure and cut the next. Edge-band the two raw edges that meet, then repeat the procedure for the next panel.

13 Place crumpled newspaper behind each drawer and replace the drawers. They should stick out about 1/2 in. beyond the cabinet front.

14 Apply four beads of construction adhesive to the drawer boxes and restack the drawer fronts, spacing them with two quarters (coins).

15 Lay a board across each edge of the fronts and clamp overnight. Then drive four 1-in. screws through each box into the fronts.

16 Set cabinet on blocks and center it in closet. Plumb it, shimming as needed, and drill 1/8-in. pilot holes through the cleats into studs or drywall.

NO STUD

HANGING STRIP

STUD

MARK EDGE ON WALL

HANGING STRIP

the cabinet and the drawer boxes square. If using drawer slides other than the ones shown here, be sure to read the directions before building the drawers. They'll give the necessary height and side-to-side clearances.

To build a square drawer, pin together the sides and then square them up with the plywood bottom before the glue dries (Photo 9). Accurate side-to-side dimensions are crucial. Shim out the drawer slides if the drawers are a little narrow, but if they're too wide, they'll have to be rebuilt.

Now is a good time to finish ripping and edge-banding the adjustable and fixed shelves. Don't cut them to final width until the cabinet is mounted so they can be measured and cut to exact widths to fit their selected positions. Stain and finish everything at the same time prior to installation. This project shows an oil-based honey maple stain, top-coated with two coats of satin polyurethane.

Making it fit in your closet

The cabinet unit is 78 in. tall, so it will fit in any closet with 8-ft. walls, even with the 6-in. gap at the floor. Alter the height for a lower ceiling.

Set the cabinet aside before mounting it to install drywall anchors, unless the cabinet falls in front of two studs. Position the cabinet in the closet, then plumb and mark the wall (Photo 17) so the pilot holes line up with the anchors after resetting it. Then measure to the wall to determine the final length for the top shelf—don't forget to add 1 in. for the left-side overhang. Place cleats and shelves anywhere. Build the cabinet taller, wider or with more drawers. Drawer sizes can be easily altered too—make deeper ones for sweaters or shallower ones for socks. The project how-to's shown will work for any configuration.

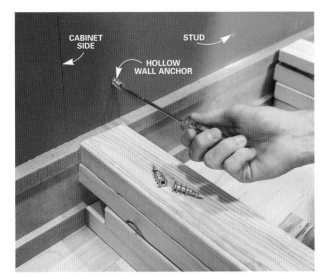

17 Remove the cabinet and screw drywall anchors into the holes without stud backing. Reposition the cabinet and screw it to the wall.

18 Build the shoebox about 1/2 in. short of the wall. Screw a cleat to the wall, then screw the box to the cabinet and nail it to the cleat.

19 Screw the closet rod brackets to the cleats and the cabinet, then install the clothes rods. Cut the top shelves and fasten them to cleats (Figure A, p. 84).

20 Add the drawer pulls and adjustable shelves, then fill it up. *Still* not enough space? Donate whatever doesn't fit!

Super stuff sacks

Ever try, unsuccessfully, to fit 10 lbs. of blankets into a 5-lb. bag? Space-saving storage bags make it possible.

These bags can double storage capacity. Just fill the bag with clothes or bedding, seal the top, and pull the air out using a vacuum. Then, seal the vacuum port. The bags can be reused for summer and winter clothes.

No matter how items are stuffed into the bag, the vacuum suction will compress them. However, the more neatly the bag is filled, the flatter it will end up. Various sizes are available to match the size to the items being stored.

Several brands of these bags are on the market. The one pictured here is a Spacemaker Bag, available only on the Web at target.com. A set of three costs $30.

Target, target.com

Small-closet organizer

M ost bedroom closets suffer from bare minimal organization—stuff on the floor; a long, over-loaded closet rod; and a precariously stacked, sagging shelf. The simple shelving system shown here cleans up some of that clutter. It provides a home for shoes; several cubbies for loose clothing, folded shirts, sweaters or small items; and a deeper (16-in.-wide) top shelf to house the stuff that keeps falling off the narrow shelf. Besides the storage space it provides, the center tower stiffens the shelf above it as well as the clothes rod, since it uses two shorter rods rather than a long one.

This section shows how to cut and assemble this shelving system from a single sheet of plywood (for a 6-ft.-long closet), including how to mount drawer slides for the shoe trays. Birch plywood is used because it's relatively inexpensive ($35 to $40 per 4-ft. x 8-ft. sheet) yet takes a nice finish. The edges are faced with 1x2 maple ($40) for strength and a more attractive appearance. The materials for this project cost $125 at a home center.

The key tool for this project is a circular saw with a cutting guide for cutting the plywood into nice straight pieces (Photo 1). An air-powered brad nailer or finish nailer makes the assembly go much faster, and a miter saw helps produce clean cuts. But neither is absolutely necessary.

BEFORE

AFTER

Cut the birch plywood to size

First, rip the plywood into three 15-3/4 in. x 8-ft. pieces (Photo 1), then cut the sides and shelves from these with a shorter cutting guide. For an average-size closet—6 ft. wide with a 5-1/2-ft.-high top shelf—cut all the sides and shelves from one piece of 3/4-in. plywood. Making the shelving wider means settling for fewer shelves/trays or buying additional plywood. Be sure to support the plywood so the pieces won't fall after completing a cut, and use a guide to keep the cuts perfectly straight. Use a plywood blade in a circular saw to minimize splintering. Cut slowly on the crosscuts, and make sure the good side of the

1/2" PARTICLE-BOARD GUIDE

A

B

2x4 SUPPORTS

A

E

E

D

C

E

D

BEST SIDE
FACING DOWN

1 Cut the sheet of plywood into three equal widths using a saw guide. Then crosscut the sections into the pieces shown in Figure A, using a shorter guide.

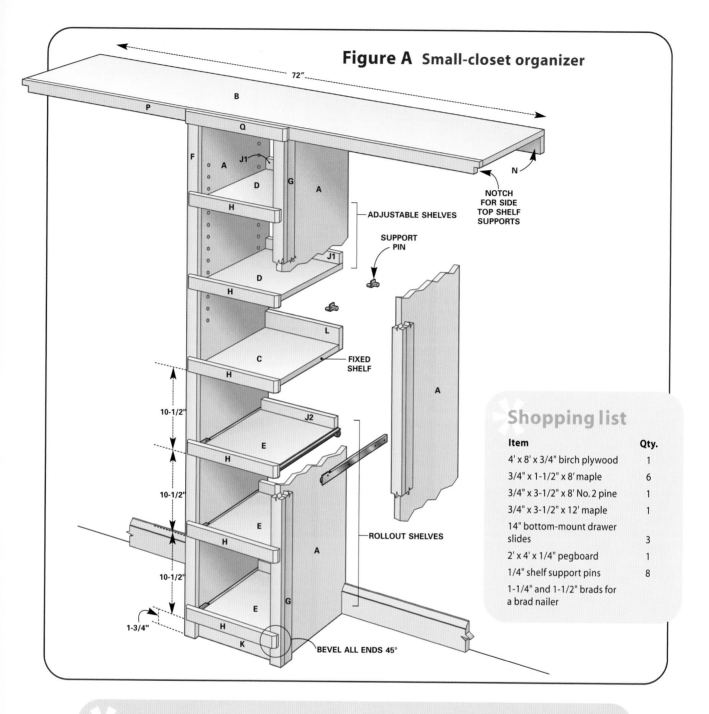

Figure A Small-closet organizer

72"

B

P

Q

F

A

J1

D

G

A

H

N

NOTCH
FOR SIDE
TOP SHELF
SUPPORTS

ADJUSTABLE SHELVES

D

SUPPORT
PIN

H

J1

L

C

FIXED
SHELF

H

J2

10-1/2"

E

A

H

10-1/2"

E

E

ROLLOUT SHELVES

H

G

A

10-1/2"

E

G

1-3/4"

H

K

BEVEL ALL ENDS 45°

Shopping list

Item	Qty.
4' x 8' x 3/4" birch plywood	1
3/4" x 1-1/2" x 8' maple	6
3/4" x 3-1/2" x 8' No. 2 pine	1
3/4" x 3-1/2" x 12' maple	1
14" bottom-mount drawer slides	3
2' x 4' x 1/4" pegboard	1
1/4" shelf support pins	8
1-1/4" and 1-1/2" brads for a brad nailer	

Cutting list

Key	Pcs.	Size & description
A	2	15-3/4" x 65-1/4" plywood (sides)
B	1	15-3/4" x 72" plywood (top shelf)
C	1	15-3/4" x 12" plywood (fixed shelf)
D	2	15 3/4" x 11-7/8" plywood (adjustable shelves)
E	3	15-3/4" x 11" plywood (rollout shelves)
F	2	3/4" x 1-1/2" x 64-1/2" maple (vertical front trim)
G	2	3/4" x 1-1/2" x 65-1/4" maple (vertical side trim)
H	6	3/4" x 1-1/2" x 14-1/2" maple (shelf fronts)
J1	2	3/4" x 1-1/2" x 11-7/8" maple (shelf backs)

Key	Pcs.	Size & description
J2	3	3/4" x 1-1/2" x 11" maple (rollout shelf backs)
K	1	3/4" x 1-1/2" x 12" maple (base)
L	5	3/4" x 3-1/2" x 12" pine (bracing)
M	2	3/4" x 3-1/2" x 24" maple (side top shelf supports—not shown)
N	2	3/4" x 3-1/2" x 29-1/4" maple (rear top shelf supports)
P	1	3/4" x 1-1/2" x 72" maple (top shelf edge)
Q	1	3/4" x 1-1/2" x 15-3/4" maple (top trim)

PROFILE GAUGE

SLIDING PINS CAPTURE PROFILE

2 Make an outline of the baseboard with a profile gauge and, using a jigsaw, cut out the pattern on the lower back side of the two shelving sides (see Figure A and Photo 4).

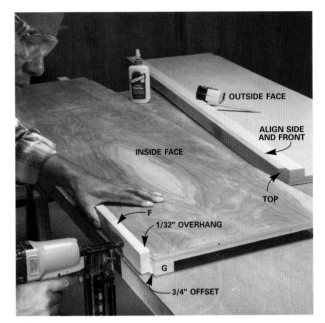

OUTSIDE FACE

ALIGN SIDE AND FRONT

INSIDE FACE

TOP

F

1/32" OVERHANG

G

3/4" OFFSET

3 Cut the 1x2s to length. Then glue and nail them to the plywood sides (Figure A) with 1-1/4-in. brads. Note the slight (1/32-in.) overhang along the inside.

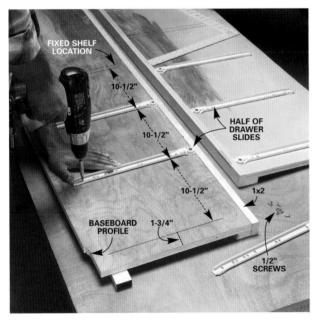

FIXED SHELF LOCATION

10-1/2"

10-1/2"

HALF OF DRAWER SLIDES

10-1/2"

1x2

BASEBOARD PROFILE

1-3/4"

1/2" SCREWS

4 Mark the center and rollout shelf locations using a framing square. Then mount half of each of the two-piece drawer slides even with the 1x2 on each side.

TOP OF FIXED SHELF

2-1/4" FROM BACK OF PLYWOOD

1-1/2" FROM FRONT OF PLYWOOD

1/4" PEGBOARD

DRILL STOP

5 Drill 1/4-in. matching holes 3/8 in. deep for the adjustable shelf pins using a pegboard template. Flip the pegboard when switching sides.

plywood is down—the plywood blade makes a big difference, but the thin veneer will splinter if rushing the cut.

Mark and cut the baseboard profile on the plywood sides, using a profile gauge ($8; Photo 2) or a trim scrap to transfer the shape, or remove the baseboard rather than cutting the plywood and reinstalling it later. Either method works fine.

> **tip** Hold the brad nailer perpendicular to the grain whenever possible so the rectangular nailheads will run with the grain instead of cutting across it. This makes them less prominent.

Attach the maple edges

Glue and nail the side 1x2s (G) to the best-looking side of the plywood (so it faces out), holding them flush with the front edge (Photo 3). Be sure to use 1-1/4-in. brads here so the nails don't go completely through the side. Use 1-1/2-in. brads everywhere else.

Then attach the front 1x2s (F). These 1x2s should be flush with the bottom of the sides, but 3/4 in. short of the top. The 1x2s will overlap the edge slightly because 3/4-in. plywood is slightly less than a full 3/4 in. thick. Keep the overlap to the inside.

Lay out the locations for the drawer slides and the fixed cen-

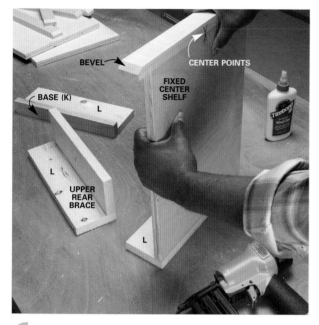

6 Assemble the shelves and shelving braces using glue and 1-1/2-in. brads. Align the centers of each piece for accurate positioning.

Labels in image: BEVEL, CENTER POINTS, FIXED CENTER SHELF, BASE (K), L, UPPER REAR BRACE, L, L

7 Attach the other halves of the slides to the rollout shelves with 1/2-in. screws. Butt them against the front 1x2.

Label in image: FRONT 1x2

ter shelf before assembling the cabinet—the 12-in. width is a tight fit for a drill. Use the dimensions in Photo 4, p. 93, and Figure A, p. 92, for spacing. Vary any of these measurements to better fit shoes or other items. Then take the drawer slides apart and mount them on the tower sides (Photo 4). Remember that one side of each pair is a mirror image of the other.

To position the shelf support pins for the two adjustable shelves, align the bottom of the 1/4-in. pegboard with the fixed shelf location, then drill mirror-image holes on the two sides (Photo 5). Mark the holes to be used on the pegboard—it's all too easy to lose track when flipping the pegboard over to the second side. Use a brad point drill bit to prevent splintering, and place a bit stop or a piece of tape for a 5/8-in. hole depth (1/4-in. pegboard plus 3/8 in. deep in the plywood). Most support pins require a 1/4-in. diameter hole, but measure to make sure.

> **tip** Make sure the pegboard has square sides.

Cut the bevels and assemble the shelves

Cut the bevels in all the 1x2 shelf fronts, then glue and nail them to the plywood shelves, keeping the bottoms flush (Photo 6). Nail 1x2 backs (J1 and J2) onto the adjustable and rollout shelves. Next, nail together the bracing (L) and the base piece (K), which join the cabinet. And add the slides to the rollout shelves (Photo 7).

Assembling the shelving tower is straightforward (Photo 8). Position the L-shaped bracing at the top and braces at the bottom, add glue to the joints, then clamp and nail. Because of the slight lip where the 1x2 front trim (F) overlaps the plywood, it requires chiseling out a 1/32-in.-deep x 3/4-in.-wide notch so the fixed shelf will fit tightly (Photo 9).

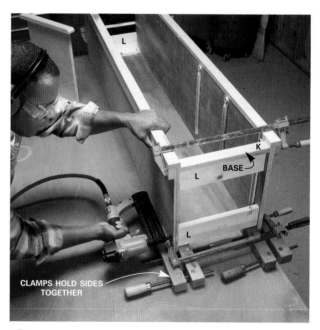

Labels in image: L, K, BASE, L, L, CLAMPS HOLD SIDES TOGETHER

8 Set the sides on edge, glue and clamp the braces (L) in place and nail the assembly together with 1-1/2-in. brads. Make sure the braces are square to the sides.

Set the cabinet in the closet

Remove the old closet shelving and position the new cabinet. If there's carpeting, it's best to cut it out under the cabinet for easier carpet replacement in the future (Photo 10). For the cleanest look, pull the carpet back from the closet wall, cut out the padding and tack strip that fall under the cabinet, and nail new tack strips around the cabinet position. Then reposition the cabinet, push the carpet back against it and cut the carpet. Or, simply cut out the carpet and tack strip under the cabinet and tack the loose carpet edges to the floor (but it won't look as nice).

9 Chisel shallow slots in the 1x2 overhang, then slide the center shelf into place. Nail at the front, back and sides.

10 Center the cabinet in the closet against the back wall, mark its position and cut the carpet out around it. Tack the loose edges of carpet to the floor.

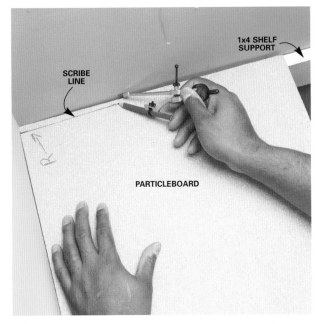

11 Shove a 16 x 24-in. sheet of particleboard into the shelf corners and scribe a line. Cut along the scribe line and use the particleboard as a pattern. Nail the shelf to the supports and cabinet top.

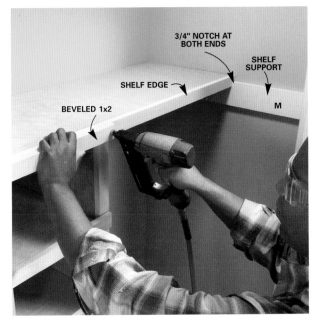

12 Notch the 1x2 shelf edge over the end supports and nail it into place. Then trim the top of the cabinet with a beveled 1x2.

Plumb and level the cabinet, then screw it to the wall. Use hollow wall anchors if the studs are hard to find. The cabinet will be firmly anchored by the upper shelf anyway.

Scribe the top shelf for a tight fit

Closet shelves are tough to fit because the corners of the walls are rarely square. To cut the shelf accurately, scribe a leftover 16-in. wide piece of particleboard or plywood in both corners (Photo 11) and use it for a template for cutting the ends of the shelf. Then the shelf will drop right into place and rest on 1x4 supports nailed to the side walls and back wall. Make sure the front of the shelf is flush with the front of the tower and nail it to the top. If the back wall is wavy, scribe the back of the shelf to the wall and trim it to make the front flush. Then cut and notch the front 1x2 and nail it to the shelf (Photo 12).

Lightly sand all the wood and apply a clear finish. When it's dry, mix several shades of putty to get an exact match to your wood and fill the nail holes. Add another coat of finish and let it dry. Screw on the clothes rod brackets, aligning them with the bottom of the 1x4. Then pile on the clothes.

Melamine
closet organizer

For about the price of a dresser, this modular closet organizer practically doubles storage space and looks great too. The units are constructed of particleboard with a durable melamine coating. Although wire shelves are more economical, the modular systems offer several advantages. They look like a built-in unit, offer adjustable shelves and closet rods, and allow you to add drawers or shelves in the future.

Installing a modular closet system is a great weekend project. The melamine units assemble easily with special locking hardware.

This project requires a tape measure, a level, a No. 3 Phillips screwdriver, an electric drill with a No. 2 Phillips bit and 3/16-in. wood and 1/2-in. spade bits, a circular saw with a 140-tooth plywood blade and a hacksaw with a 24-tooth-per-in. blade. An electronic stud finder would be handy, but rapping

on the wall or looking for nails in the baseboard are great low-tech methods.

Sketch out a master plan

Start by carefully measuring the closet's width, depth and height. Use graph paper to make scaled drawings of the floor plan and each wall where there will be shelves. Include the width and position of the door on the plan. Let each square equal 6 in. This allows sketching in and trying out different storage unit options.

The knock-down storage units are available in standard widths, with 12, 18 and 24 in. being the most common. Depths range from 12 to 18 in. depending on the manufacturer. Some units rest on the floor and reach a height of about 84 in.; others, like the ones shown here, hang from a cleat or rail mounted to the wall.

1 Draw a level line on the back wall of the closet to indicate the bottom of the hanging cleats. Refer to the instructions for the height of this line. Locate the studs along this line and mark the wall.

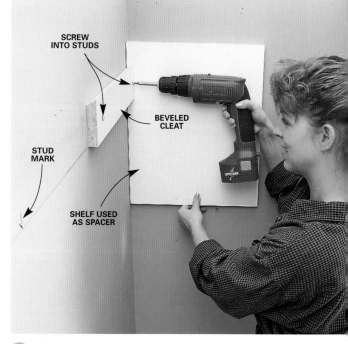

2 Drill 3/16-in. screw clearance holes through the cleat at the stud locations. Then screw the cleat to the wall with 3-in. pan head screws, leaving them a little loose. Use a shelf to space the cleat from the end wall to allow room for the side panel of the storage unit.

Each storage unit consists of two side panels drilled for shelf pins and connecting bolts, one or two hanging cleats and some fixed shelves (Photo 4, p. 98). The parts are connected with ingenious two-part knock-down fasteners consisting of a connecting bolt that screws into the side panels and a cam mechanism mounted in each fixed shelf and cleat. To assemble, just screw the connecting bolts in the right holes, slide the parts together, and turn the cam clockwise to lock the parts together. There are systems available at home centers and discount stores that simply screw together, but they're harder to assemble and not nearly as sturdy.

The basic units are essentially boxes with a lot of holes drilled in the sides. Complete the system by adding adjustable shelves, drawers and closet rods. All the components are designed to fit into or attach to the predrilled holes, so very little additional drilling is required.

The biggest difference among brands is in the quality of the drawer slides, closet poles and mounting system and in the range of unit sizes and available options. Better-quality units also have a more durable surface.

Check the yellow pages under "Closet Accessories" and make a few calls to see who sells modular closet systems locally, or check with the suppliers listed in the Buyer's Guide on p. 98. Some closet specialists insist on installing their systems, while others will help with the design and provide the storage units, hardware and instructions needed to do the installation. Take the sketch along and get estimates on a couple of different systems.

The closet system shown here cost $550. Using standard-

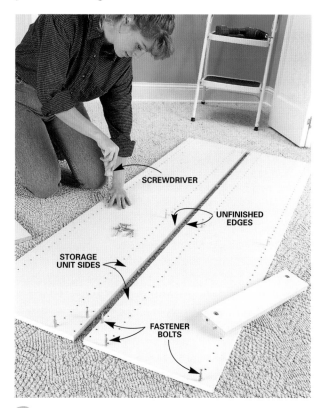

3 Lay the sides of the first storage unit on a carpet or dropcloth with unfinished edges together. Screw fastener bolts for the fixed shelves and cleats into the predrilled holes. The instruction sheet will show which holes to use.

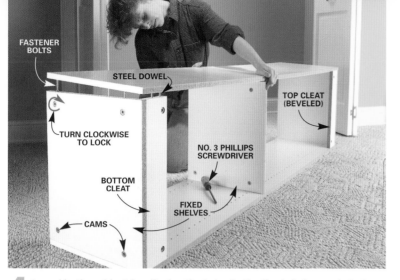

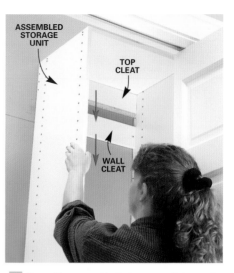

4 Assemble the cabinet by aligning the holes in the fixed shelves and cleats with the fastener bolts. Lock them together by turning the cams clockwise. Then position the second side and lock it in. Face the cams where they'll be least visible when the cabinet is hung.

5 Hang the assembled storage unit by pushing it tight to the wall and sliding it down onto the interlocking cleat.

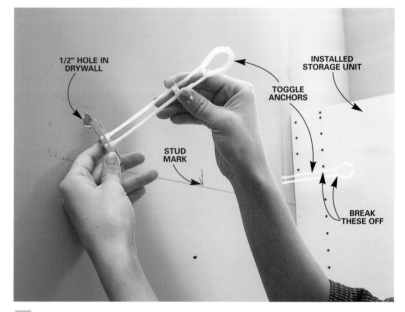

6 Check the side panel to make sure the cabinet is plumb and screw through the bottom cleat into a stud to secure it.

7 Install toggle anchors for additional support if cleats land on only one stud. Hold the cleat in position and drill a 3/16-in. hole through the cleat and the drywall or plaster to mark the location of the toggle anchor. Remove the cleat and enlarge the hole in the wall to 1/2 in. Then install the anchor and attach the cleat, making sure to leave a space for the side panel of the next storage unit.

sized, floor-standing, modular storage units would have saved about $150, but that would have required settling for a less efficient plan and doing more assembly work. Also, hanging the units on the wall avoids the extra work of cutting around or removing baseboards or dealing with uneven floors and has the advantage of keeping the floor clear for cleaning.

Although melamine-coated shelving is a great product for an affordable, prefinished storage unit, it does have some limitations. The particleboard core will not stand up to moisture. Wire shelving may be a better choice in damp places. The melamine coating is more durable than paint but not as tough as the plastic laminate used on countertops, so don't expect this stuff to tolerate the same abuse as kitchen counters.

Storing books or heavy objects may cause the particleboard to sag over time. Consider stronger plywood or metal shelves if storing heavy items.

Buyer's Guide

The following companies manufacture modular closet organizing systems.

Rubbermaid: 3320 West Market Street, Fairlawn, OH 44333, (888) 895-2110, rubbermaid.com

Schulte Corp.: 3100 East Kemper Road, Cincinnati, OH 45241; (800) 669-3225. schultestorage.com

Techline Closets: A Division of Marshall Erdman and Associates, 500 S. Division St., Waunakee, WI 53597. For the nearest Techline Studio, call (800) 356-8400. techlineusa.com

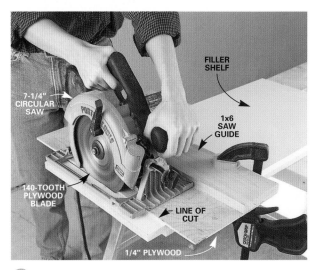

8 Mark the oversized filler shelf for cutting by laying it on top of the storage units and drawing lines along each side panel onto the shelf.

9 Cut the filler shelf with a 140-tooth plywood blade in a circular saw. Clamp a cutting guide so it just covers the line, and run the saw against it to provide a straight cut with a minimal amount of chipping. Construct the cutting guide by screwing a straight 1x6 to an oversized piece of 1/4-in. plywood. Run the saw against the 1x6 fence to cut the plywood at the exact blade location.

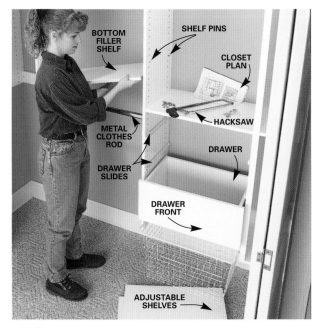

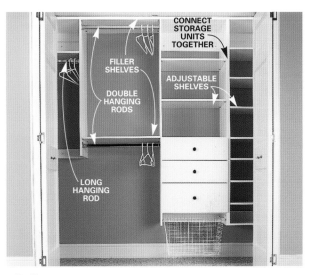

10 Tilt in the filler shelves, resting them on shelf support pins. Cut the metal closet rods with a 24-tooth-per-inch hacksaw.

11 Complete the installation by tightening all of the mounting screws after adjacent units are connected with the two-part fasteners provided. Install the drawers and drawer fronts and set the adjustable shelves on the shelf support pins.

Design tips

- Divide clothes into short (about 40 in. in length including the hanger) and long (up to 70 in.). To save closet space, the rods for shorter clothes can be stacked in a "double-hanging" arrangement. Allow about 1 in. of hanging space for every garment. A good rule of thumb is one-third long-hanging to two-thirds double-hanging rods.
- Set long-hanging rods about 72 in. from the floor and double-hanging rods at 42 in. and 84 in. Another option is a medium-hanging rod for slacks at 60 in. high. Use the space above for shelving.

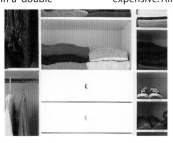

- Compartments for shoes may look tidier, but closely spaced adjustable shelves are more efficient and less expensive. Allow about 7 in. of shelf width for each pair of women's shoes, and 9 in. for men's.
- Keep dirty laundry corralled with a wire basket.
- Don't put drawers against the end walls of the closet, and make sure they will open fully without hitting a wall or door. Drawers are expensive. Install adjustable shelves and add the drawers later, to save money, if necessary.

Sports
equipment storage

Sports rack

A wall-mounted rack will keep bats and balls from getting lost in the recesses of any room. Just cut 6-in.-diameter holes in the top 1x10 shelf and 3-in. holes in the bottom 1x6 shelf. Then screw the bottom shelf to the top shelf from below. Attach a 1x2 cleat to the back and screw it to the wall studs. Customize the size and shape to fit individual needs.

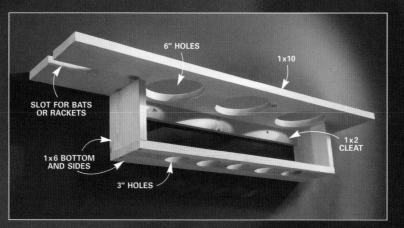

6" HOLES

1x10

SLOT FOR BATS OR RACKETS

1x6 BOTTOM AND SIDES

3" HOLES

1x2 CLEAT

Under-joist shelf

Create extra storage space by screwing wire closet shelving to joists in your garage or basement. Wire shelving is see-through, so you can easily tell what's up there. Depending on the width, wire shelves cost from $1 to $3 per foot at home centers.

Stay-put balls

Keep sport balls off the floor and out of the way by resting them in flowerpot drip trays (80¢ at home centers). Screw the trays down to an inexpensive shelving unit. The balls will stay put.

Ski and pole organizer

Keep your skis up and easy to find with this simple 2x4 rack. Drill 3/4-in.-diameter holes spaced 3/4 in. apart. Glue 4-1/2-in. lengths of 3/4-in. dowel into the holes and then mount the 2x4 to the wall studs. Space the groupings about 8 in. apart to make room for ski bindings. Now you'll spend less time looking for your skis and more time on the trails.

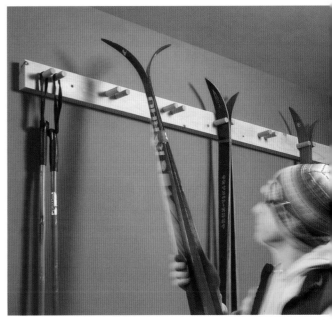

Baseball equipment organizer

If you have a family with one or more future big-league baseball or softball players, build this bat-and-ball organizer to keep the equipment tidy. Use PVC pipe and boards as shown. Then anchor them to a wall or the back of a closet door.

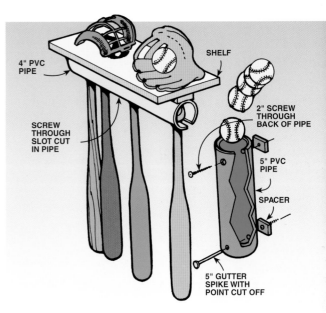

Telecommuting and in-home theater systems have created the need for well-organized home offices and media rooms. The projects in this chapter help address that need. They offer detailed how-to information for building a desk, modular bookcase and shelving, as well as setting up a home Internet café.

Chapter 4

organize your home office & media room

Simple
computer desk

Build this desk in two days with simple tools for only $175. It's designed so it won't require a lot of carpentry experience to build. Take a close look at Figure A. Just cut eight panels from 3/4-in. birch plywood and apply some easy-to-use iron-on edge banding (see p. 109 for buying info). The rest of the project consists of drilling holes, cutting the pieces and assembling them with special fasteners. It takes a weekend with time left over to apply the first coat of finish.

This project requires only basic power and hand tools: a circular saw, hacksaw, drill, screwdriver, hammer, tubing cutter, utility knife, some wrenches and an old clothes iron. The thin-veneer edge banding that covers the exposed edges of the plywood can be trimmed carefully with a sharp utility knife or a double-edge trimmer ($17).

Make precision plywood cuts

Cut the plywood pieces as precisely as possible. To make it easy, build a simple jig like the one shown in Photo 1 (p. 107) using two strips of plywood. For precise cuts, go to a full-service lumberyard and ask to have it cut, usually for a small fee. Just insist that the lumberyard use a fine blade in the panel saw so the crosscuts (the cuts opposite the grain) don't splinter the surface veneer. Offer to buy them a new plywood-cutting blade (about $6) if the first cut looks bad.

Accurate cuts are the key to making sure the panels all fit precisely with the special knockdown fasteners. The fastener will still work if the cuts are off by 1/16 in., but any more than that spells trouble during assembly.

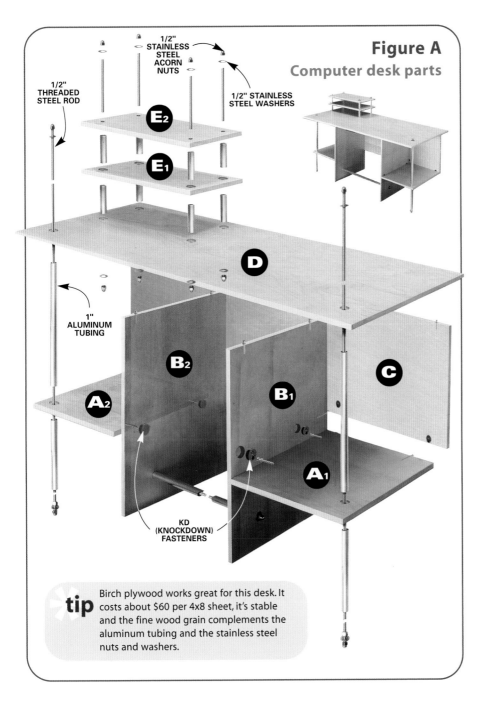

Figure A
Computer desk parts

1/2" STAINLESS STEEL ACORN NUTS

1/2" THREADED STEEL ROD

1/2" STAINLESS STEEL WASHERS

E2

E1

D

1" ALUMINUM TUBING

B2

B1

C

A2

A1

KD (KNOCKDOWN) FASTENERS

tip Birch plywood works great for this desk. It costs about $60 per 4x8 sheet, it's stable and the fine wood grain complements the aluminum tubing and the stainless steel nuts and washers.

Shopping list

Qty.	Description
2	3/4" x 4' x 8' birch plywood
60'	13/16" adhesive-backed birch edge banding
12'	1"-dia. aluminum tubing with 1/16" thick wall
14	1/2" stainless steel acorn nuts (No. 13) and washers
2	standard 1/2-in. nuts (No. 13)
16	25mm KD fasteners (see p. 106)
1 qt.	polyurethane varnish
1	1" Forstner drill bit
1	25mm Forstner drill bit
1	3/16" twist drill bit (metal)
1	3/16" brad point drill bit (wood)

Cutting list

Key	Qty.	Size & description
A1	1	3/4" x 22" x 16-3/4" lower shelf
A2	1	3/4" x 22" x 16-3/4" lower shelf
B1	1	3/4" x 22" x 29-1/4" upright leg panel
B2	1	3/4" x 22" x 29-1/4" upright leg panel
C	1	3/4" x 19" x 63-1/2" back panel
D	1	3/4" x 30" x 68" top
E1	1	3/4" x 12" x 24" upper shelf
E2	1	3/4" x 12" x 24" upper shelf

Aluminum tubing

- Cut two pieces 1" O.D. aluminum tubing (1/16" wall) at 18-3/4" (upper front leg).
- Cut two pieces 1" O.D. aluminum tubing (1/16" wall) at 9-5/8" (lower front leg).
- Cut eight pieces 1" O.D. aluminum tubing (1/16" wall) at 4" (upper shelf supports).
- Cut one piece 1" O.D. aluminum tubing (1/16" wall) at 29" (footrest).

Threaded rod

- 1/2" steel threaded rod No. 13
- Cut two pieces 30-1/4" (front legs)
- Cut four pieces 10-1/4" (shelf rods)
- Cut 1 piece 31" (footrest rod)

Apply the edge banding

The simplest way to cover exposed plywood edges is to use adhesive-backed birch edge banding (available at a home center). A hot clothes iron melts the adhesive and bonds it directly to the plywood. If the adhesive oozes out on the sides, it may ruin a good iron, so buy a secondhand unit from a thrift store. Before starting, cut the 7/8- or 13/16-in.-wide edge banding about 1/2 in. longer than needed on each side.

Preheat the iron on the cotton setting. Place the iron on top of the edge banding as shown in Photo 3, p. 107. Move the iron about 2 in. per second along the veneer; ironing too slowly scorches the wood. Go from end to end, then make a second ironing pass. The veneer should be hot to the touch. After the second pass, secure the veneer in place by pressing a 4-in. block of 2x4 back and forth along the entire length to ensure a good bond. If the glue fails at any time before finishing, go back and reheat it (or even replace a damaged strip).

Trim the edge banding once it cools. Put the veneer face down on a workbench and cut the ends flush with a utility knife. Then trim the edges as shown in Photo 4, p. 108, with a utility

Figure B Fastener location guide

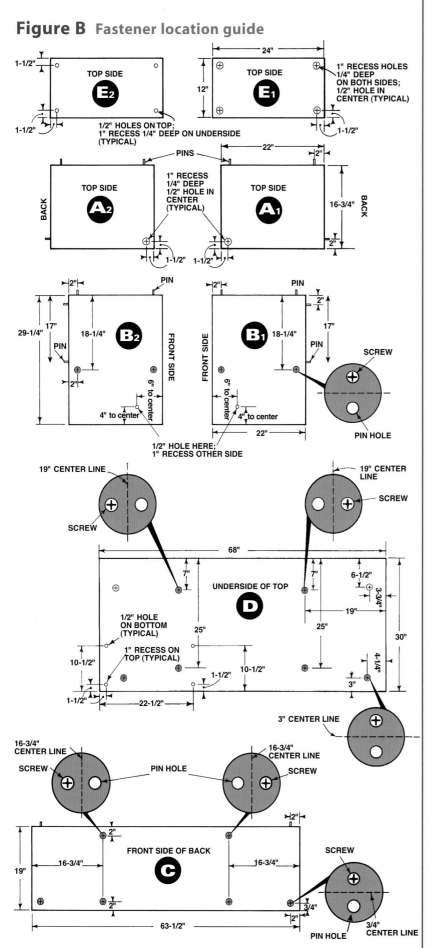

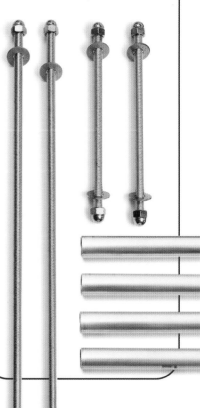

KD FASTENER (KNOCKDOWN)

KD PINS

Order the hardware kit

The kit includes all the 1/2-in. threaded rod, stainless steel nuts and washers, 1-in. aluminum tubing, the special KD fasteners and a 25mm bit. Cut the threaded rod and tubing to size. A keyboard tray is not included in the kit.

The cost of the Computer Desk Hardware Kit is $70, plus shipping. Order from The Family Handyman, P.O. Box 83695, Stillwater, MN 55083-0695, or call (800) 492-3715. (Include your street address; there is no delivery to P.O. box addresses.) Credit card orders welcome. Satisfaction guaranteed or your money back. Allow three to five weeks for delivery.

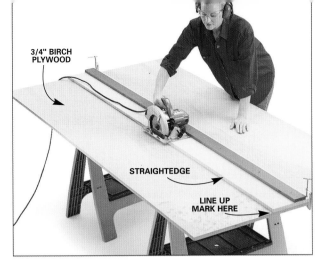

1 Cut the plywood shapes from 3/4-in. sheets of hardwood plywood. Use a homemade straightedge made from 3/4-in. plywood strips clamped to the sheet for super-straight cuts.

2 Sand the edges of the plywood smooth and flat to make an even surface for the thin adhesive-backed birch edge banding. Be careful not to round the edges.

blade or the special double-edge trimmer. Don't trim the overhanging edges of the banding all at once; do it in several passes. And don't try to trim too closely; clean up the edges with a sanding block and 150-grit sandpaper, if needed.

Measure accurately when drilling holes for the fasteners

The knockdown fasteners have a main body that fits into a 25-mm-dia. hole drilled into the plywood surface. The mating plywood panel has a pin that fits into a hole in the body of the fastener. To tighten these two panels together, a screw turns an internal cam in the fastener body that snugs the pin into the fastener body, similar to tightening a nut on a bolt. Exact placement is critical. Measure the locations as shown in Figure B. Then be sure to tap them in the correct orientation.

> **tip** Be sure to mark the hole locations and then use an awl (Photo 5) to push a small starter hole into the surface. This shallow starter hole will help align the small spur on the bottom of the Forstner drill bit.

The hole for the fastener body is about 9/16 in. deep, which leaves less than 3/16 in. of plywood at the bottom. This is touchy stuff; a hole driven too deeply can pop through the other side and ruin a panel. To avoid breaking through, mark the fastener height onto the side of a carpenter's pencil. Check the depth during drilling by dropping the pencil in the hole as shown in Photo 5, p. 108.

Drill holes for the tubing and threaded rod

Accurately mark the locations for the tubing and threaded rod as shown in Figure B. Notice that the lower shelves, A1 and A2, as well as E1, have recessed holes on the top *and* bottom. In contrast, the top (D) and the upper shelf (E2) have recessed holes *on one side only.* Carefully visualize how the pieces fit together before drilling each one.

Now drill the recessed holes for the tubing and the holes for the rod as shown in Photo 8, p. 109, into the top (D) and small

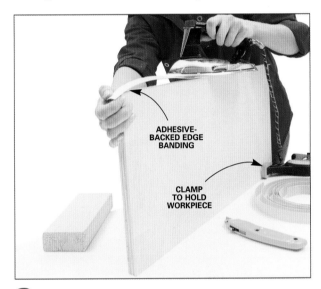

3 Iron on the adhesive-backed edge banding using the cotton setting. Heat the veneer until it's hot to the touch. Cut each piece of edge banding so it's about 1/2 in. overlong on each end and trim it flush with a utility knife once the glue sets. Keep pressure on the edge banding after ironing by running a small 2x4 block back and forth until the glue sets (about 20 seconds).

upper shelves (E1, E2). Make a heavy paper template to get the centers of all the holes exactly placed. This will ensure perfectly aligned shelves.

Assemble plywood panels, then insert tubing and threaded rods

The two lower shelves (A1 and A2) must be attached to the two upright panels (B1 and B2) first. Insert the pins of the fasteners into the holes and turn the screws until they're tight. Next, attach these two assemblies to the back (C). To complete the desk frame, lay the top upside down on the floor (a carpeted area works best) and attach the top in the same manner.

Now, insert the long tubes between the top and the lower shelf as shown in Photo 12, p. 109. Push the top and the lower shelf apart slightly to fit the tube into the recesses. Next, thread a standard nut onto the bottom of each of the long rods and push the rod through the lower leg tube and then through the upper

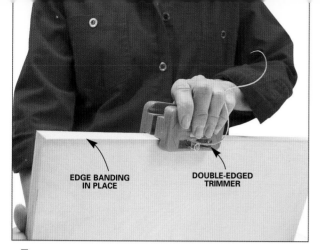

4 Trim the edges of the edge banding flush with the front and back surfaces of the plywood with a double-edge trimmer or a utility knife.

EDGE BANDING IN PLACE

DOUBLE-EDGED TRIMMER

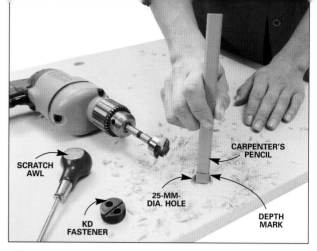

5 Mark the hole centers with a scratch awl, then drill the holes for the knockdown fasteners with a special 25mm Forstner bit.

SCRATCH AWL

CARPENTER'S PENCIL

25-MM-DIA. HOLE

KD FASTENER

DEPTH MARK

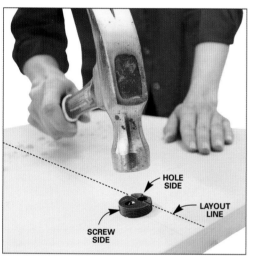

6 Position each fastener correctly and then tap it in place; there's only one chance at it because there's no getting them out once they're in. (See Figure B, p. 106, for details.)

HOLE SIDE

LAYOUT LINE

SCREW SIDE

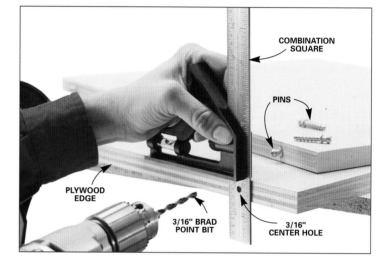

7 Make this simple hole-alignment jig from a combination square: Just drill a 3/16-in. hole in the center of the square blade anywhere along the length. Set the square so the hole lines up with the center of the ply-wood edge. Lock it in place. Now drill through this hole about 1 in. deep into the plywood edge with a 3/16-in. brad point drill bit.

COMBINATION SQUARE

PINS

PLYWOOD EDGE

3/16" BRAD POINT BIT

3/16" CENTER HOLE

long tube. Play with the rod a bit to get it to come through the top. Finally, slide the washers onto each end and thread on the acorn nuts. Make sure the tubing is still in the recessed holes. Tighten the nuts firmly without crushing the wood. (This is a desk, not a pickup truck frame.)

Finally, attach the upper shelves, E1 and E2, to the desktop. Fit the tubes into the recesses and fish the rod through the tubes and holes in the shelves. Slide the washers in place and thread the nuts onto the ends of the rods.

Apply two coats of urethane

An oil-based polyurethane gives the desk a tough finish that'll enhance and slightly darken the birch into a beautiful warm color. For a clear coating, choose a water-based finish.

Take the desk apart and sand all the surfaces with 220-grit

tip A brad point drill bit is different from other twist bits. It has a center point that extends past the bit to position itself into the wood. This keeps the bit from wandering during drilling.

sandpaper. Wipe the surfaces with a regular cloth and then a tack cloth to remove all of the dust. Brush on the urethane, watching for any drips and smoothing them out with your brush as they appear on the surface.

The next day, lightly sand the entire surface with 220-grit sandpaper to remove any bumps or trapped dust. Wipe with a tack cloth and apply your second coat. Let it dry for two days before assembling the desk.

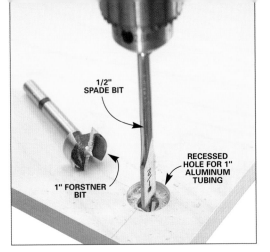

8 Drill the shallow holes for the tubing first at the locations shown in Figure B. Then drill the 1/2-in.-dia. holes for the threaded rod.

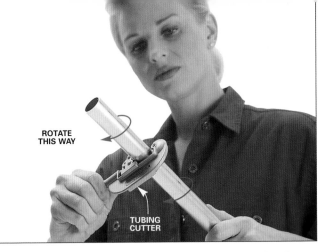

9 Cut the aluminum tubing with a plumber's tubing cutter. Adjust it to the size of the tube, then rotate the handle as shown. After each revolution, turn the knob about a quarter turn until the pipe is cut. Resist the temptation to screw the cutter down too hard and cut too fast.

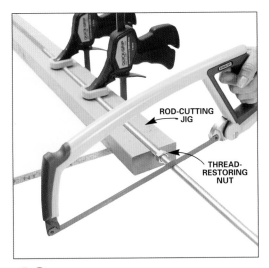

10 Saw the 1/2-in. threaded rod with a hacksaw. Clamp the threaded rod in a vise; just don't mar the threads within 2 in. of each end. Or support the rod with a 2x4 block with a groove cut in it and some soft-grip clamps as shown.

Buyer's Guide

▓ One-inch aluminum tubing is available from Outwater Plastics. Call (800) 631-8375 for a catalog. Web site: outwater.com. You can also get 1-in. aluminum tubing through your local hardware store by special order.

▓ Half-inch stainless steel acorn nuts should be available by special order from your local hardware store. They are included in our hardware kit.

▓ The following items are available from Rockler (800-279-4441, rockler.com):

– Knockdown fasteners (KD) Part No. 34900 (eight per pack, $10)

– Keyboard slide No. 39851 ($48)

– Keyboard platform No. 91463 ($35)

– 25mm Forstner drill bit No. 21263 ($9)

– 1-in. Forstner drill bit No. 21200 ($6.50)

– Double-edge trimmer No. 43208 ($18)

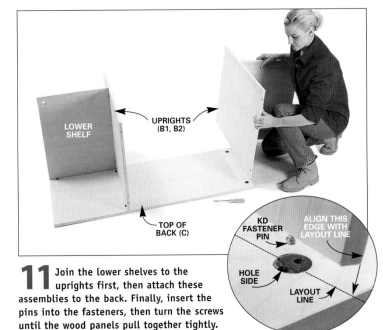

11 Join the lower shelves to the uprights first, then attach these assemblies to the back. Finally, insert the pins into the fasteners, then turn the screws until the wood panels pull together tightly.

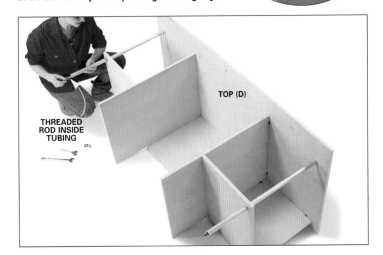

12 Assemble the front legs. The bottom of each leg has an extra standard nut that fits inside the tube to keep the rod centered (Figure A). Once both legs are attached, lower the desk and check to be sure both legs and upright panels are contacting the floor at the same time. If they aren't, trim the tubing or add a washer or two at the bottom.

Add home office outlets

Surface wiring is a system of channels and boxes that allow outlets, switches or light fixtures to be put anywhere—without the hassle of cutting into walls, fishing wire and patching holes. And it can look much less messy, since the parts can be painted to match the walls. Mount outlets low on walls where they'll be hidden by furniture.

All the parts are available in metal or plastic at home centers. This project uses plastic because it is easier to cut. All it takes for the project is wire, connectors, outlets and cover plates. The total bill for the added outlets shown here was $60. (Use a similar system to run low-voltage wiring for a telephone, TV or computer.)

Add outlets to an existing circuit unless a device that draws a lot of power, such as an air conditioner or a space heater, will be plugged in to the same circuit. An electrical inspector will review the plan before approving a permit. Be sure to have the work inspected when it's complete.

Start by mounting a box base at an existing outlet (Photo 1). Cut out the back panel of the box with a utility knife before screwing it to the junction box. Then use a stud finder to locate studs and mark them with masking tape.

Run channel to the first outlet location (Photo 2). If the channel won't have to make any turns or run around corners, just cut it to length with a hacksaw. But if the channel turns up or down or goes around a corner, miter the adjoining ends at a 45-degree angle. A power miter saw will do this fast, although a miter box guiding a hacksaw blade will also work ($7 at home centers and hardware stores). To mount the channel base, drill 1/8-in. holes at each stud and 1/2 in. from the ends. Wherever an end doesn't land on a stud, use a drywall anchor.

With the first section of channel in place, fasten a box base to the wall. *Don't* cut out the back panel. If the base lands on a stud, simply screw it to the stud. If not, use two drywall anchors. Continue adding channel and boxes.

Next, run wire from the existing junction box to each box base. The size of the wire added must match the size of the existing wire. Use the labeled notches on a wire stripper to check the gauge of the existing wire (14-gauge is most common, but it may have 12-gauge wire). Use only individual wires labeled "THHN,"

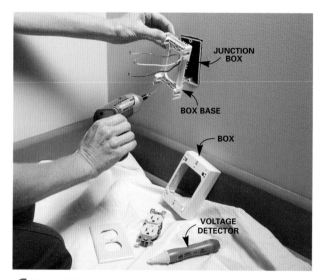

1 Turn off the power and make sure it's off using a voltage detector. Remove the old outlet and screw a box base to the junction box.

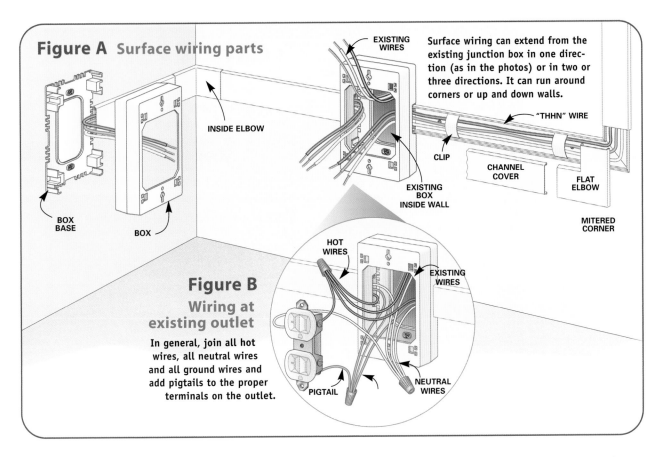

Figure A Surface wiring parts

EXISTING WIRES

Surface wiring can extend from the existing junction box in one direction (as in the photos) or in two or three directions. It can run around corners or up and down walls.

INSIDE ELBOW

"THHN" WIRE

CLIP

CHANNEL COVER

FLAT ELBOW

BOX BASE

BOX

EXISTING BOX INSIDE WALL

MITERED CORNER

HOT WIRES

EXISTING WIRES

Figure B

Wiring at existing outlet

In general, join all hot wires, all neutral wires and all ground wires and add pigtails to the proper terminals on the outlet.

PIGTAIL

NEUTRAL WIRES

which is sold in spools or by the foot at home centers and hardware stores. Get three colors: green for the ground, white for the neutral, and red or black for the hot wire. *Don't* simply buy plastic-sheathed cable and run it inside the channel.

Cut channel covers to length (no need to miter them). At turns or corners, hold an elbow in place when measuring for the covers—the elbow will overlap about 1/4 in. of the cover. Snap the covers onto the channel base followed by the elbows and boxes (Photo 3). Wiring the outlets is similar, whether several outlets are added or only one. If two channels run from the existing junction box (as in Figure A), there will be two new sets of wire to connect to the old wiring (Figure B). If channel runs only one direction from the box (as in these photos), there will be fewer wires, but the process is the same: Join all the hot wires together, all the neutrals together and all the grounds together. Wiring is similar at the new outlet boxes that fall between sections of channel (Photo 3 shows "pigtails" ready for an outlet). At the last box in the run, there will be only three wires (see Figure A); connect them directly to the new outlet.

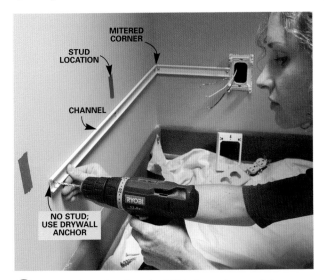

MITERED CORNER

STUD LOCATION

CHANNEL

NO STUD; USE DRYWALL ANCHOR

2 Cut the channel to length, drill holes and screw it to studs. If the ends don't land on studs, fasten them with drywall anchors.

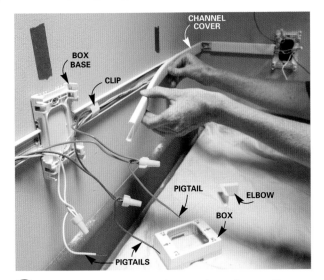

CHANNEL COVER

BOX BASE

CLIP

PIGTAIL

ELBOW

BOX

PIGTAILS

3 Mount a box base on the wall. Run wire and secure it with clips. Snap the cover and elbows over the channel. Then snap the boxes onto the bases. Add outlets.

"Anywhere" home office

tip Use the new Wi-Fi system to wirelessly network all the computers in the household. That allows sharing files and even printers. An adapter card is needed for each computer. Most WAPs can handle at least four computers connected to the Internet at the same time.

With a laptop and access to the Internet via a high-speed broadband or DSL connection, a Wi-Fi (wireless fidelity) system in the home gives the ability to roam the home or yard at will. (Sorry, this system won't work for dial-up connections.) Call up those chat rooms, place online trades or deal with e-mail with the same speed and security as before, but without being chained to a specific location by a cable. Instead, with laptop in hand, lounge by the pool, relax in the screen room or sprawl in a favorite recliner.

To get the convenience of a wireless café at home, purchase two items: a WAP (wireless access point, often less than $100) and a laptop adapter card (also less than $100) if your computer doesn't already have built-in wireless capacity. The WAP plugs into the DSL or broadband router box (supplied by the high-speed Internet provider). The WAP sends and receives signals from the adapter card that plugs into the side of the laptop. Setup only takes minutes and then the connection is wireless! Follow the directions on the CDs included with the equipment.

As any computer junkie knows, wireless systems have been around for years. But the equipment available now is more affordable and has dramatically greater range than ever before. With the gear shown on this page, the laptop had a fast, clean Internet connection 200 ft. away from the WAP, even though the signal had to penetrate three concrete block walls and a moving van. So consider upgrading an older Wi-Fi system to new gear for bettter quality, speed and range.

LAPTOP CARD:
Plugs into the laptop's card port to send and receive signals from the WAP (wireless access point).

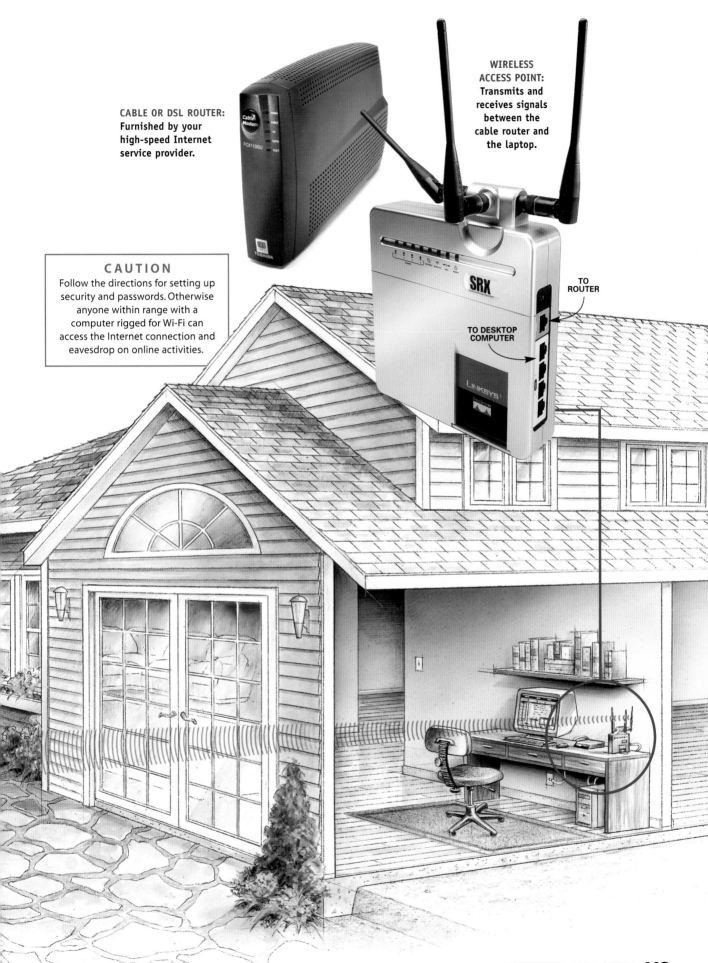

CABLE OR DSL ROUTER: Furnished by your high-speed Internet service provider.

WIRELESS ACCESS POINT: Transmits and receives signals between the cable router and the laptop.

CAUTION
Follow the directions for setting up security and passwords. Otherwise anyone within range with a computer rigged for Wi-Fi can access the Internet connection and eavesdrop on online activities.

TO ROUTER

TO DESKTOP COMPUTER

Modular bookcase

ome bookcases have plenty of charm but are shy on actual shelf space. Others will house stacks of books but are short on looks. This elegant design does it all, featuring more than 43 ft. of shelf space.

The multi-component system has two 7-ft.-tall end bookcases plus a shorter center cabinet with glass doors to create dust-free storage for electronics or favorite collectibles. The total width is just over 10 ft., but can be built narrower or wider with individual components to custom-size it to fit nearly any room. Build it into a corner, center it along a wall, or build it wall to wall. The total cost was $1,500 for the bookcase shown here.

Don't confuse this project's elegance with complexity. The step-by-step building process is well within an intermediate skill level. As far as special tools go, a portable table saw is a must. The flat homemade moldings and dentils are simply cut from 3/4-in.-thick boards. The face frame and door joints are made with an inexpensive pocket hole jig and can be assembled in minutes. A power

miter saw also is a real timesaver, and buying or renting an air-powered finish nailer will save even more time and get better results.

Cherry isn't available at home centers. Find a specialty hardwood lumber supplier that stocks cherry boards and plywood. If cherry isn't available, consider another hardwood like oak, maple or birch.

Sizing up the room

Trying to decide where to install the shelves? First make sure the ceiling height is adequate and there's enough wall space. If needed, change the dimensions of the project a bit to accommodate the space. Second, check the locations of the electrical outlets. Make sure they don't fall directly behind one of the cabinet sides. If they do, adjust the placement of the cabinets or move the receptacle. If the receptacle is directly behind one of the tall cabinets, cut an opening in the back of the cabinet to expose the receptacle and install a box extender.

Start with simple boxes

Cut the plywood for the sides, top and bottom to width on a table saw. Notice in the Cutting list (p. 117) that the outer plywood sides (E) are 1/4 in. wider than the inner plywood sides (A). This additional width covers the 1/4-in. plywood back nailed to the back of the inner sides to get a nice, right-to-the-wall look viewed from the side.

Drill the shelf support holes into the inner sides using a homemade jig like the one shown in Photo 2. It takes a bit of work to make this simple jig, but it'll find tons of uses in the shop. The jig will ensure that each row of the shelf bracket holes will be level with each other. Don't bother drilling holes within the top and bottom foot of the sides, since they'll never be used that high or low; see Figure A (p. 116) for hole placement.

Screw the sides to the top and bottom panels (Photo 3) with 1-3/4-in.-wood screws. Next cut the 1/4-in. plywood back to the dimensions in the Cutting list. Use the factory edges of the plywood back to square up the cabinet as it's nailed to the back sides of parts A and B.

Thicken box sides for function and looks

The bookcases don't need to have double-thick side walls, but thick walls look more substantial and keep books from being hidden behind the wide face frame front.

With the simple box completed, add straight 2x2s to the sides as shown in Photo 4 on p. 118. Apply yellow wood glue to the edge and hold it firmly against the side of the box as it's nailed with a nail gun from inside the box. Use 1-1/2-in. nails. Be sure the front 2x2 is flush with the inner side (A) and the outer side (E). The back 2x2 is best placed slightly in from the back edge of the outer side so it won't keep the cabinet away from the wall as it's screwed in place later.

Once the outer plywood sides are glued and nailed to the 2x2s (Photo 4), cut the cabinet top to the dimensions in the Cutting list. If customizing the cabinets to a different size, cut this top piece 2-1/4 in. deeper and 3-1/2 in. wider than the outer dimensions of the top of each cabinet assembly. Now get somebody to help carry these two cabinet boxes into the room and get ready to tip them up into place. Be sure to remove the baseboard around the bookcase location, and save the pieces to recut them to fit against the bookcase sides once the project is finished.

1/4" BRAD POINT BIT

STOP BLOCK

DEPTH STOP

1 Cut 3/4-in. plywood sides and tops using a circular saw and a cutting guide. Support the workpiece with 2x4s beneath to keep the cut from buckling and pinching the blade.

SQUARE CUTTING GUIDE

2x4 SUPPORTS

2 Make a drilling guide jig for the shelf supports from 1/8-in.-thick steel from a hardware store. Drill holes every 2 in. and carefully place the jig on each panel (A) for uniformly spaced holes 1/2 in. deep. Use a stop block to control the depth positioning. See Figure A for positioning details.

STOP BLOCK

A

JIG

SHELF PIN HOLE GUIDE

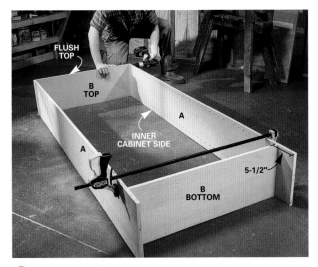

3 Predrill and screw the inner side panels (A) to the top and bottom (B) with 1-3/4-in. wood screws. Nail the 1/4-in.-plywood back to the inner side panels and the top and bottom to square up the box.

FLUSH TOP

B TOP

A

INNER CABINET SIDE

A

5-1/2"

B BOTTOM

Figure A

Bookcase details

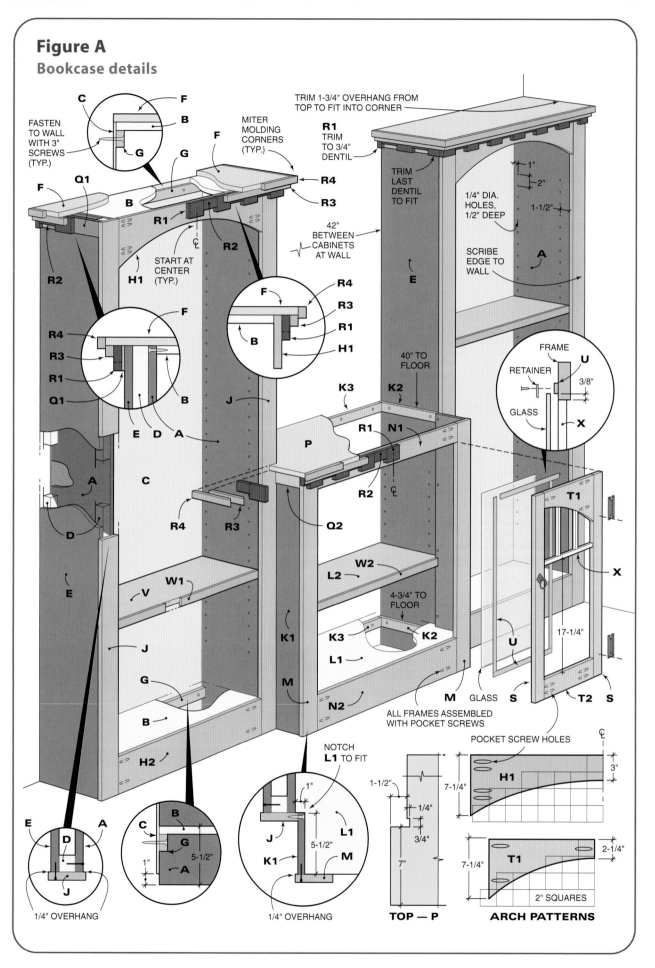

FASTEN TO WALL WITH 3" SCREWS (TYP.)

C
F
B
G

F
MITER MOLDING CORNERS (TYP.)
F
G
G

TRIM 1-3/4" OVERHANG FROM TOP TO FIT INTO CORNER

R1 TRIM TO 3/4" DENTIL

TRIM LAST DENTIL TO FIT

1"
2"
1-1/2"

1/4" DIA. HOLES, 1/2" DEEP

SCRIBE EDGE TO WALL

A

F
Q1
B
R1
R2

R4
R3

42" BETWEEN CABINETS AT WALL

E

R2
H1
START AT CENTER (TYP.)

F
B
R4
R3
R1
H1

FRAME
U
RETAINER
3/8"
GLASS
X

R4
R3
R1
Q1

F

B

E D A

C

A

D

R4
R3

J

P
R1
N1
R2

Q2

T1

E

W1
V

W2
L2

K3
K1
L1
M

4-3/4" TO FLOOR
K3
K2

X

U
17-1/4"

J

G

B

H2

N2

M GLASS
S
T2 S

ALL FRAMES ASSEMBLED WITH POCKET SCREWS

40" TO FLOOR

K3
K2

NOTCH L1 TO FIT

1"
J
K1
L1
5-1/2"
M

POCKET SCREW HOLES

3"
H1
7-1/4"

1-1/2"
1/4"
3/4"
7"

T1
2-1/4"
7-1/4"

2" SQUARES

E
D
A
J
1/4" OVERHANG

C
B
G
5-1/2"
A
1"

1/4" OVERHANG

TOP — P

ARCH PATTERNS

Cutting list

Key	Pcs.	Size & description
A	4	3/4" x 11-5/8" x 84" inner plywood cabinet sides
B	4	3/4" x 11-5/8" x 33" plywood cabinet top, bottom
C	2	1/4" x 34-1/2" x 83" plywood cabinet backs
D	8	1-1/2" x 1-1/2" x 84" pine
E	4	3/4" x 11-7/8" x 84" outer plywood cabinet sides
F	2	3/4" x 14-1/8" x 42-1/2" plywood cabinet tops
G	4	3/4" x 1-1/2" x 33" upper and lower fastening strips
H1	2	3/4" x 7-1/4" x 32-1/2" face frame arch
H2	2	3/4" x 5-1/2" x 32-1/2" face frame base
J	4	3/4" x 3-1/2" x 84" face frame sides
K1	2	3/4" x 5-1/2" x 40" center cabinet side wings
K2	4	3/4" x 1-1/2" x 11-7/8" cabinet cleats
K3	2	3/4" x 1-1/2" x 40-1/2" wall cleats
L1	1	3/4" x 17-3/8" x 42" plywood center cabinet floor*
L2	1	3/4" x 11-7/8" x 42" plywood center cabinet shelf*
M	2	3/4" x 3-1/2" x 40" center face frame sides
N1	1	3/4" x 3" x 35" center face frame top
N2	1	3/4" x 5-1/2" x 35" center face frame base
P	1	3/4" x 19-5/8" x 45" plywood center cabinet top*
Q1	4	1/4" x 2-1/4" x 11-7/8" cabinet side fillets
Q2	2	1/4" x 2-1/4" x 4-3/4" cabinet side fillets
R1	32	3/4" x 3-1/6" x 2-1/4" dentils
R2	28	3/4" x 1-1/2" x 3-1/16" dentil spacers
R3	16'	3/4" x 1" upper molding
R4	16'	3/4" x 1" top molding
S	4	3/4" x 2-1/4" x 31-1/2" door stiles
T1	2	3/4" x 7-1/4" x 12-15/16" arched door rails
T2	2	3/4" x 3" x 12-15/16" bottom door rails
U	17'	3/16" x 3/4" glass edging*
V	10	3/4" x 11" x 32-13/16" plywood shelves
W1	10	1/2" x 1-1/4" x 32-13/16" shelf nosing
W2	1	1/2" x 1-1/4" x 40" shelf nosing
X	5'	5/8" x 5/8" door muntins*

* Cut to fit

Use a pocket hole jig to help join face frames and door frames

Unlike dowel and biscuit assembly, pocket hole joinery doesn't have messy glue or clamps. Just set the jig on the back side of the rail (top or bottom horizontal piece), squeeze the locking plate pliers, drill the holes, remove the jig and then drive the screws through the angled pilot holes into the face frame sides. For the best results, be sure to hold the two pieces down firmly on a clean, flat surface so the screw drives precisely for perfect alignment.

KREG POCKET HOLE CLAMP

SCREW PILOT DRILL

SCREWHEAD CLEARANCE DRILL

DEPTH STOP

ANGLED DRILL GUIDES

Cut the curves for the top rails of the face frames and the door frames using a jigsaw and the pattern shown in Figure A. Clamp the cut piece to the side of the workbench or saw-horse and then use a belt sander to carefully smooth the irregularities of the cut. Then just cut the lower rails to length with a miter saw and pocket-screw them together as shown in Photos 6 and 7 on p. 118.

Plumb, shim and screw side bookcases to the wall

Chances are the walls and floor have some irregularity, like a corner that's not exactly square or a wall slightly out of whack. Start with the corner cabinet and get it reasonably plumb and level with shims. Close is good enough because the project design is somewhat forgiving. Leave about a 1/8-in. gap between the side wall and the cabinet to make room for the face frame to overhang a bit. Screw the corner cabinet to the wall (Photo 9, p. 119).

Once the first cabinet is set, draw a plumb line 42 in. away from this cabinet. Slide the next wall cabinet over to this line and shim it to be perfectly level with the first cabinet. Screw the cabinet to the wall through the fastening strips at the top and bottom into the wall studs.

With the tall side cabinets securely fastened, bring the face frames into the room and check their fit against the faces of wall

Shopping list

Description	Qty.
3/4" cherry plywood	5
1/4" cherry plywood	2
1x4 x 7' cherry	12
1x6 x 8' cherry	5
1x8 x 8' cherry	1
Door hinges (see Buyer's Guide)	2 pr.
3/16" tempered door glass (measure to fit)	2
Magnetic door catches	2
Yellow wood glue	1 pt.

Description	Qty.
Door glass retainers	12
No. 4 brass screws	12
1/4" shelf supports	44
Pneumatic gun nails (3/4", 1-1/4", 1-1/2")	
1-1/4" wood screws, box of 100	1
1-3/4" wood screws, box of 100	1
Epoxy glue	1
Watco Cherry Finish	2 qts.

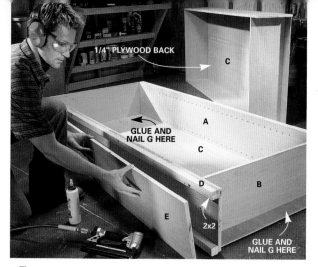

4 Glue and nail the 2x2 spacers to the sides from inside the box with a nail gun. Complete the cabinet box by gluing and nailing the outer plywood panels to the 2x2. Glue and nail fastening strips (G) in place at this time.

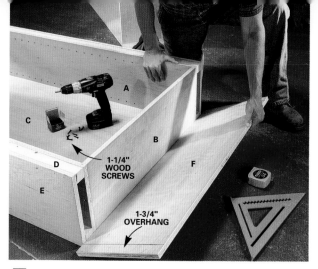

5 Screw the finished top (F) to the top of the cabinet with 1-1/4-in. wood screws. Make the back flush with the back of E and space the sides evenly. If the cabinet goes against the wall, cut off the wall side of the top flush with E.

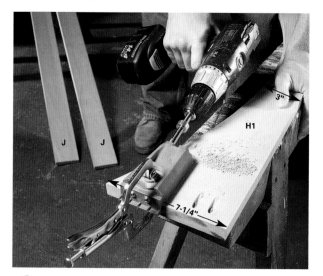

6 Cut the arched curves with a jigsaw, smooth them with a belt sander, then drill the back side of the arched front using a pocket hole jig.

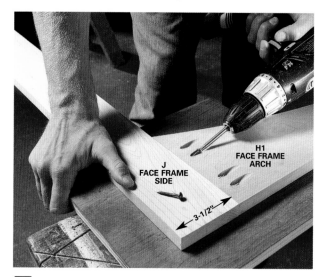

7 Hold the sides of the frame so the edges are flush and drive the screws into the mating piece with special pocket hole screws. This makes for a super-strong, fast, glue-free joint.

cabinets. If installing one of the cabinets against the side wall, scribe and trim the face frame a bit before installing it if needed (Photo 10). Trim or sand if necessary and then apply glue to the front of each cabinet and nail each face frame assembly in place with a finish nailer (Photo 11).

SCRIBE

Build the center cabinet in place

Unlike the flanking side cabinets, the center cabinet relies on the outer cabinets for part of its structure, so build it right in the room. Cut the flanking side wing pieces (K1), align them with the edges of the face frames, drill a pilot hole and screw them in place as shown in Photo 12. Next cut the support strips (K2 and K3) and screw them to the cabinet sides and back wall as supports for the center cabinet floor and the top (Photo 13). Cut and notch the floor piece (L1) and nail it to the cleats. Next, position the center face frame over the side wings, leaving a 1/4-in. overhang on each side. Then glue and nail it (1-1/2-in. nails) to the wings (K1) and to the front edge of the plywood floor (Photo 14).

Be sure to cut the top (P) so it projects 1-3/4 in. past each side wing (K1) and 1-1/2 in. out from the face frame in the front. If the top projects a bit farther than this, all the better, since it can be sanded flush with the upper molding strip (R3) later. This way the top strip (R4) will fit against the plywood top.

Mass-produce the dentils and spacers ahead of time

Rip a 1x4 board to 3-1/16 in. on a table saw and another to 1-1/2 in. wide. Mark a line on a miter saw to cut the wider board into 2-1/4-in. lengths to make the dentils. Change the mark to cut the narrower board into 3-1/16-in. lengths to make the spacers. Next rip a couple of 1x4 boards to 1-in. widths to make the upper moldings R3 and R4.

Mark the top center of each cabinet, then grab three dentils and mark the center bottom of each. Align the marks and nail the dentils right in the middle of the cabinets up against the projecting plywood tops. Next, nail a spacer on each side and work to

8 Set the cabinet boxes in the room. Space them 42 in. apart. Shim as necessary to get them both plumb and level. Cover spaces or gaps at the bottom with base shoe molding later.

9 Locate the studs and screw the cabinet through the horizontal fastening strip into the wall. Make sure there's enough room next to the side wall for the face frame.

10 Scribe the preassembled face frame to the side wall if the wall is uneven. Make sure the face frame overlaps the inner panel by 1/4 in. on each side.

11 Center the second face frame assembly on the box, mark it, then glue and nail it to the front of the cabinet.

12 Screw the side wings (K1) of the center cabinet to the edges of the face frames of the side cabinets. Drill pilot holes and use 1-1/4-in. wood screws.

13 Level and screw the cleats (K2 and K3) to the cabinet sides and wall studs with wood screws (1-1/4-in. screws on the sides and 2-1/2-in. screws into the wall studs).

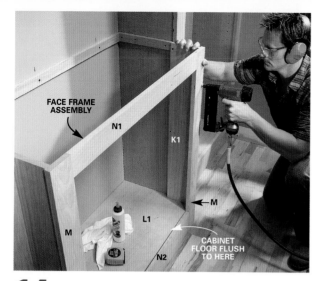

14 Cut and nail the center cabinet floor (L1) to the lower cleats, then glue and nail the center face frame assembly to the side wings (K1) and floor (L1). Then cut and nail on the top (P).

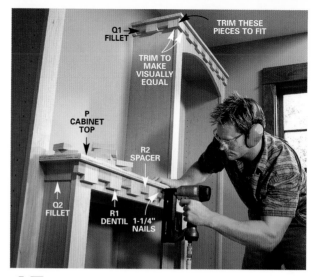

15 Mark the center of each cabinet. Center the first dentil (R1) over the mark and then nail the dentil spacers (R2) between each pair of dentils. Use 1-1/4-in. brads in a nail gun. Trim the dentils at the corners to ensure even wraps around each side of the corner.

the side of each side cabinet. Nail a 1/4-in. x 2-1/4-in. fillet on the side of each cabinet to fur out the dentil moldings to keep them aligned. Measure and cut this piece carefully so it ends up flush with the overhanging face frame. **Note:** Make the dentils visually equal at the corners (Photo 15). To achieve this, trim the side corner 3/4 in. less than the front corner dentil.

To finish the top cornice of each bookcase, cut the molding strips to length on the miter saw and nail them with 1-1/2-in. nails. After the first strip is in place, check the overhang of each top. The top edge should be flush with the face of R3. If the pieces aren't flush, sand them flush with a belt sander.

Get the spacing right on the inset doors

Inset doors are often considered difficult to install because they have to fit precisely inside the face frame. First, cut the pieces, then assemble each door using the pocket hole jig. Next, clamp the doors together at their center stiles with spacers between them and set the assembly up to the opening (Photo 17). Trim an edge or two with the table saw, and for fine adjustments, use a belt sander.

To hang the door, use simple face-mount hinges (see Buyer's Guide, p. 121). Just shim the doors as shown and then drill pilot holes holding the hinge in place. Work in one screw at a time to get perfect hinge placement. Once the doors are mounted, remove the hinges until after finishing.

Shaping a recess for glass along the inside of the door can be a hassle. To keep things simple, this project uses a much easier method than routing it out. Cut strips and glue and nail them to the back side of the door. Leave a 3/8-in. lip for the glass to sit on and then buy simple glass retainers at a hardware store. Then order the glass. Get tempered glass from a glass supplier because regular double-strength glass is prone to breaking.

16 Miter the ends of the upper trim strips R3 and R4 and nail the first strip to the dentils and the upper strip to the cabinet top.

The final step to great-looking doors is to make the muntins that overlay the glass (Photo 20). Measure up 17-1/4 in. from the bottom of the door glass opening and then measure, cut and place the first horizontal piece so the bottom edge of it aligns with the mark. Mark these strips to get three equal glass sections. Cut angles on the tops to follow the curve. Once they fit into place, mark the muntin placement onto the door, mix up some clear epoxy (Photo 20) and glue the assembly to itself and the door edge. **Note:** Place wax paper under joints to keep the epoxy off the glass. Once the glue is set, clean up any excess at the joints with a file or sandpaper.

17 Cut the door stiles (S) and the door rails (T1 and T2) and assemble them with pocket holes and screws as shown in Figure A. Trim the doors and set the top and side clearance. Use tablet backer board from a legal pad for spacers. Use double spacers at the top, bottom and center and use single spacers at the sides against the face frame. Install the face-mount hinges and magnetic catches.

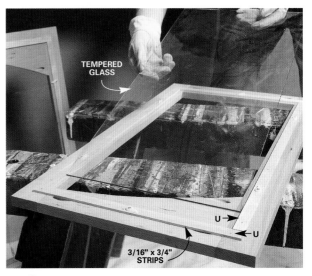

18 Cut 3/16-in. strips from 3/4-in.-thick material, then glue and tack it (5/8-in. brads) to the inside of the door. Leave a 3/8-in. lip for the tempered glass panels.

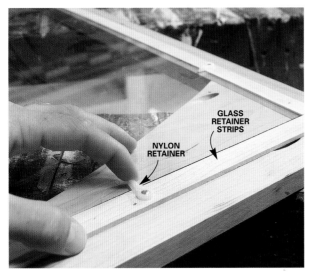

19 Buy nylon storm-window glass retainers from a hardware store along with No. 4 brass screws to secure the glass.

20 Cut muntin strips on the table saw and glue them to the ends of the rails and stiles with epoxy. Be careful not to slop glue on the wood faces or it will block the finish stain.

Cut the shelves from 3/4-in. plywood

Rip the plywood and then cut it to length (3/16 in. less than the inside measure) for the shelf blanks. To give the shelves a solid wood look, rip strips 1-1/4 in. wide and then 1/2 in. thick, cut them the same length as the shelf blanks and glue and nail them to cover the plywood edge.

The center shelf is made the same way. Just rip the plywood to 11-7/8 in. wide and cut the solid edge strip and nail it in place so the strip falls between the inside faces of the side wings (K1). Drill holes into the center cabinet sides for the shelf supports.

Cherry can be fussy to finish

To help get the Watco Cherry Finish as even as possible, Minwax Pre-finish Wood Conditioner was used first and then the color was applied. This cut down on the blotchiness, and sanding lightly over trouble spots gave a good look. After three days, apply satin polyurethane for a nice, even, durable sheen. Or, apply a clear oil or varnish and the cherry will darken naturally with age.

Buyer's Guide

Buy hinges, door pulls, shelf supports, magnetic catches and a Kreg jig from Rockler Hardware (800-279-4441, rockler.com) or other woodworking specialty stores.

Leaning
tower of shelves

This stylish but sturdy shelf unit will neatly hold lots of stuff and can be built in a day. The unit may look light-weight and easy to topple. But don't be fooled. It's a real workhorse. The 33-1/2-in. x 82-3/4-in. tower features five unique, tray-like shelves of different depths to hold a wide variety of items up to 13-1/4 in. tall. Despite its 10-degree lean, the unit is surprisingly sturdy, and its open design won't overpower a room.

Select the type of wood and stain or paint to dress it up to fit the look of any room. All the materials can be purchased in home centers or lumberyards. The only special tools needed are a power miter box for crisp angle cuts and an air-powered brad nailer for quick assembly and almost invisible joints. And rustle up an old clothes iron for applying oak edge-banding material. The shelf unit can be built in one afternoon.

Buying the wood

This unit is built with red oak and oak veneer plywood and fin-ished with two coats of red oak stain. The beauty of this project is that any wood species will work. To paint it, select alder or aspen for the solid parts and birch for the plywood.

One note when buying boards: Use a tape measure to check the "standard" dimensions of 1x3s and 1x4s. They sometimes vary in width and thickness. Also check the two full-length 1x4s to be used as the uprights to be sure they're straight, without warps or twists. And always examine the ends, edges and surface for blemishes or rough areas that won't easily sand out.

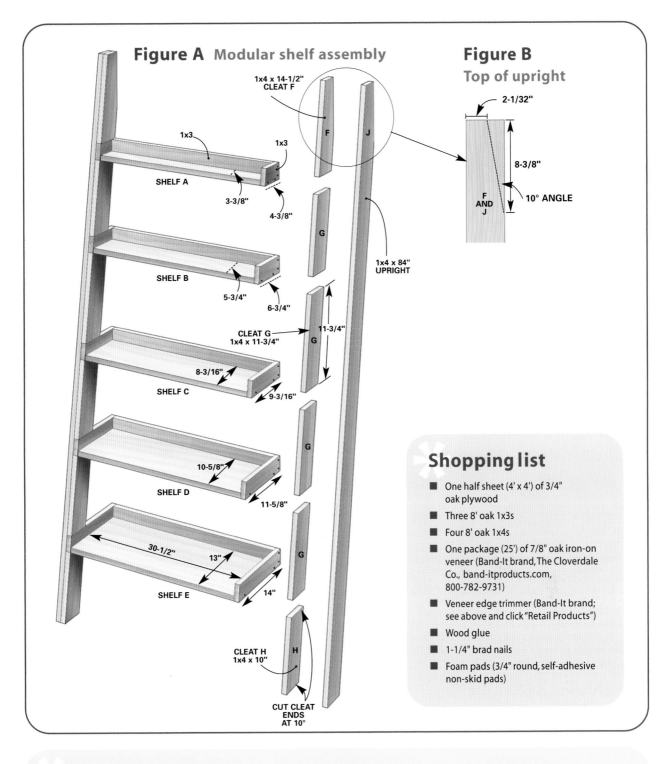

Figure A Modular shelf assembly

1x4 x 14-1/2"
CLEAT F

1x3

SHELF A

1x3

3-3/8"

4-3/8"

F

J

SHELF B

5-3/4"

6-3/4"

G

CLEAT G
1x4 x 11-3/4"

11-3/4"

G

8-3/16"

9-3/16"

SHELF C

1x4 x 84"
UPRIGHT

G

10-5/8"

11-5/8"

SHELF D

30-1/2"

13"

G

14"

SHELF E

CLEAT H
1x4 x 10"

H

CUT CLEAT
ENDS
AT 10°

Figure B
Top of upright

2-1/32"

8-3/8"

F
AND
J

10° ANGLE

Shopping list

- One half sheet (4' x 4') of 3/4" oak plywood
- Three 8' oak 1x3s
- Four 8' oak 1x4s
- One package (25') of 7/8" oak iron-on veneer (Band-It brand, The Cloverdale Co., band-itproducts.com, 800-782-9731)
- Veneer edge trimmer (Band-It brand; see above and click "Retail Products")
- Wood glue
- 1-1/4" brad nails
- Foam pads (3/4" round, self-adhesive non-skid pads)

Cutting list

Pcs.	Size & description
1	3/4" x 3-3/8" x 30-1/2" oak plywood (shelf **A** base)
1	3/4" x 5-3/4" x 30-1/2" oak plywood (shelf **B** base)
1	3/4" x 8-3/16" x 30-1/2" oak plywood (shelf **C** base)
1	3/4" x 10-5/8" x 30-1/2" oak plywood (shelf **D** base)
1	3/4" x 13" x 30-1/2" oak plywood (shelf **E** base)
2	3/4" x 2-1/2" x 4-3/8" oak (shelf **A** sides)*
2	3/4" x 2-1/2" x 6-3/4" oak (shelf **B** sides)*
2	3/4" x 2-1/2" x 9-3/16" oak (shelf **C** sides)*

Pcs.	Size & description
2	3/4" x 2-1/2" x 11-5/8" oak (shelf **D** sides)*
2	3/4" x 2-1/2" x 14" oak (shelf **E** sides)*
5	3/4" x 2-1/2" x 30-1/2" oak **A - E** (shelf backs)
2	3/4" x 3-1/2" x 14-1/2" oak shelf cleats **F** (cut with 10-degree angles)
8	3/4" x 3-1/2" x 11-3/4" oak shelf cleats **G** (cut with 10-degree angles)
2	3/4" x 3-1/2" x 10" oak shelf cleats **H** (cut with 10-degree angles)
2	3/4" x 3-1/2" x 84" oak uprights **J** (cut with 10-degree angles)

*Front part of side cut at 10 degrees

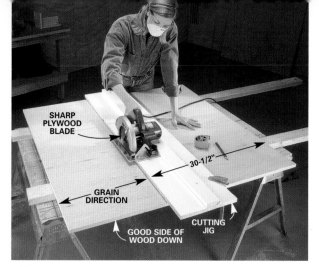

1 Cut 3/4-in. shelf plywood to width first, using a circular saw and a homemade jig for exact cuts. Use a sharp plywood blade and cut with the best side of the wood facing down to minimize splintering.

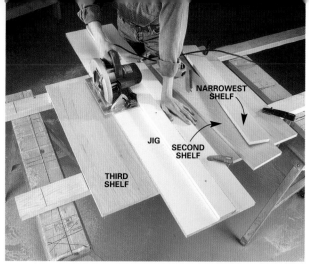

2 Cut the individual shelves, beginning with the narrowest, using the jig for perfectly straight cuts.

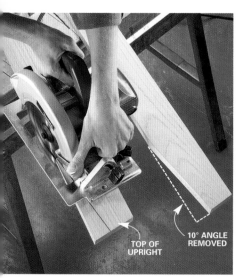

3 Cut both shelf uprights to length with a miter saw. Clamp to sawhorses. Mark the 10-degree angle at the top (dimensions in Figure B), then cut with a circular saw.

4 Iron edge-banding veneer to the front edge of all five shelves. Roll the entire surface to ensure a solid bond, and trim the edges.

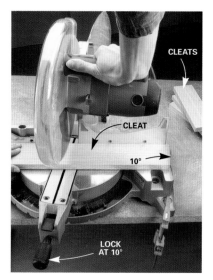

5 To maintain accuracy, lock the miter box at 10 degrees, then cut all angled pieces—uprights, cleats and one end of shelf sides—without changing the table.

Cut plywood shelves first

Lay a couple of 2x4s across sawhorses (Photo 1) to cut the half sheet of 3/4-in. plywood cleanly and without pinching the saw blade. Since all five shelves are 30-1/2 in. wide, cut this width first, making sure the grain will run the long way across the shelves. Remember to wear safety glasses, earplugs and a dust mask. Make a homemade jig to fit the circular saw and clamp it to the plywood.

Next, cut all five shelf depths, starting with the smallest shelf (3-3/8 in.) first. Cut smallest to largest so there will be enough wood to clamp the jig. **Important:** Make sure to account for the width of the saw blade when cutting each shelf.

Now mark and cut the top of all four 1x4 uprights (the end that rests against the wall), according to Photo 3 and the two dimensions provided in Figure B. Use a sharp blade in the circular saw to prevent splintering. Then stow the sawhorses and move to the workbench.

Select the best front of each plywood shelf, clamp it to the bench on edge and sand it smooth with 150-grit paper on a sanding block. Then preheat a clothes iron to the "cotton" setting and run it over the top of the edge-banding veneer, making sure the veneer extends beyond all edges (Photo 4). Roll it smooth immediately after heating. Let each shelf edge cool for a couple of minutes before trimming and sanding the edges.

Cut uprights and shelf frame next

Now use a miter saw to make all the 90-degree straight cuts first (five shelf backs and 10 shelf sides; see Cutting list). **Important:** Remember that one end of each shelf side has a 10-degree cut, so first cut them square at their exact length, then cut the angle carefully so the long edge of each piece remains the same.

Next, rotate the miter saw table to the 10-degree mark and cut all the angle pieces. First cut the bottom of both uprights so each upright rests flat against the floor and wall (see Figure A, p. 123).

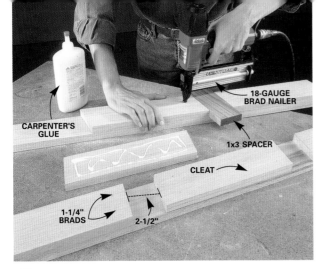

CARPENTER'S GLUE

18-GAUGE BRAD NAILER

1x3 SPACER

CLEAT

1-1/4" BRADS

2-1/2"

6 Glue and nail the shelf cleats to the uprights using a 1x3 spacer. Hold each cleat tight to the spacer.

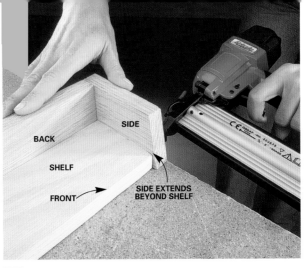

SIDE

BACK

SHELF

FRONT

SIDE EXTENDS BEYOND SHELF

7 Glue and nail the shelf backs, then attach the sides to the plywood shelves. Position the sides to overlap the shelf base as shown.

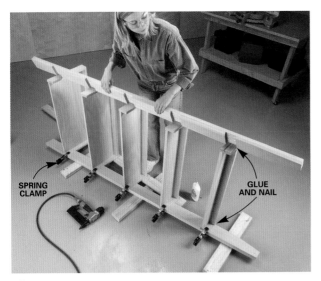

SPRING CLAMP

GLUE AND NAIL

8 Clamp the shelves into one upright. Spread glue in the shelf notches of the other upright, position it flush with the front of the shelves and nail. Flip the unit over and attach the other upright.

BAR CLAMP

1/2" GAP

9 Set the shelf unit against a straight wall, check for square and apply three bar clamps until the glue dries.

Then trim the top of the upright to match the bottom, being careful to maintain the 84-in. total length. Next, cut the cleats based on the Cutting list dimensions, which are measured edge to edge (Photo 5 and Figure A). Leave the top cleats long and cut them to exact fit during assembly. Then, to speed finishing, use an orbital sander with 150-grit sandpaper to smooth all pieces before assembly.

Assemble uprights first, then the shelves

To begin assembly, lay out both uprights and all cleats to ensure that the angles are correct so the shelves will be level when the unit is against the wall. Then glue and nail the first cleat flush with the base of each upright (using five or six 1-1/4-in. brads) on each cleat. Work upward using 1x3 spacers (Photo 6). Make sure the spacer is the exact same width as the shelf sides! Set these aside to dry.

For shelf assembly, first glue and nail on the shelf backs. Next, apply the sides with glue and nails (Photo 7).

For final assembly, lay one upright on 2x4s, then clamp on the shelves as shown in Photo 8. Apply the glue, position the second upright on top flush with the front edge of the shelves, then sink four 1-1/4-in. brads into each shelf from the upright side. Carefully turn the unit over and repeat the process to attach the second upright. Work quickly so the glue doesn't set. Lift the ladder shelf and place it upright against a straight wall. Check it with a framing square and flex it if necessary to square it up and to make sure that the uprights rest flat against the floor and wall (assuming the floor is level). Attach three bar clamps as shown in Photo 9 while the glue dries.

The shelf is highly stable as designed, but once it's stained or painted, add self-adhesive foam gripping pads to the bottom of the uprights. The unit's width is perfect for screwing the top of the uprights into wall studs if desired.

NON-SKID FOAM PAD

DVD
storage cabinet

This cabinet is 42 in. wide and holds about 60 DVD cases. Go ahead and expand or shrink the width to better hold a personalized collection or to fit a particular spot on the wall. The construction techniques will be the same no matter the width. The simple cutting and joining techniques shown here will produce fine cabinet-quality results, and making clean and accurate crosscuts, rabbets (grooves on edges) and miters, results in a spectacular finished product.

This project does require a table saw. To get good, true, splinter-free results, buy a 40-tooth carbide blade. Use a pneumatic nailer with 1-1/2-in. brads to fasten the cabinet parts and 1-in. brads to nail the cornice. This will speed up the assembly and give better results than hand nailing. All told, the actual cutting and assembly only take a few hours, plus time spent finishing. Expect to spend about $65 for all the hardwood.

Choose the wood to match the decor

This cabinet is made of oak and finished with oil stain (Minwax "Golden Oak") and shellac. Make the cabinet from whatever wood best matches the room's decor. But be aware that if you choose wood other than poplar, oak or pine, the home center probably won't stock matching molding for the top and bottom. If paint will be the finish, select poplar boards and clear pine molding.

Rip the parts to width first, then to length

Begin by ripping the two 6-ft.-long 1x8s to 6 in. wide, then cross-cut the end and top and bottom boards to length (Figure B). Go ahead and rip the divider panels to the final 5-in. width, but hold off on cutting the dividers and top cap to length for now.

The key to clean tight joints is to make matching pairs of parts *exactly* the same length.

The small fence that comes with the miter gauge isn't much good for holding wood square to make accurate cuts. Extend it by screwing a 24-in.-long fence extension to the miter gauge, with the right side hanging a bit past the blade (Photo 1, p. 128). (There are holes in the miter gauge just for this task.) One of the leftover pieces from the previous rips will work great for the extension fence. Choose screw lengths that penetrate the wood about 5/8 in. after allowing for the miter gauge wall thickness.

Don't trust the angle indicators on the miter gauge; they're bound to be inaccurate. Instead, square the miter gauge to one of the miter gauge slots with a carpenter's square (Photo 1). When it's square, tighten up the locking handle. Raise the blade and cut off the end of the fence and it's ready to crosscut. The end of the fence perfectly marks the saw blade's path. Line up measurement marks with that end and you'll know exactly where to place the board for cutting.

Nest the wood against the miter gauge clear of the blade, start up the saw, and push the wood all the way past the blade. To be safe, shut off the saw before removing both parts.

Cut the rabbets

Now cut the 3/8-in.-deep, 1/4-in.-wide rabbets on the back of the bottom, top and sides to create a recess for the 1/4-in.-thick ply-wood back (Photo 3, p. 128). First lower the blade below the

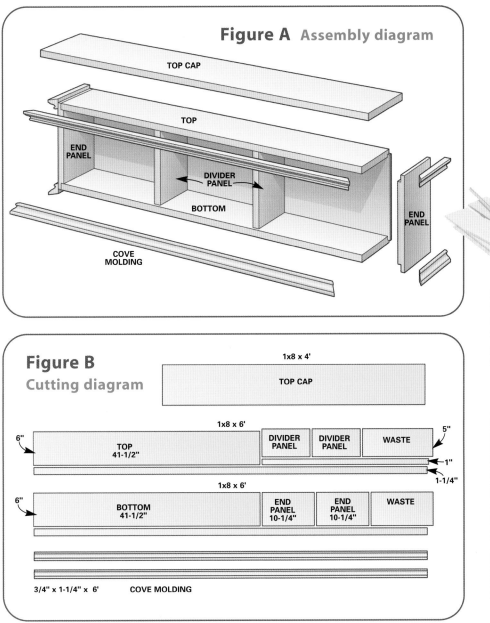

Figure A Assembly diagram

TOP CAP

TOP

END PANEL

DIVIDER PANEL

BOTTOM

END PANEL

COVE MOLDING

Build this project from three boards, a little plywood and 12 ft. of trim.

Figure B
Cutting diagram

1x8 x 4'

TOP CAP

1x8 x 6'

6"

TOP
41-1/2"

DIVIDER PANEL

DIVIDER PANEL

WASTE

5"

1"

1-1/4"

1x8 x 6'

6"

BOTTOM
41-1/2"

END PANEL
10-1/4"

END PANEL
10-1/4"

WASTE

3/4" x 1-1/4" x 6'   COVE MOLDING

Materials list

- Two 6-ft. 1x8s: Cabinet top and bottom, end panels and center dividers.
- One 4-ft. 1x8: Top cap
- Two 6-ft. lengths of 3/4-in. x 1-1/4-in. cove molding: Top and bottom trim
- 2 x 4-ft. 1/4-in. plywood: Back panel (not shown)

throat plate and clamp a straight 3/4-in.-thick sacrificial board to the saw fence. Position the clamps at least an inch above the table so the 3/4-in. boards can slide under them. Move the fence over the blade so it will cut about 1/8 in. into the sacrificial board, then lock the fence, turn on the saw and slowly raise the blade into the board until it's about 1 in. above the table to cut a clearance slot (Photo 3). Lower the blade to 3/8 in. above the table to start cutting the rabbets.

Nudge the fence about 1/16 in. away from the blade and make cuts on all four boards (Photo 3). Be sure to hold the boards tight to the fence and the table for smooth, complete cuts. And keep hands well away from the blade, because the guard has to be removed to make this cut. Continue moving the fence in 1/16-in. increments and making cuts until approaching the final 1/4-in. depth of the rabbet. Then check the depth with 1/4-in. plywood and make fine adjustments in the fence to make a final cut. The plywood should fit flush with the back edge of the board.

Leave the depth setting on the blade and use the miter gauge to cut the rabbets on the end panels. Set the fence to cut

3/4 in. wide (measured to the far edge of the blade). Make a series of cuts at each end (Photo 4, p. 128). Push the wood completely through and stop the saw before pulling the miter gauge back. Smooth any saw marks with a sharp chisel for a cleaner-looking, tighter-fitting joint (Photo 5, p. 129).

Sand all the surfaces up to 120 grit for open-grain woods like oak, pine, cherry and walnut. Sand to 220 grit for closed-grain woods like maple and birch.

Stain before assembly

If staining, stain the parts at this point because it's tough to get into inside corners after assembling the cabinet. For stronger glue joints, cover the surfaces of the rabbets with masking tape to keep stain off (Photo 6). Cut the plywood back about 1/2 in. larger than the opening, prefinish it at the same time and cut it to exact size later along with the center dividers.

This step gives better finishing results, but it will add to the project completion time because it means letting stains dry before assembly.

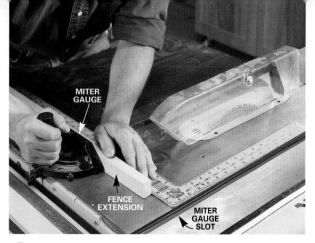

1 Screw a 2-ft.-long extension fence to the miter gauge. Square the miter gauge with the miter gauge slot.

2 Rip the boards to width (use Figure B, p. 127 for cutting dimensions), then cut the top, bottom and sides to length.

CAUTION: You must remove the blade guard for these rabbeting techniques, so be careful!

3 Set the blade to cut 3/8 in. deep. Make a series of passes along the back edge of each board, moving the fence away from the blade with each pass until the width is 1/4 in.

4 Set the fence 3/4 in. from the far edge of the blade and make a series of 3/8-in.-deep overlapping saw kerfs to rabbet the top and bottom of the end panels.

Assemble the sides, dividers and back

Glue and nail each end panel to the top and bottom boards. Four 1-in. brads, two at the top and two at the bottom, are plenty. Then clamp the assembly together to pull the joints tight (Photo 7). Check for square right away before the glue sets. It requires clamps that are at least 5 ft. long. Use blocks to spread the pressure over the whole joint. If one of the diagonal measurements is longer than the other, gently squeeze another clamp across those corners to pull the frame square. Or, instead of using long clamps, just glue and clamp the joints together with a few extra brads. (The joints might not fit as tightly as clamped ones, but plug slim gaps with wood filler later.) Measure and cut the back to fit, then glue and nail it in place with 1-in. brads spaced every 6 in. (Photo 8).

Save the dividers for last. Measure and cut them to fit, then space them equally in the cabinet and nail them through the top and bottom with 1-1/2-in. brads (Photo 9). No glue is needed.

Add the cove trim and top cap

Cut and install the cove molding starting at one end, then the long front piece, then the other end. To get perfect final lengths (Photo 11), cut 45-degree bevels on a short piece of molding to

use as a test block when fitting and cutting. Use the miter gauge to cut the bevels. The technique is the same as crosscutting, only with the saw blade set to 45 degrees (Photo 10). Leave 3/16 in. of "reveal" (exposed cabinet edge) for a nice look. Or go with a wider or narrower reveal as long as it's consistent. Fasten the molding to the cabinet with glue and 1-in. brads.

Center the top cap on either side of the molding and flush with the back, then glue and pin it to the molding with 1-1/2-in. brads (Photo 12). Place the brads carefully over the thick part of the trim. It's easy to accidentally blow through the narrower, contoured front.

Clear-coat the cabinet with finish. It's easier to apply smooth coats of finish with a spray can than with a brush, especially when finishing the interior. This project used three coats of shellac. It dries quickly so it can be completely finished (all three coats) in one day. It's also the least hazardous of all finishes. Do the spraying in a dust-free room to eliminate sanding between coats.

Hang it on the wall

Hang the 42-in. cabinet with 2-1/2-in. screws driven through the back and into two studs. But if only one stud can be found, use drywall anchors near the end farthest from the stud.

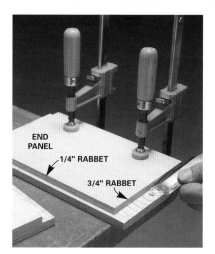

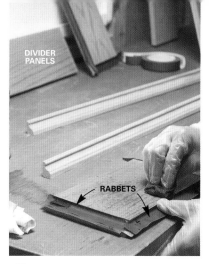

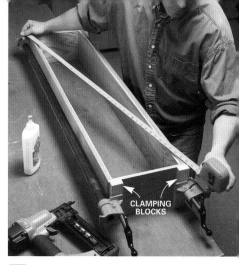

5 Smooth the saw marks by shaving the rabbets flat with a sharp chisel.

6 Cover the rabbets with masking tape and apply stain to all the cabinet parts.

7 Glue and nail the end panels to the top and bottom. Then clamp the assembly and check for square.

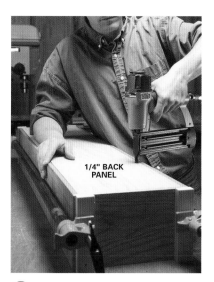

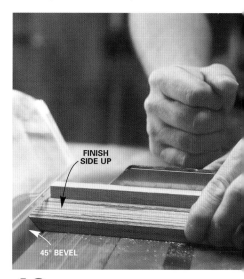

8 Cut the back panel to fit, then glue and nail it into the rabbets with 1-in. brads.

9 Measure and cut the center dividers to fit. Then space them equally and nail them with 1-1/2-in. brads.

10 Cut the moldings to length using the miter gauge with the saw blade set at a 45-degree bevel.

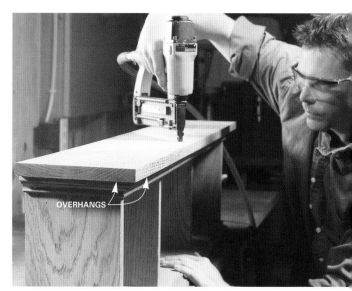

11 Use a scrap of cove molding to test-fit lengths. Glue and nail the molding with 1-in. brads.

12 Cut the top cap to length so that the end overhangs match the front. Then glue and nail the top cap to the molding with 1-1/2-in. brads.

Stackable shelving

Looking for a way to maximize the storage on a wall? Look no further. These shelves are easy to build, stylish enough to display a collection of favorite things, yet strong enough to hold plenty of books. In addition, they can be easily customized to fit around windows, doors, desks and other features and make every inch of wall space count.

This section shows how to make these handsome shelves with plywood and iron-on edge veneer. Then it shows how to mount them in simple grooved 1x2 uprights that are fastened to the walls.

Cutting the groove in the uprights (Figure B) and making square, splinter-free crosscuts on the plywood are the only tricky parts of the project, and the how-to steps show foolproof methods for both. Even though the shelves are simple, they require cutting out a lot of parts, so plan to spend a weekend on this project. Allow a few more days for staining and finishing.

Use a circular saw with a sharp 40-tooth carbide blade for cutting the plywood. To cut the groove in the 1x2, use a table saw and standard blade. The edge-trimming tool shown isn't manda-tory (a sharp utility knife and patience give good results), but it simplifies the job. The Veneer Edge Trimmer No. 147456 is available at Woodcraft for $9 (800-225-1153 or woodcraft.com).

The project uses 1-1/2 sheets of 3/4-in. plywood to build the 8-ft.-long section. Add the edging, 1x2s and hardware, and the cost of these shelves comes to about $150. For a contemporary look, these oak shelves are stained black with two coats of sealer, but any paint or stain color will work.

Cut the plywood and iron on the edge veneer

Start by cutting the 4 x 8-ft. sheet of plywood into four 10-in.-wide strips (Figure C). Cut the 4 x 4-ft. sheet into five 8-in.-wide strips. Sand any saw marks from the edge of the plywood strips, being careful not to round over the corners. Then vacuum the edges to remove the sawdust.

The next step is to cover one long edge of each plywood strip with veneer tape (Photo 1, p. 132). Find iron-on veneer tape at

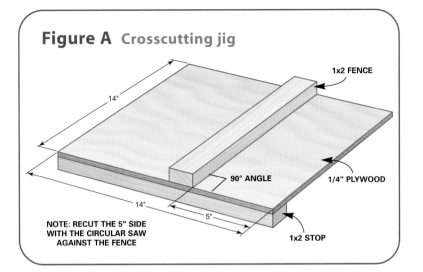

Figure A Crosscutting jig

1x2 FENCE

14"

90° ANGLE

1/4" PLYWOOD

14"

5"

1x2 STOP

NOTE: RECUT THE 5" SIDE
WITH THE CIRCULAR SAW
AGAINST THE FENCE

Materials list

Item	Qty.
3/4" x 4' x 8' A1 grade plywood	1
3/4" x 4' x 4' A1 grade plywood	1
1x2 x 6' oak	3
1x2 x 4' oak	1
3/4" or 7/8" iron-on veneer tape	60 ft.
1-5/8" flathead screws	32
2-1/2" flathead screws	20
1-1/4" trim head screws	4
3/4" x 3" mending plates	12
3/4" x 1-1/2" angle braces	4
3/4" x No. 6 flathead screws	52

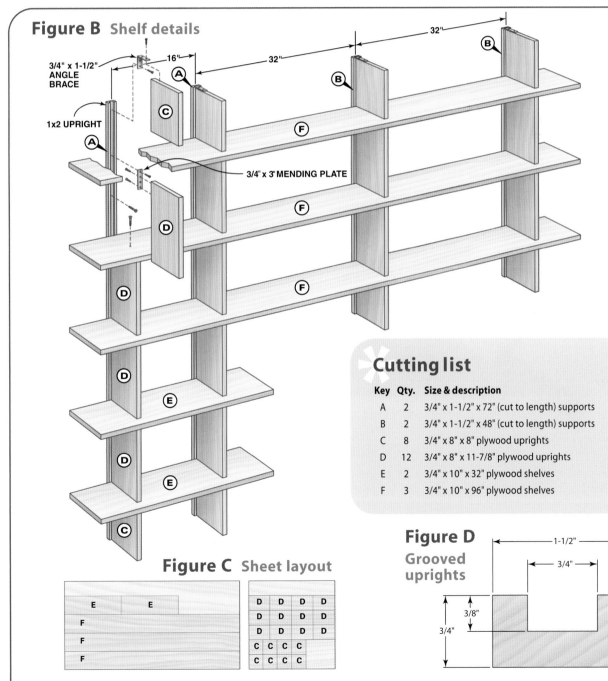

Figure B Shelf details

3/4" x 1-1/2"
ANGLE
BRACE

16"

32"

32"

1x2 UPRIGHT

3/4" x 3' MENDING PLATE

A
B
C
D
E
F

Cutting list

Key	Qty.	Size & description
A	2	3/4" x 1-1/2" x 72" (cut to length) supports
B	2	3/4" x 1-1/2" x 48" (cut to length) supports
C	8	3/4" x 8" x 8" plywood uprights
D	12	3/4" x 8" x 11-7/8" plywood uprights
E	2	3/4" x 10" x 32" plywood shelves
F	3	3/4" x 10" x 96" plywood shelves

Figure C Sheet layout

E	E
F	
F	
F	

D	D	D	D
D	D	D	D
D	D	D	D
C	C	C	C
C	C	C	C

Figure D
Grooved uprights

1-1/2"

3/4"

3/8"

3/4"

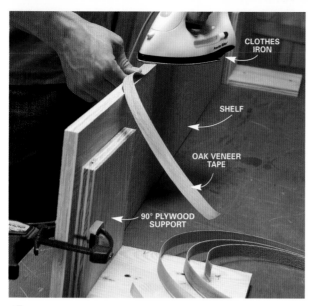

1 Rip the plywood to width and iron on the veneer tape. Align one edge with the plywood edge, set the iron to "cotton" and move it slowly along the veneer to melt the glue.

2 Trim the ends flush with a utility knife. Then trim the long edges flush with a special trimming tool. Finish by lightly sanding the edges flush with 220-grit paper.

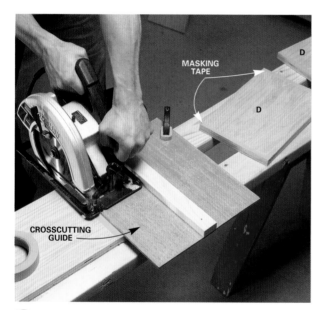

3 Crosscut the 8-in.-wide strips of plywood. Use a cross-cutting jig with a circular saw to get perfectly square cuts. Masking tape minimizes splintering.

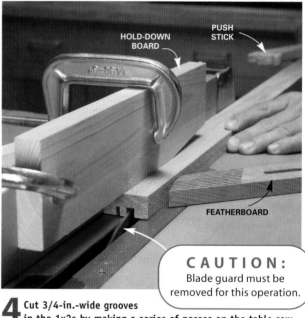

CAUTION: Blade guard must be removed for this operation.

4 Cut 3/4-in.-wide grooves in the 1x2s by making a series of passes on the table saw. Practice on a scrap to set the exact width and depth of the cut.

woodworking stores and home centers. Start by cutting strips of veneer tape a few inches longer than the plywood. Then align one edge of the tape with the face of the plywood and press the tape into place with a hot iron. Move the iron slowly enough to melt the glue, but fast enough to avoid scorching the veneer. An 8-ft. strip should take about 10 seconds. While the glue is still hot, rub a small chunk of wood along the tape to press and seal it to the plywood. Inspect the seam between the tape and the plywood for gaps, and reheat and press any loose areas. Use a sharp utility knife to trim the ends of the tape flush. Then use a special trimmer (Photo 2), a utility knife or a block plane to trim the long edges flush. Finish by sanding the edges of the tape flush to the plywood. Wrap 220-grit sandpaper around a small block of wood

and angle it slightly when sanding to avoid scuffing through the thin veneer on the plywood face. Cover the ends of the shelves with veneer tape later, after cutting the short shelves (E) to length.

Build a jig for accurate crosscutting

It may take a half hour to build, but an accurate crosscutting jig is essential for perfectly square, splinter-free cuts (Figure A, p. 131). Start by cutting a 14-in. square of 1/4-in. plywood on the table saw. Align a 1x2 stop with the edge of the plywood and attach it with 3/4-in. screws. Keep the screws 3 in. from the ends to avoid sawing through them. Countersink the screw heads.

5 Predrill, glue and screw one 8-in.-square upright piece to each 1x2, making sure to keep the bottom of the upright aligned with the bottom of the 1x2.

6 Cut the 1x2s to length. Then locate the studs, plumb the first 1x2 support and screw it to a stud. Predrill and space the screws every 16 in.

7 Level the top of the next 1x2 support to the first 1x2 and fasten it near the top. Then use the level to plumb the sides and screw it to the stud every 16 in.

8 Check the 1x2 supports for dips and bows with a straight-edge. Remove screws and shim behind the 1x2s with 1-in.-diameter washers to straighten them if necessary.

9 Center the first shelf with an equal overhang at each end. Square the upright (C) to the front of the shelf and predrill and drive a 1-5/8-in. screw through the shelf into the upright.

On the opposite side, attach another 1x2 perpendicular to the first one and about 5 in. from the edge of the plywood. Use a Speed square or combination square to align this 1x2 90 degrees to the first one. Clamp the jig to a scrap of plywood. With the saw's base tight to the fence, saw through the jig and plywood (check for screws in the path of the blade before cutting). Check the test cut on the plywood with a framing square. If it's not perfectly square, adjust the position of the stop slightly. Make new screw holes for each adjustment, or use the jig as a measuring guide for the longer uprights by cutting the jig to 11-7/8 in. wide on the table saw. For repetitive cuts without measuring, line up one end of the jig with the end of the plywood and cut along the opposite end.

To avoid splintering the plywood, press high-adhesive masking tape over the cutting path (Photo 3) and cut slowly with a sharp, thin-kerf 40-tooth carbide blade.

Use a table saw to cut a groove for the uprights

There are many ways to cut the grooves in the 1x2s. Use a router mounted in a router table to cut the groove, or a table saw with a standard blade or a set of dado blades.

The first step is to use a scrap of wood to set the exact width of the groove. Cut a 16-in. length from one of the 6-ft. 1x2s as a practice piece. Adjust the height of the blade to 3/8 in. above the saw's table and set the fence 11/16 in. from the blade. Set up a

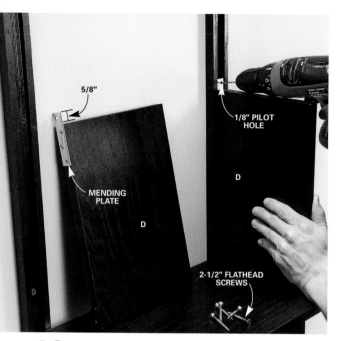

10 Screw a mending plate to the back of each upright. Set the uprights into the groove, predrill and drive a screw through the mending plate and 1x2 into the stud.

11 Rest a long shelf across two uprights. Align the bottom short 1x2 supports with the shelf, plumb them and screw the supports to studs.

featherboard and clamp a hold-down board to the fence (Photo 4, p. 132). Run the 1x2 through the saw. Use a push stick when the board gets within 6 in. of the blade. Rotate it end-for-end and run it through again to get a groove that's about 1/8 in. wide. Move the fence about 1/8 in. closer to the blade and make two more cuts on the 1x2. Repeat this process to make the groove progressively wider. When the groove gets close to 3/4 in. wide, make finer adjustments with the fence. Test after each pair of passes until the 1x2 fits snugly over the edge of the plywood. Make sure the mending plates also fit in the groove (Photo 10). With the width of the cut perfectly set, cut the grooves on the 1x2 uprights in reverse, starting from the outer edges and moving in (Photo 4). Run each 1x2 through the saw twice, once in each direction. Then move the fence about 1/8 in. farther from the blade and repeat the process until the groove is complete. Remove slivers of wood from the grooves with a sharp chisel.

Prepare the 1x2s and mount them on the wall

First attach the 8-in.-tall plywood uprights to the low end of the 1x2s (Photo 5). Determine the length of each 1x2 by literally stacking uprights and scraps of plywood in the groove to simulate the desired shelving system. Then cut the 1x2s to length.

Photos 6 – 8 show the process for mounting the 1x2s to the wall. Start by locating the studs with a stud finder. Mark the studs with a strip of masking tape centered about 80 in. from the floor. Then screw the long 1x2s to the studs (Photos 6 and 7). If the wall has a stud that's bowed, the 1x2 will be crooked and the shelves won't fit well. To avoid this problem, hold a straightedge against the face of the 1x2 after screwing it to the wall. If it's crooked, back out the screw near the low spot and add washers to shim the 1x2 straight (Photo 8).

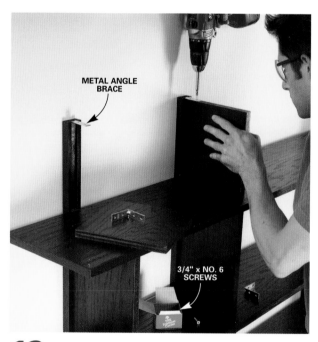

12 Stack the remaining shelves and uprights following the procedure in Photos 9 and 10. Secure the top upright to the 1x2 with a metal angle brace.

With the long 1x2s in place, add shelves and uprights to get to the level of the first long shelf. Photo 11 shows how to make sure the long shelf will be straight when mounting the short 1x2s. The rest is simple. Stack the parts and screw them together until reaching the top. Photo 12 shows how to anchor the top shelf with an angle brace. To anchor the bottom of the final upright, drive a trim screw at an angle through the shelf from underneath.

Clever Cord Storage

Wire roundup

Use a short length of gutter to corral that clutter of wires hanging down behind a computer desk or stereo cabinet. It keeps them off the floor.

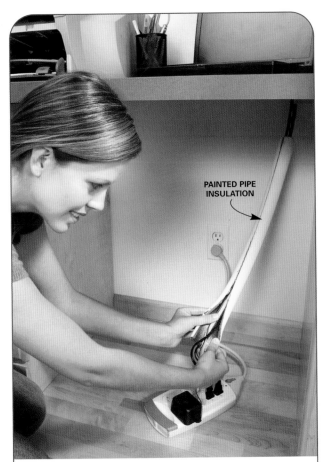

PAINTED PIPE INSULATION

Cord holder

Here's a good way to tidy up lamp cords or speaker wires and keep them up off the floor. Slit short lengths of clear plastic tubing and fasten them to your baseboard with a staple or tack.

Wire organizer

Clean up that jungle of computer, TV, DVD, receiver and other wires by wrapping them in an old-style coiled telephone cord. Just clip the snap-in plugs off the ends and wrap the coils around the wires.

Cord control

Tame that cord jungle under your desk with a length of 1/2-in. foam pipe insulation. Paint it the color of your wall and it will virtually disappear.

It's amazing how fast things accumulate in the garage. Before you know it, there's no longer room for vehicles. This chapter features easy-to-build storage projects that allow you to organize your garage—not just shuffle stuff from one side to the other.

organize
your
garage

Storage cabinet system

Garage storage conjures up images of flimsy metal shelves or crude plywood cabinets. But take a moment to think outside the box. Better yet, think about a different kind of box—because that's really what this storage system is: a series of simple boxes screwed to the wall. Open shelves fill the gaps between the boxes and rest on adjustable supports mounted in the box sides. This design maximizes storage space, saves labor and requires less material than a standard wall of cabinets.

Read on for everything needed to build this system. Adapt the design to suit any special needs. Build one cabinet or a dozen, build tall floor-to-ceiling cabinets or shorter ones that cover only part of the wall. Or adapt this system for a laundry room, basement or closet.

Tools, materials and money

Just a few hand tools, a drill and a circular saw are needed to build this system, but a table saw will save lots of time. The skills needed are just as basic as the tools.

This whole system is made from just two materials: plastic-coated particleboard, usually called "melamine," and construction-grade pine 1x4s. (Melamine is the type of plastic used as the coating.) It's okay to use 3/4-in. plywood or particleboard, but this project shows melamine because it doesn't require a finish. The melamine coating is tougher than most finishes and easy to clean.

The materials for the floor-to-ceiling system cost about $37 per linear foot of wall space. That's less than it costs for wimpy "utility" cabinets at a home center. The garage walls shown here are 10 ft. tall. For ceilings about 8 ft. tall, eliminate the deep upper cabinets. That will lower the cost to about $27 per linear foot. If you want completely open shelving and want to eliminate the cabinet doors, the cost will drop to about $20 per linear foot.

Plan the system to suit

This system is easy to adapt to the space available in the garage. Start the planning process with a tape measure and notepad. Survey the garage, basement, attic and any other place that currently holds stuff to be stored in the cabinets. Jot down the measurements of larger items (like luggage or boxes that hold holiday decorations).

Then go to the wall where the cabinets will be installed. Roughly block out the cabinet locations on the wall. Remember to space out the cabinets to leave room for shelves in between. Experiment with different cabinet widths and spacing to find a layout that works well. Follow these guidelines:

- Each cabinet must have at least one stud behind it to fasten the cabinet securely to the wall.
- Limit door widths to 24 in. To cover an opening wider than that, install double doors. Limiting most of the doors to 12-in. widths makes it easier to open them even when the car is parked in the garage.
- Shelves longer than 2 ft. often sag. To make them longer, stiffen the melamine by screwing 1x4 cleats to the undersides.
- If possible, size and space the cabinets so the shelves inside and between cabinets are the same length. That way, all the shelves will be interchangeable and faster to cut out.
- Size the cabinets to make the most of a full sheet of

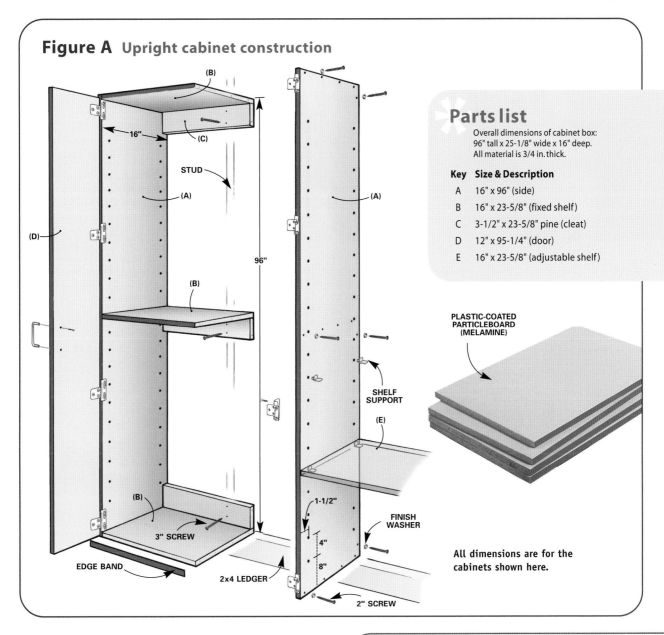

Figure A Upright cabinet construction

(B)

(C)

16"

STUD

(A)

(A)

(D)

96"

(B)

SHELF
SUPPORT

(E)

(B)

1-1/2"

FINISH
WASHER

3" SCREW

4"

8"

EDGE BAND

2x4 LEDGER

2" SCREW

Parts list

Overall dimensions of cabinet box:
96" tall x 25-1/8" wide x 16" deep.
All material is 3/4 in. thick.

Key	Size & Description
A	16" x 96" (side)
B	16" x 23-5/8" (fixed shelf)
C	3-1/2" x 23-5/8" pine (cleat)
D	12" x 95-1/4" (door)
E	16" x 23-5/8" (adjustable shelf)

PLASTIC-COATED
PARTICLEBOARD
(MELAMINE)

All dimensions are for the
cabinets shown here.

melamine. By making the cabinets 16 in. deep, for example, three cabinet sides can be cut from each sheet with no wasted material (see Figure A for other dimensions). Don't forget that the saw blade eats up about 1/8 in. of material with each cut. Most sheets of melamine are oversized by about 1 in. to account for this.

Buying melamine

Most home centers carry melamine in 4 x 8-ft. sheets ($30), usually only in white. For colors other than white, try a lumberyard that serves cabinetmakers (look in the yellow pages under "Cabinets, Equipment and Supplies" or "Hardwoods"). These suppliers often charge more (about $40 per sheet) and might sell only to professionals, so call before visiting. Some cabinet suppliers stock a few colors like gray, black and almond. Others carry a dozen or more colors. Manufacturers produce hundreds of colors, but unusual colors are only available in large quantities (30 or even 60 sheets).

Plastic iron-on edge banding is available at home centers, usually only in white. Cabinet suppliers carry other colors, but be sure to get banding that can be ironed on.

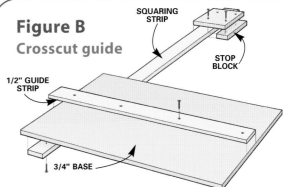

Figure B
Crosscut guide

SQUARING
STRIP

STOP
BLOCK

1/2" GUIDE
STRIP

3/4" BASE

This guide takes a few minutes to make but saves time when cutting the fixed shelves (Photo 5, p. 140) and even more time later when cutting the rest of the shelves (Photo 14, p. 143). This system required 30 shelves. To make a crosscut guide, screw a guide strip to the base and run the saw against the guide strip to trim the excess off the base. Add a squaring strip positioned perpendicular to the guide strip. Position the stop block to set the length of the parts.

1 Cut melamine to width and iron on edge banding. Position the banding so it overhangs the ends and sides. Let the banding cool before trimming.

2 Hold a wood block firmly over the end and carefully slice off the excess banding. Use a sharp new blade in a utility knife.

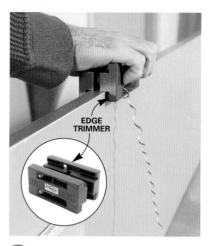

3 Slice off the excess banding width with an edge trimmer. Test the trimmer on a banded scrap first; adjust the blades for a perfect cut.

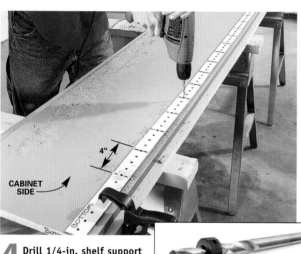

4 Drill 1/4-in. shelf support holes through cabinet sides using a scrap of pegboard as a guide. For end panels that won't have to support shelves on one side, place a stop collar on the drill bit.

5 Cut parts to length using a crosscut guide. A stop block screwed to the guide helps mass-produce identical lengths. Support the melamine on both sides of the cut with 2x4 scraps.

Working with melamine

With the cabinet dimensions in hand, begin cutting the melamine into parts. Cut the material into equal widths for the sides and the fixed and adjustable shelves, but don't cut the stretchers and shelves to length until they're edge-banded. Here are some pointers:

Get help. Melamine is too heavy to handle solo. It's usually better to slice a sheet into manageable sections with a circular saw first. Then make finish cuts on the table saw.

Wear gloves when handling large pieces. The edges of melamine are sharp enough to slice your hands.

Avoid scratching the melamine surface. If the workbench has a rough surface, cover it with cardboard or old carpet. Pad sawhorses the same way. Run a few strips of masking tape across the base of the circular saw so it doesn't mar the melamine.

Be careful with edges. They're easy to chip. When standing parts on edge, set them down gently. Don't drop or drag sheets across the floor.

Plan for chip-out. Saw blades often leave slightly chipped edges in the melamine coating. A new carbide blade will chip

less than a dull one, but can't completely prevent chips. Chipping is worse on the side where the saw teeth exit the material. When running melamine across a table saw, the underside of the sheet is particularly prone to chipping. When using a circular or jigsaw, chipping is worse on the face-up side. Plan cuts so that all the chipped edges are on the same side of the part. Then hide them during assembly by facing them toward the insides of cabinets.

Iron on the edge band

The first rule of edge banding is to buy a cheap iron (less than $10). Set the iron to the "cotton" setting and iron the banding on in two or three passes (Photo 1). On the first pass, run the iron quickly over the banding just to tack it into place. Center the banding so it overhangs on both sides. Make a second, slower pass to fully melt the glue and firmly adhere the banding. Then check the edges for loose spots and make another pass if needed.

Trim the ends of the banding with a utility knife (Photo 2) before trimming the edges. It's possible to trim the edges with a utility knife if the banded edge is set face down on a flat surface. But for faster, better results, use a trimmer ($13) that slices off

6 Predrill and screw 1x4s to melamine to form the fixed shelves. Screw all the fixed shelves to one cabinet side, then add the other side to complete the cabinet.

FIXED SHELF

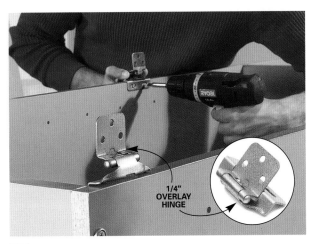

7 Screw hinges to cabinets. Position top and bottom hinges 1/4 in. from each corner and space the others equally apart.

1/4" OVERLAY HINGE

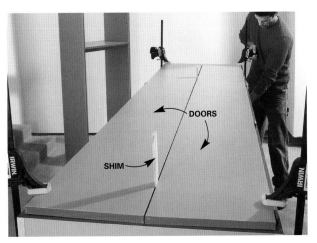

8 Position the doors over the hinges using shims to maintain a 1/8-in. gap. Use clamps or weights to hold the doors in place. A self-centering drill bit (right) makes positioning screw holes easy.

DOORS

SHIM

SELF-CENTERING BIT ($7)

9 Predrill with a self-centering bit and drive one screw through each hinge from inside the cabinet. Add the other screws with the doors open.

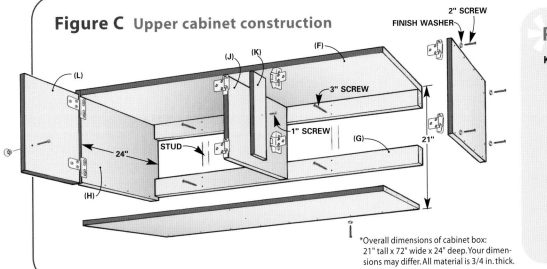

Figure C Upper cabinet construction

2" SCREW
FINISH WASHER

(L)

(J) (K) (F)

3" SCREW

1" SCREW

STUD

24"

(H)

(G)

21"

Parts list*

Key Size & description

F   24" x 70-1/2" (top/bottom panel)

G   3-1/2" x 70-1/2" pine (cleat)

H   21" x 24" (side panel)

J   19-1/2" x 23-1/4" (divider)

K   4" x 23-1/4" (hinge spacer)

L   17-7/16" x 20-1/4" (door)

*Overall dimensions of cabinet box: 21" tall x 72" wide x 24" deep. Your dimensions may differ. All material is 3/4 in. thick.

STUDS
SPACED
EVERY 16 OR
24 INCHES

LEDGER

10 Fasten a 2x4 ledger to the wall framing with 3-in. screws. Choose a straight 2x4 and make sure the ledger is level.

LEDGER

11 Set the cabinet into place and screw it to the ledger. Then level the cabinet and fasten it to the wall with pairs of 3-in. screws driven through the upper and middle cleats into studs.

both sides with one pass (Photo 3, p. 140). If the banding is damaged while trimming, just reheat it, pull it off and start over.

Drill shelf support holes

The adjustable shelves rest on shelf supports that fit into holes drilled into the cabinet sides (Photo 4, p. 140). Drill all the way through the sides that will support shelves inside and outside the cabinet. Drill holes 3/8 in. deep in cabinet sides that form the outer ends of the shelf system. Tape wrapped around a drill bit makes a good depth marker when drilling just a few holes, but a stop collar ($4) is better for this job.

Check the shelf supports before drilling. Some require 1/4-in. holes; others require 5mm holes. Use a brad point drill bit for a clean, chip-free hole. To limit blowout where the bit exits the melamine, set a "backer" underneath. Just about any material makes a good drilling guide, but a strip of pegboard is a perfect ready-made guide (a 4 x 8-ft. sheet costs $8). Label the bottom of the guide and the bottoms of the cabinet sides so all the holes will align. This will eliminate teeter-totter shelves.

Build fixed shelves and assemble the cabinets

The fixed shelves that fit between cabinet sides (A) are made from melamine panels (B) and pine 1x4s (C). Paint the 1x4s to match the melamine. Cabinets less than 4 ft. tall need only top and bottom fixed shelves. Taller cabinets also need a middle fixed shelf. To make the fixed shelves, just cut melamine and 1x4s to identical lengths and screw them together (Figure A, p. 139).

Assembling the cabinets is a simple matter of fastening the sides to the fixed shelves (Photo 6). Predrill and drive a screw near the front of each fixed shelf first, making sure the banded edges of the fixed shelf and side are flush. Then drill and drive another screw near the back side of the cabinet to hold the fixed shelf in position before adding the other screws. Handle the completed cabinet boxes with care—they're not very strong until they're fastened to the wall.

Hang the doors

Make the doors *after* the cabinet boxes are assembled. To hang the doors, first screw hinges to the cabinets (Photo 7, p. 141). This project uses a "wrap" hinge because it wraps around the corner at the front edge of the cabinet. This design has two big advantages: It mounts more securely to the cabinet and it allows the doors to be perfectly positioned (Photo 8, p. 141) before they're fastened (Photo 9, p. 141). Be sure to buy 1/4-in. "overlay" hinges (the door covers 1/4 in. of the cabinet edge). Hinges with a larger overlay will protrude beyond the outer edge of the cabinet.

Use four hinges for each of the 12-in.-wide double doors. If opting for a single wide door, use at least five hinges. The hinges themselves are strong enough to hold much more weight, but they're fastened with just two screws each. The particleboard core of melamine doesn't hold screws very well. So when in doubt, add more hinges.

With the hinges in place, measure between them to determine the door width (with double doors, allow a 1/8-in. gap between them). To determine the length, measure the cabinet opening and add 3/4 in. Cut the doors and set them in place to check the fit before banding the edges. When the doors are complete and screwed to the hinges, label each door and cabinet. Then unscrew the doors to make cabinet installation easier.

Mount the cabinets

Don't install the cabinets directly on the garage floor. Water puddles from dripping cars will quickly destroy particleboard. Mount the cabinets about 6 in. off the floor—just enough space for easy floor sweeping. This height also allows leveling the ledger and fastening it to the wall framing (Photo 10) rather than to the concrete foundation. Drive screws into the studs and sill plate (the board over the foundation, inside the wall).

Use a helper to install the cabinets (Photo 11). Install the two end cabinets first, then position the others between them, leaving equal spaces for the shelves that fit between the cabinets.

12 Build the upper cabinets with the same techniques and materials used for the uprights. Install a blank panel where cabinets will meet at a corner.

13 Set the upper cabinets on top of the lower cabinets and screw the uppers together with 1-1/4-in. screws. Then screw them to the wall studs and to the lower cabinets.

Watch out for obstructions that prevent cabinet doors from opening. End cabinets that fit into corners, for example, should stand about 1/2 in. from the adjacent wall. This project shows mounting an end cabinet about 1-1/2 in. from the wall to allow for the trim around the entry door (see Photo 11).

Upper cabinets

The upper cabinets provide deep, enclosed storage space and tie the upright cabinets together so they can't twist away from the wall. Instead of installing upper cabinets, simply run a long shelf across the tops of the upright cabinets, if desired.

The upper cabinets are simply horizontal versions of the upright cabinets; use the same techniques and materials (see Figure C, p. 141). Here are some building tips:

- Minimize measuring and math errors: Build the upper cabinets *after* the upright cabinets are in place.
- To allow easy installation, leave a 1/2-in. gap between the ceiling and the upper cabinets. It's okay to leave the resulting gap open, if desired. To cover it: Rip 1x4s into 1-in.-wide strips, paint the strips to match the edge band and screw the strips to the tops of the cabinets. After the uppers are installed, cut trim strips from 1x4, paint them and use them to cover the gap.
- Build upper cabinet sections up to 8 ft. long. For strength and ease of installation, size the sections so they meet over the upright cabinets, not over open shelves.
- Remember to add hinge spacers (K) to dividers (J) to install hinges back to back.

Shelves and hardware come last

Cut the shelves at the very end of the project (Photo 14). Take exact measurements inside and between shelves and use up any scraps. Decide on the number of shelves to put in the cabinets. Install cabinet knobs or pulls after the doors are in place to make drilling a hole in the wrong location just about impossible.

14 Measure the spaces inside and between cabinets. Subtract 1/4 in. and cut shelves using the crosscut jig.

SHELF
SUPPORT

CABINET
BUMPER

Buyer's Guide

All the tools and materials used in this project are available at most home centers. Most of the materials can also be ordered from Woodworker's Hardware, (800) 383-0130, woodworkershardware.com.

- Finish washers, No. SCWCF08, $5 for 100
- Shelf supports, No. G111NI, $4 for 20
- 1/4-in. overlay hinges, No. A 07566, $1.66 per pair
- Edge tape in white, black, gray and almond, $33 for 250 ft.
- Double-sided edge band trimmer, No. VIAU93, $21

Garage megashelf

The average two-car garage has the upper regions of three 24-ft.-long walls ready and available for big-time storage. Add a continuous 2-ft.-deep shelf on all three walls and the result is a huge, accessible storage platform that doesn't take up any floor space whatsoever. This project will work on just about any garage, although it may have to be customized a bit for individual garages. (More on adapting it later.) This project is in a garage with finished walls, but the assembly techniques will also work on garages with open studs.

While these shelves aren't sturdy enough to store an anvil collection, they're plenty strong enough for off-season clothes, sporting goods and camping gear. In short, just about anything a person would want to hoist up onto an 8-ft.-high shelf and get out of the way. In general, keep the weight under about 30 lbs. per linear foot.

The 23-in.-high apron under the shelf is a great place to drive nails and hooks for hanging garden tools, cords and hoses—

all that stuff that clutters up the garage. Add a closet rod between a couple of braces for a convenient place to hang jackets, rain-coats or other clothes.

Cutting and installing the parts for an entire garage will only take a weekend. As for skills, it's a project any weekend do-it-yourselfer can tackle. A circular saw, a screw gun and basic hand tools are all that's needed. For the cleanest look, use a miter saw to cut the trim. And to speed up the job, use a brad nailer for most of the nailing.

Choosing the materials

This shelving system, made from oak plywood and solid oak trim, costs about $55 per 8 ft. of length. To whittle down the cost to about $40 per 8-ft. section, choose 3/4-in. CDX (construction grade) plywood and pine trim. The shelves are prefinished with two coats of polyurethane. Roll the finish on the full sheets of plywood and brush the finish on all of the trim boards before cutting. That'll take much less time than finishing it later. Of course, the shelves can be left unfinished, if desired.

Measure the overall length of shelving to be built and then use the dimensions in Figure B to help calculate the materials needed.

Lay out the walls and mount the aprons

Rip each sheet into one 23-in.-wide apron and one 24-in.-wide shelf. Use the factory edge of a "freehand" cut shelf as a saw guide for straight cuts on the other shelves and aprons (Photo 1, p. 146).

Snap a line on the wall to mark the top of the apron and then mark all of the studs with masking tape. Be patient with this step; it's important that the apron nails anchor into solid framing, since they support the entire weight of the shelf. To be sure, poke nails through the drywall (just below the line, where holes will be hidden) to find the centers of studs. Start the first apron somewhere in the middle of the wall, making sure that both ends fall

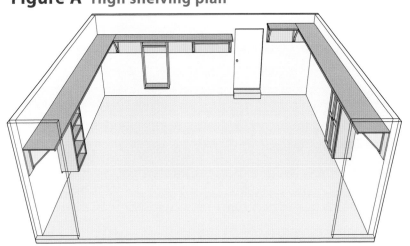

Figure A High shelving plan

Position shelves in all unobstructed zones along the ceiling. Customize by varying heights and adding shelves, racks and cabinets for special items.

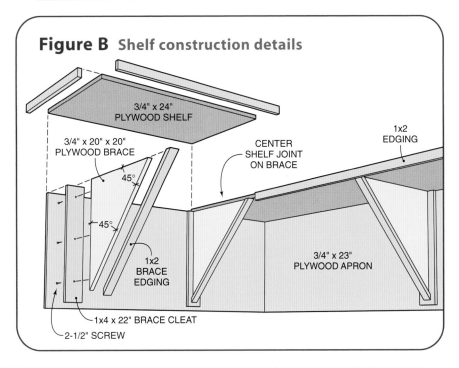

Figure B Shelf construction details

- 3/4" x 24" PLYWOOD SHELF
- 3/4" x 20" x 20" PLYWOOD BRACE
- CENTER SHELF JOINT ON BRACE
- 1x2 EDGING
- 45°
- 45°
- 1x2 BRACE EDGING
- 3/4" x 23" PLYWOOD APRON
- 1x4 x 22" BRACE CLEAT
- 2-1/2" SCREW

Planning the shelves

There are no magic heights or widths for the shelves; customize them for the garage and any personal needs. The best strategy is to build a 3-ft.-long mockup of the shelf shown here and hold it against the walls in various positions to test the fit. It just takes a little effort and may help prevent headaches later. Then decide what height and size the shelves need to be to clear obstacles.

Some rules of thumb for sizing and positioning:

- Choose shelf heights that'll allow for enough space between the ceiling and the shelf for the tall items to be stored.

- Make sure that shelves *and braces* will clear obstructions like garage doors, garage door tracks and service doors.
- In foot traffic areas (near car doors, for example), keep braces above head level and back from doorways, so people don't bump into them.
- If driving an SUV or a pickup truck, make sure the braces won't obstruct the doors.
- To build narrower shelves, just shrink the plywood braces and shelves by the same amount.

1 Rip 24-in.-wide shelves and 23-in.-wide aprons from each 3/4-in. sheet of plywood. Use a factory edge as a straight-edge guide.

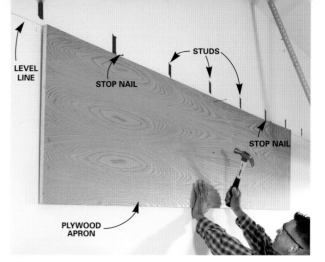

2 Snap a chalk line to mark the top of the apron and then mark the stud locations. Hold the plywood apron even with the line and nail it with 16d finish nails, four to each stud.

3 Rip 20-in.-wide lengths of plywood and cut them into 20-in. squares. Draw a diagonal line and cut the triangular braces. Use a sharp blade to minimize splintering.

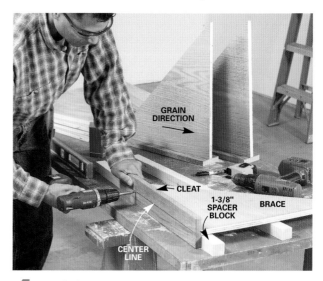

4 Rest the braces on 1-3/8-in.-thick spacer blocks, then mark the center of each 1x4 cleat. Predrill 1/8-in. holes and screw them together with three 2-1/2-in. screws.

on the centers of the studs. Then work toward the corners where the freehand crosscut ends will be hidden. If working alone, partially drive a couple of "stop" nails at the chalk line to help align the apron (Photo 2). That'll eliminate any guesswork. Prestart a couple of nails at stud locations before hoisting the apron into place.

Cut and mount the braces

Cut the triangular braces from 20-in. squares (Photo 3). It's okay to cut the diagonal freehand because the trim will hide minor cutting flaws. Use two 1-3/8-in.-wide spacers to center and support the brace while screwing the 1x4 brace cleat to the back side (Photo 4). Drill 1/8-in. pilot holes into both pieces and countersink holes in the cleats to prevent splitting. Use three 2-1/2-in. screws, one about 2 in. in from each end and one more centered. For the best appearance, run the wood grain the same direction on each brace.

Drill four pilot holes in the cleats, two 1-1/2 in. from the top and two more 3 in. up from the bottom. Then screw each brace assembly to the apron (Photo 5). Use finish washers under the screws for a polished look. Position them directly over each apron seam and then place one more in the center so no shelf span is

more than 4 ft. Make sure they're flush and square with the top of the apron. When shelving turns a corner, center a brace exactly 24 in. from one wall (Figure B, p. 145). This brace will support the front edge of the shelf on the adjoining wall as well as a shelf end.

Nail on the shelves and add the trim

Lay the shelves in place so joints fall over the braces and nail them to the braces and the apron with 2-in. brads spaced every 8 in. As with the apron, start somewhere in the center of each wall so factory edges will abut each other at joints and the saw cuts will be hidden at the ends. Angle the nails slightly at joints so they hit the center of the braces.

Add trim to the raw plywood edges for a nice finished look. Trim also strengthens the assembly and stiffens the shelves. Cut the brace trim to fit with opposing 45-degree bevels at each end. Then glue and nail them to each brace with 2-in. brads (Photo 7).

Starting at one end of each wall and working toward the other, cut the shelf edging to fit (Photo 8). Overlap plywood joints by at least 2 ft. for better support. The plywood will be a little wavy, but it'll straighten out as you nail on the trim.

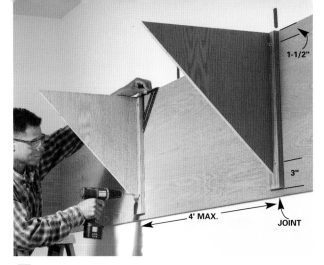

5 Fasten each brace to the apron, flush with the top, with four 1-5/8-in. screws. Space the braces at the ends and middle of each full sheet.

6 Nail the shelves to the apron and to the braces with 2-in. nails spaced every 8 in. Make sure joints meet at the center of the 3/4-in. braces.

7 Cut the 1x2 brace trim pieces to fit with opposite 45-degree bevels at each end. Glue and nail them to the braces with 2-in. brads.

8 Cut the 1x2 edge trim to length, and glue and nail it to the front edge of the shelf with 2-in. brads.

Customizing the shelves

It's easy to customize this shelving to fit special items like golf clubs, hanging clothes or anything else that's best stored in a cabinet or on open shelving. Just assemble a cabinet box like the one shown here so that the sides fall over the wall studs. Go as narrow as 16 in. or as wide as 4 ft., but make sure to attach the cleats directly to wall studs. Attach those cleats to the back of the cabinet with 2-in. screws placed every foot, like with the braces, and then screw the assembly to the wall. The cabinet sides replace the 45-degree braces and support the shelf. A simple unit like this one takes no more do-it-yourself skill than the shelves require.

Garage wall
storage system

There are lots of ways to create more storage space in the garage, but few are as simple, inexpensive or versatile as this one. It begins with a layer of plywood fastened over drywall or bare studs. Then a variety of hooks, hangers, shelves and baskets are simply screwed on, to suit individual needs. That's it. The plywood base handles any kind of storage hardware in any spot—no searching for studs. And because hardware can be placed anywhere (not only at studs), items can be arranged close together to make the most of wall space. As needs change, the versatility of this storage wall allows the hardware location to change too; just unscrew shelves or hooks to rearrange the whole system.

This system uses three types of storage hardware: wire shelves, wire baskets, and a variety of hooks, hangers and brackets (see p. 149). Selecting and arranging these items can be the most time-consuming part of this project. To simplify that task, outline the dimensions of the plywood wall on the garage floor with masking tape. Then gather all the stuff to be stored and lay it out on your outline. Arrange and rearrange items to make the most of the wall space. Then make a list of the hardware needed before heading off to the hardware store or home center.

Money, materials and planning

The total materials bill for the 6 x 16-ft. section of wall shown here was about $200. Everything that's needed is available at home centers. The project uses 3/4-in.-thick "BC" grade plywood, which has one side sanded smooth ($27 per 4 x 8-ft. sheet). It's okay to save a few bucks by using 3/4-in. OSB "chip board" (oriented strand board; $16 per sheet) or MDF (medium-density fiberboard; $23 per sheet). But don't use particleboard; it doesn't

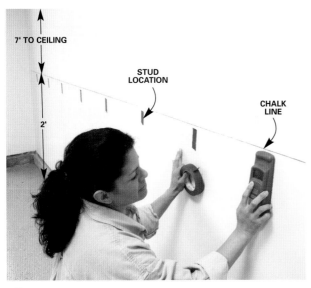

7' TO CEILING

STUD LOCATION

CHALK LINE

2'

1 Snap a level chalk line to mark the bottom edge of the plywood. Locate studs and mark them with masking tape.

2-1/4" SCREW

SUPPORT BLOCK

2 Screw temporary blocks to studs at the chalk line. Start a few screws in the plywood. Rest the plywood on the blocks and screw it to studs.

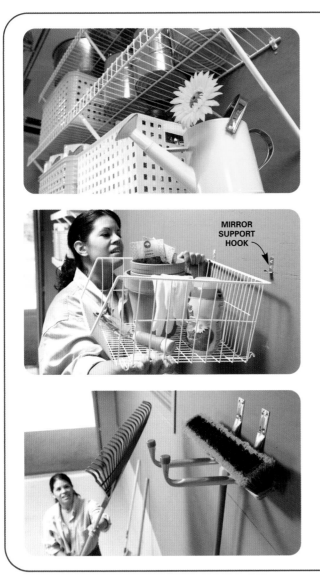

MIRROR SUPPORT HOOK

Storage supplies for every need

Wire closet shelves are sturdy and inexpensive, and they don't collect dust like solid shelving. They come in lengths up to 12 ft. and can be cut to any length using a hacksaw or bolt cutters. Standard depths are 12, 16 and 20 in. A 12-in. x 12-ft. shelf costs about $10. Get more shelving for the money by cutting up long sections than by buying shorter sections. Brackets and mounting clips (Photo 4, p. 150) are usually sold separately.

Wire baskets are perfect for items that won't stay put on shelves (like balls and other toys) and for bags of charcoal or fertilizer that tend to tip and spill. They're also convenient because they're mobile; hang them on hooks, then lift them off to tote all the tools or toys to the garden or sandbox when needed. Baskets are available in a variety of shapes and sizes at home centers and discount stores. The large baskets used in this project cost about $10 each. Just about any type of hook will work to hang baskets. Heavy-duty mirror supports fit these baskets perfectly.

Hooks, hangers and brackets handle all the odd items that don't fit on shelves or in baskets. Basic hooks ($1 to $4) are often labeled for a specific purpose, but can be used in other ways. Big "ladder brackets," for example, can hold several long-handled tools. "Ceiling hooks" for bikes also work on walls. Don't write off the wall area below the plywood—it's prime space for items that don't protrude far from the wall.

3 Set the upper course of plywood in place and screw it to studs. Stagger the vertical joints between the upper and lower courses.

VERTICAL JOINT

12" SCREW SPACING

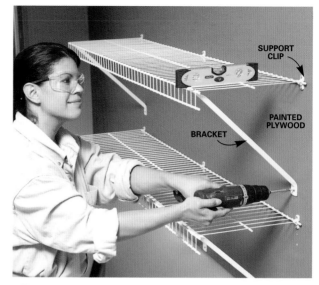

4 Fasten the back edge of shelves with plastic clips. Set a level on the shelf and install the end brackets. Then add center brackets every 2 ft.

SUPPORT CLIP

PAINTED PLYWOOD

BRACKET

hold screws well enough for this job. Aside from standard hand tools, a drill to drive screws and a circular saw to cut plywood is needed to complete this project.

This project doesn't require much planning; just decide how much of the wall to cover with plywood. Cover an entire wall floor-to-ceiling or cover any section of a wall. This project left the lower 3 ft. of wall and upper 18 in. uncovered, since those high and low areas are best used for other types of storage. To make the most of the plywood, combine a course of full-width sheets with a course of sheets cut in half. If ceiling height is 9 ft. or less, a single 4-ft.-wide course of plywood may work.

Cover the wall with plywood

After determining the starting height of the plywood, measure up from the floor at one end of the wall and drive a nail. Then measure down to the nail from the ceiling and use that measurement to make a pencil mark at the other end of the wall. (Don't measure up from the floor, since garage floors often slope.) Hook your chalk line on the nail, stretch it to the pencil mark and snap a line (Photo 1, p. 149).

Cut the first sheet of plywood to length so it ends at the center of a stud. Place the cut end in the corner. That way, the factory-cut edge will form a tight joint with the factory edge of the next sheet. Be sure to place the rough side of the plywood against the wall. Fasten the plywood with 10d finish nails or screws that are at least 2-1/4 in. long (Photo 2, p. 149). This project shows trim screws, which have small heads that are easy to cover with a dab of spackling compound. Drive screws or nails every 12 in. into each stud. To add a second course of plywood above the first (Photo 3), cut the plywood to width. Use a circular saw or a table saw. Some home centers and lumberyards cut plywood for free or for a small charge.

Garden

5 Acrylic photo frames make great label holders. Just slip in your labels and hot glue the frames to wire baskets. Frames cost about $2 each at office supply and discount stores.

Sports

Beach

Lawn

Auto

With all the plywood in place, go ahead and mount the hardware, or take a few extra steps to dress up the wall: One option is to add 3/4-in. cove molding along the lower edge of the plywood. This gives a neater look and covers up the chalk line and screw holes left by the support blocks. Framing the window trim with doorstop molding hides small gaps between the trim and the plywood. Then caulk gaps between the sheets of plywood and fill screw holes. For a finished appearance, prime the plywood, lightly sand it with 100-grit sandpaper and paint it.

Handy hooks

Elaborate hangers designed to hold specific toys and tools are available at home centers. These specialty hooks are neat, but require spending $10 or more just to hang a bike or garden tools. With a little ingenuity, it's possible to hang just about anything on simple screw-in hooks that typically cost about $1. Place hooks anywhere on the plywood wall, or locate them at studs.

Drill a hole at a 45-degree angle and turn in a screw hook to hang a bicycle by the front wheel.

Hang ladders on hooks below the plywood for easy access.

Now's the time to add outlets

The National Electrical Code requires only one outlet in a garage—and a single outlet is all most builders install.

If the garage has bare stud walls, adding outlets is easy anytime. But if the walls are covered, this plywood storage wall makes adding outlets or extra circuits easier because big holes cut in the drywall to run wire will be covered with the plywood. No patching needed. Since the plywood itself will be covered with shelves and hangers, place new outlets below it for easier access. If an existing outlet gets covered by the wall, cut a hole in the plywood about 1/8 in. larger than the junction box and add a box extender (see photo). All garage outlets must be either GFCI outlets or connected to a circuit that's GFCI-protected.

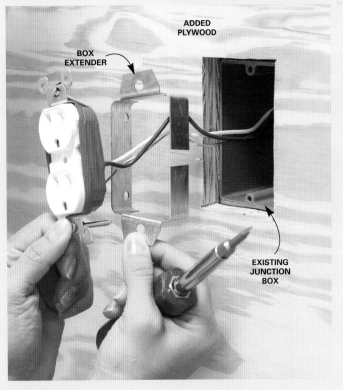

ADDED PLYWOOD

BOX EXTENDER

EXISTING JUNCTION BOX

1-hour tips
for garage workshops

Instant workbench

Take an hour to build this sturdy, simple workbench from a single sheet of 3/4-in. plywood. Then spend only a couple of seconds tapping it together whenever you need it. It can hold heavy power tools, large project assemblies or an old outboard motor.

Cutting list

- Two 38-in. x 8-in. stretchers
- Two 27-1/2-in. x 23-in. legs
- One 48-in. x 30-in. top
- Two 26-in. x 3/4-in. x 3/4-in. side cleats
- Two 12-in. x 3/4-in. x 3/4-in. end cleats

Saw 4-in. x 3/4-in. notches in the legs and stretchers, spacing them 3 in. in from the edge on the legs and 4 in. in from the ends on the stretchers. Tap them together to create an interlocked base. Lay the top upside down on the floor, then position the base so the top overhangs all four sides equally. Screw cleats on the top so they will fit just inside the base. Position them slightly away from the base to make assembly easy. Stand everything right side up and put the instant workbench to work!

8"
4"
4"

STRETCHER
(38" x 8")

4" 3"

LEG
(27-1/2" x 23")

3/4" THICKNESS

TOP
(48" x 30")

CLEATS

Rugged-and-ready pipe clamp rack

T his sturdy, easy-to-build pipe clamp rack eliminates the fuss when hanging up clamps, and they're just as easy to take down when needed. Plus, the generous width and depth of the 2x4 won't let a clamp fall off the rack if it's bumped on the bottom end.

Build the rack from scrap pieces of 2x4 and a 3/4-in.-thick backer board of whatever length is needed. Cut 6-in. lengths of 2x4, then saw a 45-degree corner on the bottom ends so it's easier to slide the clamps into the rack. Measure the outer diameter of the pipes, then add 1/8 in. for clearance between blocks. Space and screw the 2x4s along the backer board, creating gaps 1/8 in. wider than the pipe's outside diameter. Finally, screw the backer board to the wall and load it up!

BACKER BOARD

6"

2x4 BLOCK

SPACE BLOCKS 1/8" WIDER THAN PIPE O.D.

Glue-go-round

H ere are four good reasons to build this glue caddy for the shop. First, no more hunting for the right type of glue; they'll all be readily accessible. Second, it stores the containers upside down. That keeps the glue near the spout—no more shaking down half-filled bottles. Third, upside-down storage helps polyurethane glues last longer without hardening because it keeps the air out. Last, the caddy is so *dog-gone* handsome.

Here's how to make it:

First, arrange all the glue bottles in a circle with 1-in. spacing between the bottles. Add 2 in. to the circle diameter and cut out two 3/4-in. plywood discs. Drill 7/8-in. holes in the center of each one. Measure the various bottle diameters and drill storage holes around the top disc a smidgen larger than the bottles. Glue the discs on a 12-in.-long, 7/8-in. dowel, with a 5-in. space between the discs.

Add a knob on top, load up the glue, and get a grip on every type of sticky problem that comes along.

Studly clamp storage

C lamps scattered and hard to find? Here's a way to keep them in one spot. Hang bar clamps on horizontal scraps of 2x4 screwed between open-wall studs. Add another board or two for glue bottles, dowels and biscuits. To hold C-clamps and spring clamps, drill holes in the studs and install lengths of 3/16-in. threaded rod, tensioned with 1/4-in. fender washers and nuts.

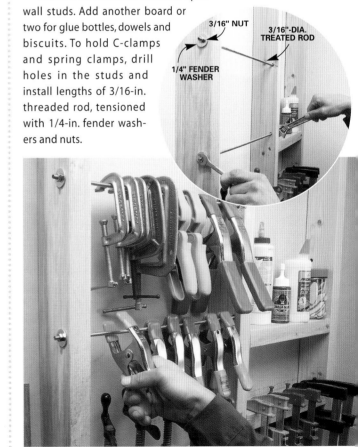

3/16" NUT

3/16"-DIA. TREATED ROD

1/4" FENDER WASHER

Simple utility cabinets

Build 'em and fill 'em. These sturdy cabinets are designed for simple assembly. Just glue and screw plywood together to make the basic box, then add a premade door, actually an inexpensive bifold door panel. Since bifolds are readily available in several styles, including louvered and paneled, it's easy to make a wide range of practical yet handsome cabinets without the time and hassle of making the doors.

Make the cabinets big and deep to store clothing and sports gear; shallow and tall for shovels, rakes, skis or fishing rods; or shallow and short to mount on walls for tools, paint cans and other small items. Or mount them on wheels and roll the tools right to the job. The only limitation is the size of standard bifold doors.

Here you'll learn how to build one of the smaller hanging wall cabinets. Use the same techniques and the Cutting lists on pp. 155 and 158 to build others.

Advanced skills or special tools are not needed to build this entire set of cabinets. However, it does require cutting a lot of plywood accurately. A table saw helps here, but a circular saw with a guide works fine too. Add a drill or two, a couple of clamps and some careful advance planning, and start building!

Buying the bifolds and plywood

When planning the cabinets, begin by choosing the bifold door and build the rest of the cabinet to match its dimensions. Standard bifolds are 79 in. high and available in 24-in., 30-in., 32-in. and 36-in. widths. Keep in mind that it takes two doors for each of these widths, each approximately 12, 15, 16 or 18 in. wide. The cabinet can be any of the single-door widths or any of the double-door widths. Or cut the doors down to make shorter cabinets, as demonstrated here. Make them any depth desired.

Bifolds come in several styles and wood species. This project shows louvered pine doors ($60 for 30 in. wide) and birch plywood ($40 per sheet) for a handsome, natural look. All the materials for the ventilated wall cabinet shown at top, p. 155, including hardware, cost about $70. The five cabinets cost $320. Cut that cost considerably by using less expensive plywood, bifolds and hinges.

Also save by using plywood efficiently. Decide on the door sizes, then lay out all the cabinet pieces on a scale drawing of a 4 x 8-ft. sheet of plywood (graph paper helps). Feel free to adjust the cabinet depths a bit to achieve best use. The five cabinets shown were built from four sheets of 3/4-in. plywood and two sheets of 1/4-in. plywood for the backs.

The "partial wrap-around" hinges may not be available at home centers or hardware stores. However, woodworking stores carry them. If exposed hinges are okay, use bifold hinges, which cost less than $1 each at home centers.

tip

Most lumberyards and home centers have a large saw (called a panel saw) for cutting sheets of plywood. For a nominal fee, they will rip all of the plywood to proper widths. (Cut the pieces to length later.) It requires planning the cabinet depths in advance, but it's quicker than ripping the plywood at home and makes hauling it a lot easier.

Cut out all the parts

Begin by cutting the bifold doors to size (Photo 1, p. 156). This will determine the exact cabinet height. Be sure to use a guide and a sharp blade for a straight, crisp cut. Center the cut on the dividing rail. Be prepared for the saw to bump up and down slightly as it crosses each stile (Photo 1, p. 156). Then trim each newly created door so that the top and bottom rails are the

Ventilated wall cabinet

TOP
(C)

DOOR
(BIFOLD
CUT OFF)
(A)

HANGING
CLEAT
(E)

11-1/4"

HINGE

6"

MAGNETIC
LATCH

FIXED
SHELF
(D)

CATCH
PLATE

KNOB

SIDE
(B)

ADJUSTABLE
SHELVES
(D)

DOOR
(BIFOLD
CUT OFF)
(A)

BACK
(F)

HINGE

43-3/4"

HANGING
CLEAT
(E)

BOTTOM
(C)

6"

29-5/8"

Cutting list

A - Two 14-3/4" x 43-3/4" doors (30" bifold)*

B - Two 3/4" x 11-1/4" x 43-3/4" sides

C - Two 3/4" x 11-1/4" x 28-1/8" top and bottom

D - Three 3/4" x 11-1/4" x 28-1/8" shelves

E - Two 3/4" x 3" x 28-1/8" hanging cleats

F - One 1/4" x 29-5/8" x 43-3/4" back

*Exact door sizes vary. Measure the doors before deciding exact cabinet dimensions.

Other cabinet options (Cutting lists and dimensions on p. 158)

Storage locker

Compact storage for long items like skis, fishing rods, long-handled tools; either on the floor or wall-hung; 12-in.-wide door and one fixed shelf.

Closet on wheels

Large storage capacity (about 32 in. wide and 22-1/2 in. deep); fixed shelf; closet rod; 3-in. swivel casters ($6 each).

Paneled wall cabinet

Shorter version of cabinet above; made from the paneled portion of partial louvered doors; one adjustable shelf.

Narrow floor or wall cabinet

Shelf version of storage locker (left); top and bottom shelves fixed; intermediate shelves mounted on adjustable shelf standards ($2 each).

DIVIDING RAIL

STILES

DIVIDING RAIL

GUIDE

1 Mark the door length and clamp a straightedge to the door to guide the saw. Cut the other cabinet pieces using the straightedge as well.

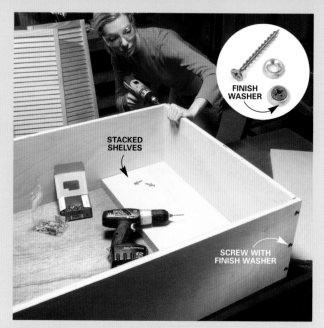

FINISH WASHER

STACKED SHELVES

SCREW WITH FINISH WASHER

2 Predrill screw holes through the sides 3/8 in. from the ends. Drive 1-5/8-in. screws with finish washers through the sides into the top and bottom. Stack extra shelves in the corners to keep the box square.

same width.

Some bifold door manufacturers use only a single dowel to attach each rail to the stile. If that's the case, one of the rails (after being cut in half) is no longer attached to the door. Don't panic. Dab a little glue on each rail and stile and clamp them back together. After 20 minutes or so, they'll be ready.

Then cut the plywood to size using a guide to keep all the cuts straight and square. If the plywood splinters a bit, score the cutting line first with a utility knife.

Assemble the box

Assemble the box facedown on a flat surface. The garage floor works well for this step.

Mark and predrill screw holes through the sides for the top and bottom pieces (Photo 2).

This project uses finish washers (8¢ each; available at full-service hardware stores) for a more decorative look.

Attach the fixed shelf next to stiffen and strengthen the box (Photo 3). Use the extra shelves as guides to help position and square the shelf. Predrill and drive three screws through each side into the fixed shelf.

Attach cleats at the top and bottom of the cabinet to use for screwing the cabinet to a wall (Photo 4). Use three or four screws across the top and bottom. Clamp the cleat into place until the screws are driven. Because the screws won't be visible on the top and bottom, skip the finish washers. Make sure the

Partial wraparound hinges

The hinges shown are available at woodworking stores such as Rockler Woodworking and Hardware (800-279-4441; rockler.com; No. 31456; $8 per pair). Less expensive styles are also available.

cleat sits flush with the side (Photo 4).

The 1/4-in. plywood back stiffens the frame and keeps it square, which is essential for the doors to fit accurately. Spread glue along the cabinet edges, including the fixed shelf and the hanging cleats (Photo 5). Carefully set the back onto the cabinet, keeping the top flush with the cabinet top. Nail in the order and direction shown in Photo 5. Align the edges carefully before nailing each side to keep the cabinet perfectly square.

Shelves, hinges and other hardware

Use a scrap of pegboard to help lay out the holes evenly for the adjustable shelf support pins. Mark each hole clearly (red circles; Photo 6) on the front and back of the pegboard. Mark each hole position on one side of the cabinet, then slide the pegboard across to the other side for marking. Don't flip the pegboard over; it can throw the pattern off and the shelves will rock rather than lie flat.

Most shelf support pins require a 1/4-in. hole, but check the pins to be sure. In addition, measure how far the pins are supposed to go into the cabinet sides. Wrap a piece of masking tape around the drill bit at this depth (photo at left). This ensures that the bit won't go completely through the side of the cabinet. Check the bit after

MASKING TAPE DEPTH GAUGE

3 Predrill, clamp and screw the fixed shelf to the sides. Use adjustable shelves as a guide to space it and keep it square.

4 Glue and clamp hanging cleats to the top and bottom. Predrill and drive screws through the top, bottom and sides into the cleats.

5 Spread a bead of glue on all back edges. Then align the plywood back with the top and nail with 1-in. brads. Align the other sides and nail in the order shown.

6 Mark shelf pin locations on both front and back sides of a pegboard template. Mark one side of the cabinet, then slide (not flip) the pegboard to the opposite side and mark matching holes. Drill the 1/4-in. pin holes.

every few holes to make sure the tape hasn't slipped.

Install the door hinges 6 in. from the top and bottom of the doors (add a third hinge on taller doors). The best type is a "partial wraparound" hinge (Photo 7, p. 158). Its hinge leaves are hidden when the door is closed, and the design avoids driving screws into the weak plywood edge grain.

Begin by installing the hinges on the door (Photo 7). Keep them perfectly square to the door edge and predrill screw holes as precisely as possible. An extra set of hands will be helpful when attaching the doors to the cabinet. Have one person align the door exactly with the top or bottom of the cabinet while the second person marks, predrills and screws the hinges to the cabinet side. Repeat for the other door. Ideally the doors will meet evenly in the center with about a 1/8-in. gap between. If not, "tweak" the

7 Screw the hinges to the cabinet doors. Align the door edges with the cabinet top and bottom. Then predrill and screw the hinges to the cabinet sides.

STILE

8 Attach cabinet knobs to the doors and install a pair of magnetic latches to hold the doors closed. For full-length doors, install latches at both the top and the bottom.

hinge positions slightly with paper shims, or plane the doors a bit to make them perfect.

Choose any type of knob and magnetic latch. However, bifold door stiles (the vertical edges) are narrow, so make sure the neighboring door will clear the knob when opened (Photo 8). If there's a rail (the horizontal door frame member), mount the knobs there.

Another potential problem: Bifold stiles are usually 1 to 1-1/8 in. thick and most knobs are designed for 3/4-in. doors. Look for longer knob screws at a local hardware store. Or try this trick: With a 3/8-in. bit, drill a 1/4-in.-deep hole on the back side of the stile to recess the screwhead.

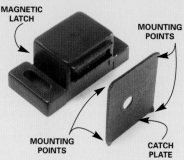

MAGNETIC LATCH

MOUNTING POINTS

MOUNTING POINTS

CATCH PLATE

To mount a magnetic latch, first mount the magnet to the underside of the fixed shelf (Photo 8). Stick the catch plate to the magnet with the "mounting points" facing out (photo above). Close the door and press it tightly against the latch. The points on the catch plate will indent the door slightly and indicate where to mount the plate.

Finishing

That's about it. These cabinets are finished inside and out with two coats of clear water-based satin polyurethane. It dries quickly (one-half hour), has little or no odor, and cleans up with soap and water. The first coat raises the wood grain a bit, so sand it lightly with fine sandpaper (150 grit or finer). Whether using a clear finish, paint or stain, it's generally faster to remove the doors and hardware first.

✳ Cutting list for cabinet styles shown on p. 155

Cutting list for cabinet styles shown on p. 155

Storage locker

Door: One 11-3/4" x 79" (half of a 24" bifold)*

Sides: Two 3/4" x 11-1/4" x 79"

Top, bottom shelf: Three 3/4" x 11-1/4" x 10-1/4"

Cleats: Two 3/4" x 3" x 10-1/4"

Front cleat: 3/4" x 3" x 10-1/4"

Back: One 1/4" x 11-3/4" x 79"

Closet on wheels

Doors: Two 15-3/4" x 79" (32" bifold)*

Sides: Two 3/4" x 22-1/2" x 79"

Top, bottom shelf: Three 3/4" x 22-1/2" x 30-1/8"

Cleats: Three 3/4" x 3" x 30-1/8"

Back: One 1/4" x 31-5/8" x 79"

Casters: Four 3"

Paneled wall cabinet

Doors: Two 14-3/4" x 32-1/4" (30" bifold)*

Sides: Two 3/4" x 11-1/4" x 32-1/4"

Top, bottom shelves: Four 3/4" x 11-1/4" x 28-1/8"

Cleats: Two 3/4" x 3" x 28-1/8"

Back: One 1/4" x 29-5/8" x 32-1/4"

Narrow floor cabinet

Door: One 11-3/4" x 79" (half of a 24" bifold)*

Sides: Two 3/4" x 11-1/4" x 79"

Top, bottom shelves: Nine 3/4" x 11-1/4" x 10-1/4"

Cleats: Two 3/4" x 3" x 10-1/4"

Back: One 1/4" x 11-3/4" x 79"

*Exact door sizes vary. Measure doors before deciding cabinet dimensions.

Roll-around
tool caddy

This simple workstation rolls right up to the job—anywhere in the work area. With specialty tools organized and within easy reach, there's no more wandering around the shop gathering materials.

As shown here, the caddy is configured for woodturning and ready to roll up to the lathe. Gearheads could build it with a flat top with bins for sockets and wrenches, and shelves below for car supplies. Woodworkers could outfit it with planes, mallets and chisels. However it's used, just roll it out of the way at the end of the job.

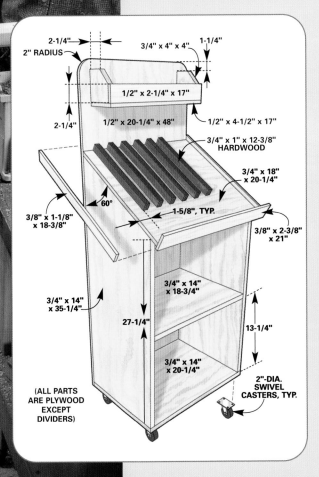

2-1/4"
2" RADIUS
3/4" x 4" x 4"
1-1/4"
1/2" x 2-1/4" x 17"
2-1/4"
1/2" x 20-1/4" x 48"
1/2" x 4-1/2" x 17"
3/4" x 1" x 12-3/8" HARDWOOD
3/4" x 18" x 20-1/4"
3/8" x 1-1/8" x 18-3/8"
60°
1-5/8", TYP.
3/8" x 2-3/8" x 21"
3/4" x 14" x 18-3/4"
3/4" x 14" x 35-1/4"
27-1/4"
13-1/4"
3/4" x 14" x 20-1/4"
2"-DIA. SWIVEL CASTERS, TYP.

(ALL PARTS ARE PLYWOOD EXCEPT DIVIDERS)

It's nice to have all of your outdoor tools in one convenient location—and this chapter shows you how to do just that. These cabinet, cart and shed projects don't take up a lot of space, but they hold and organize a wide range of tools.

Chapter 6

organize your outdoor space

Garden
tool cabinet

I magine this: Driving home with a carload of new plants and flowers, opening a new outdoor garden tool cabinet and grabbing the shovel, bulb planter, trimmer or whatever else is needed—and it's all there in plain view! This scenario doesn't have to be a dream. Just build this cabinet in one weekend and paint and organize it the next.

This cabinet is compact, but it can store a ton of garden hand tools and still have room for boots, fertilizers and accessories. Most gardeners set aside a tiny spot in their garage for their tools, which often end up tangled in a corner. Now garden tools can

have a home of their own, outside the garage. The design is flexible, so customize the interior to suit individual needs and add a lock if desired.

Read on to learn how to assemble the cabinet in the garage and then wheel it out and mount it on the garage wall. Specialty tools or advanced carpentry skills aren't required for this project.

Besides being good looking, this project is designed to last. The shingled roof will keep the rain out. And if moisture does get in, the slatted bottom and 4-in.-diameter vents near the top allow enough air circulation to dry everything out. This storage cabinet is

Figure A Garden tool cabinet

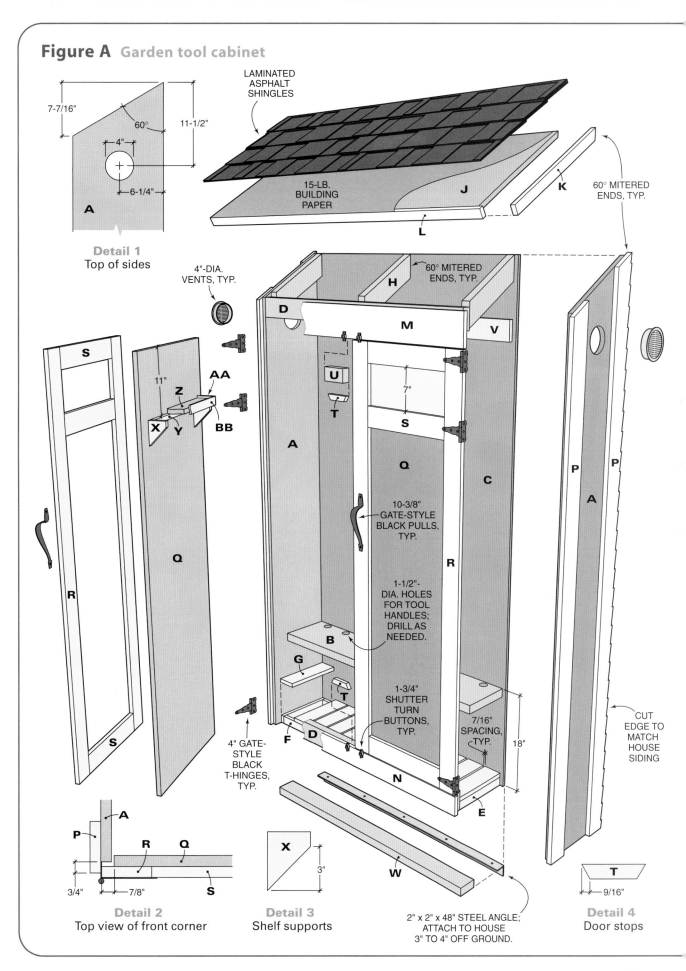

Detail 1
Top of sides

7-7/16"
60°
11-1/2"
4"
6-1/4"
A

LAMINATED ASPHALT SHINGLES

15-LB. BUILDING PAPER

J

K

60° MITERED ENDS, TYP.

L

4"-DIA. VENTS, TYP.

60° MITERED ENDS, TYP.

D

H

M

V

U

T

S

Z

AA

X

Y

BB

11"

A

Q

7"

S

Q

C

R

10-3/8" GATE-STYLE BLACK PULLS, TYP.

1-1/2"-DIA. HOLES FOR TOOL HANDLES; DRILL AS NEEDED.

B

G

T

1-3/4" SHUTTER TURN BUTTONS, TYP.

7/16" SPACING, TYP.

18"

N

E

F

D

4" GATE-STYLE BLACK T-HINGES, TYP.

P

A

R

S

P

P

A

R

CUT EDGE TO MATCH HOUSE SIDING

W

Detail 2
Top view of front corner

P
A
R
Q
S
3/4"
7/8"

Detail 3
Shelf supports

X
3"

2" x 2" x 48" STEEL ANGLE; ATTACH TO HOUSE 3" TO 4" OFF GROUND.

Detail 4
Door stops

T
9/16"

1 Cut the plywood sides and 2x10 shelf, prop up the shelf with 2x4 blocks and fasten the sides into the shelf with 2-in. deck screws.

2 Turn the assembly over and screw the back to the sides and center shelf. Use a level or straightedge to mark the shelf location on the back side of the plywood.

3 Cut the subrails (D) and the roof supports (H), then screw them into place. Use 2-in. screws for the subrails and 3-in. screws for the roof supports.

4 Glue and nail the 1x2 cleats (E and F) to the sides, back and subrail (D) and then screw the 1x4 floor slats (G) to the cleats. Start with the center slat and leave 7/16-in. gaps.

mounted on the outside of a garage, but can easily be mounted to the back of the house or to a shed.

The 4-ft. by nearly 8-ft. cabinet is made from exterior plywood with pine trim. All the materials are available at home centers and lumberyards. A huge variety of tool mounting clips and retainers for hanging rakes, shovels, clippers and everything else is available at hardware stores. Figure on spending about $250 on the materials, not including hardware or paint. So get the materials, read the photo sequence, examine the detailed drawings and text instructions, and get started.

Assemble the main box

Exterior-grade plywood is the basic building material for this project. Unfortunately, it's almost impossible to find *absolutely* flat pieces of plywood at a home center or lumberyard, but look through the pile. The flatter the plywood, the better this project

will turn out. Choose a BC grade of plywood. This will ensure one good side "B" that'll look good on the outside, and the "C" side can go inside.

Keep the plywood out of the sun at home or the flat panel will warp in no time. It's best to cut the pieces in the shade or in the garage. A long straightedge cutting guide for the circular saw will help get nice straight cuts if a full-size table saw isn't available. Look at the Cutting list on p. 165 and cut all the parts to size except the door stiles, rails and trim pieces, which are best cut to fit after constructing the main plywood box.

Choose the flattest sheet of 3/4-in. plywood for the doors. Choose the best-looking side of the plywood for the painted parts. The sides of the cabinet form a 30-degree slope for the roof. Use a Speed Square (see Photo 1) to mark the angled roof supports (H) and ends of the trim pieces that follow the roofline. It's easier to cut accurate slopes on the larger side

5 Mount the 1x2 roof trim to the 3/4-in. plywood roof, then center it and mark the position. Then temporarily screw it to the roof supports with a pair of 2-in. screws on each side.

6 Glue and screw the 1x4 side trim to the plywood sides, keeping the trim pieces 3/4 in. above the plywood at the front. Cut the 4-in.-diameter side vents.

Materials list

Item	Qty.
3/4" x 4' x 8' BC plywood	2
1/2" x 4' x 8' BC plywood	1
2x10 x 4' pine	1
2x4 x 8' pine	2
1x6 x 8' pine	1
1x4 x 8' pine	12
1x2 x 8' pine	3
2x4 x 8' treated wood	1
12" x 48" hardware cloth (1/4" grid)	1
bundle of asphalt shingles	1
3' x 5' strip of 15-lb. building paper	1
1-5/8" galv. screws	2 lbs.
2" galv. screws	2 lbs.
3" galv. screws	1 lbs.
4" T-hinges	6
Shutter turn buttons	4
4" round vents	2
1-1/4" finish nails	1 lb.
1/4" x 3" galv. lag screws and washers	9
2" x 2" steel angle	1
7/8" shingle nails	1 lb.

Cutting list

Key	Qty.	Size & description
A	2	3/4" x 12-7/8" x 90" plywood sides
B	1	1-1/2" x 9-1/4" x 46-1/2" pine shelf
C	1	1/2" x 48" x 90" plywood back
D	2	1-1/2" x 3-1/2" x 46-1/2" pine subrails
E	2	3/4" x 1-1/2" x 11-3/8" pine bottom cleats
F	2	3/4" x 1-1/2" x 45" pine bottom cleats
G	12	3/4" x 3-1/2" x 11-3/8" pine bottom slat
H	3	1-1/2" x 3-1/2" x 15-1/8" pine roof supports
J	1	3/4" x 21-7/8" x 60" plywood roof
K	2	3/4" x 1-1/2" x 21-7/8" pine roof trim
L	1	3/4" x 1-1/2" x 61-1/2" pine roof trim
M	1	3/4" x 5-1/2" x 48" pine upper rail
N	1	3/4" x 3-1/2" x 48" pine lower rail

Key	Qty.	Size & description
P	4	3/4" x 3-1/2" x 91" pine side trim
Q	2	3/4" x 23" x 72-3/4" plywood doors
R	4	3/4" x 3-1/2" x 72-3/4" pine door stile
S	6	3/4" x 3-1/2" x 16-7/8" pine door rail trim
T	2	3/4" x 1" x 4-1/2" pine door stop
U	1	1-1/2" x 2-7/16" x 4-1/2" pine door stop support
V	1	3/4" x 3-1/2" x 46-1/2" pine hang rail
W	1	1-1/2" x 3-1/2" x 48" treated mounting board
X	1	3/4" x 3" x 4" pine shelf supports
Y	1	3/4" x 3/4" x 16-1/2" pine shelf-mounting cleat
Z	1	3/4" x 3" x 20" pine shelf
AA	2	1/4" x 1-1/2" x 3" pine shelf edging
BB	1	1/4" x 1-1/2" x 20-1/2" pine shelf edging

pieces (A) by first measuring each side, marking a diagonal line from point to point and then cutting along the mark. Assemble the main box of the cabinet as shown in Figure A, p. 163, and Photos 1 – 5. Drill pilot holes for all screws with a No. 8 combination countersink and pilot bit. Use 2-in.-galvanized deck screws to fasten the sides to the shelf and 1-5/8-in. screws to fasten the back to the sides. **Note:** Cut a piece of 1/4-in. hardware cloth to fit under the floor slats of the cabinet. This wire

mesh will keep furry critters from making the tool cabinet into a cozy winter home.

Cut the roof panel (J) and trim pieces (K and L), then glue and nail the trim to the front and side edges of the roof panel. Center the panel (Photo 5) and temporarily screw it to the roof supports to install the side trim (P) and the upper rail (M). **Note:** Remove the roof and the doors after assembly to make the project light enough to move.

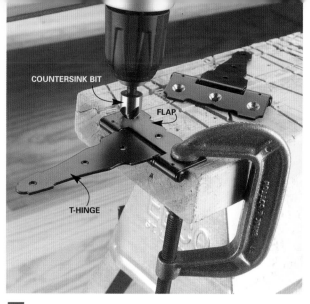

7 Countersink the holes in the inside of the hinge flaps to accept the tapered heads of the mounting screws.

8 Position the flaps of the hinges against the plywood sides at the centers of the door rail locations. Drill pilot holes and drive the screws into the side trim to secure the hinges.

Add trim and assemble the doors

Make sure to extend the front edge of each side. Set the trim (P) 3/4 in. beyond the front edge of the plywood side (Photo 6, p. 165). Next cut and nail the front upper rail (M) and the lower rail (N) to the subrails. Both ends should butt tightly to the side trim.

Even though the doors are made mainly from plywood, the rail and stile trim boards glued and screwed to the front side give the doors a handsome frame-and-panel look. Be sure to lay the doors out on a flat surface and then glue and nail the rails (long vertical pieces) and stiles (short horizontal pieces) to the plywood surface. The stile on each hinge side must hang 3/4 in. past the plywood (see Photo 10 inset).

Alter the factory T-hinge for the inset design of the doors. The hinge flap is screwed to the side trim (P) as shown in Photo 8. If the factory-supplied pan head screws are used, the door will bind on the screw heads. To solve this problem, taper the edges of the existing holes with a countersink bit. Remove just enough steel (Photo 7) so the head of the tapered No. 8 x 3/4-in. screw fits flush with the hinge flap surface.

Cut the small doorstops with a handsaw and then glue and nail them to the edges of the subrails. With the doorstops in place, set the doors into the opening. Make sure to leave a 1/8-in. gap at the top and bottom and a 3/16-in. gap between the doors. Plane or belt-sand the door edges to get a good fit, if necessary. **Note:** Because the flaps of the hinge that fasten to the side trim are about 7/8 in. wide instead of 3/4 in., the doors will sit about 1/8 in. above the side trim.

Mount the cabinet to the wall

Fasten a 4-ft. 2x4 to the top flange of a 4-ft.-long piece of steel angle (Figure A, p. 163). Hardware stores usually have steel angle that measures 1-1/2 in. x 1-1/2 in. with holes drilled every 3 in., but any steel angle that's 1/8 in. thick or larger will do.

Locate the exact position of the cabinet on the wall at least 3 in. above grade and then fasten the angle to the wall with 1/4-in. galvanized lag screws. It must be level. Cut a course or two of sid-

ing to get the angle to lie flat, if needed. This garage slab was several inches off the ground, so it was possible to drill holes into the side of the slab, install lag shields and fasten the angle. If the slab is too close to the ground, fasten the angle farther up into the wood studs of the garage. The weight of the cabinet rests entirely on this wall cleat. It's not necessary to fasten the bottom of the cabinet to it.

Measure the locations of the wall studs and transfer these to the cabinet back. Locate three 1/4-in.-diameter pilot holes in the hang rail (V) and another three holes 4 in. up from the bottom at the stud locations.

Now, strap the cabinet to a furniture dolly (with the doors and roof removed to reduce the weight) and wheel it over to the wall cleat. Set the bottom of the cabinet onto the cleat, center it and temporarily brace it against the wall. Drill 5/32-in.-diameter pilot holes into the wall studs using the existing pilot holes as a guide. Drive the 3-in. lag screws (including washers) and snug the cabinet to the wall.

Finishing touches

Lay the side trim (P) against the siding. It may need to be trimmed with a jigsaw to conform (Photo 12). Screw the roof panel to the cabinet. Staple a layer of 15-lb. building paper to the roof panel and shingle the panel using 7/8-in. roofing nails. Avoid driving shingle nails through the overhangs where the points might show. At the last course, trim the shingles to fit and run a bead of matching caulk at the siding to seal the edge.

Rehang the doors and then mount the door handles and the catches at the top and bottom of the door. Wait to add the vents until after painting. Spray-paint the vents to match the color of the sides, if desired.

Take a trip to the hardware store and shop for a variety of fasteners, from angle screws to rake and broom holders. After organizing the cabinet, prime it and then paint it to match the siding.

VENTS

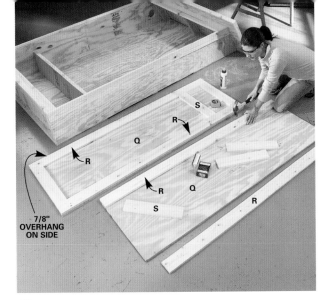

9 Glue and nail the door rail and stile trim to the 3/4-in. plywood core. Overhang the stile on the hinge side of each door 7/8 in. See Figure A for the exact placement.

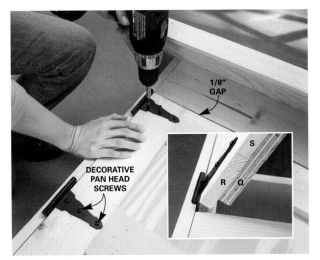

10 Install the door stops (Figure A), then set each door into its opening. Use the decorative pan head screws provided by the manufacturer for the long decorative flap on the door surface.

11 Fasten a steel angle to the foundation with a 2x4 attached to its top (Figure A, p. 163). Lift the cabinet into place and stabilize it with a 8-ft. 2x4 brace against the ground, forcing the cabinet back against the wall.

12 Scribe the 1x4 side trim to fit the siding. Cut the notches with a jigsaw. Nail it to the cabinet side. Screw on the roof panel and shingle it.

tip For vinyl, aluminum or steel siding, here's how to prevent the siding from deforming while tightening the cabinet to the wall. Instead of tightening the lag screws one at a time, gently tighten them alternately to even out the pressure as you go.

All-purpose garden cart

This simple cart is lightweight and easy to maneuver, but it works like a heavyweight. It's solid enough to carry a heavy load of soil and plants and a bunch of gardening tools to boot. It's designed so the weight will balance nicely over the axle, making it easy to push. And the large wheels easily roll loads across bumpy lawns and up and down slopes with minimal effort.

This cart is designed to look just as good 20 years from now. It's made from white ash, a tough hardwood traditionally used for garden tool handles, boats and furniture. For extra strength and longevity, it's assembled with half-lap joints, screws and exterior glue.

Read on for complete cart assembly step by step. Several joints require accurate detail work and patience, but instructions on how to build a router jig to simplify the notching process are included. The rest is straightforward: Simply cut, glue and screw the pieces together.

The project requires a miter saw, circular saw, drill and router. A table saw will also come in handy. Allow two to three full days to assemble the cart. Materials for this project will cost about $200.

Gather the materials

Look for ash at any hardwood supplier. However, other species—white oak, elm, Douglas fir, or even pine or cedar—work well too if ash isn't available. Regardless of the species, stick with knot-free wood for the best results. Ash and other hardwoods usually come in random widths, so rip it all to size before starting. (See Cutting list and Figure B, p. 170.) Most suppliers will cut the wood for a small charge if needed. (Also see Buyer's Guide, p. 162, for a list of mail order suppliers.) The Shopping List shows exact sizes, but unless the wood is already ripped and planed to size (S4S), add about 50 percent extra to account for waste.

Cut the lap joints

Cutting accurate half-lap joints is the trickiest part of this project. Figure A and Photo 1 illustrate the jig needed to make precise cuts with a router. But a table saw with a dado blade gives equally good results much faster. Whichever method is used, cut a pair of test pieces first to check the accuracy of the jig and the depth of the half-laps.

Setting up a half-lap router jig

Assemble the jig by first screwing down two lengths of 2x2 (1-1/2 in. x 1-1/2 in.) at a right angle (90 degrees) to each other in one corner of the worktable (Photo 1). This forms a squaring template, which is also used later for assembling the cart sides (Photo 4, p. 171). These pieces should be at least 2 ft. long and 1-1/2 in. thick, the same thickness as the ash handles and legs. Make the router guide portion of the jig from 2x2s and 1x3s (Figure A). Keep all pieces at right angles to each other. The router base glides against the two parallel 1x3s. Screw one into position and temporarily clamp the other while testing joint widths. The temporary piece will be screwed down in two positions, one for a 2-1/2-in. lap and the other for a 1-1/2-in. lap. The 2x2 fence screwed to the table secures the handle and leg and also provides an entry point for the router bit. Test and tinker with the setup to get accurate cuts.

To cut the half-lap joints with the router jig, place the ash tight against the squaring template, then lock it into place with the 2x2 fence screwed to the work-

tip After finding the exact 3/4-in. depth on the test piece, use this piece to set the depth of the router for subsequent cuts (unless the router has a depth stop).

table. Make the 1-1/2-in.-wide x 3/4-in.-half-lap cutouts in the handles (A) and bases (B) first (Figure C, p. 171), sliding the router guide to the proper position and screwing it into place. Clamp the workpiece down—the router will push it out of position otherwise.

A sharp, carbide-tipped 1/2-in. straight bit in the router works great, but smaller diameter straight bits will also work. In any case, make the cutouts in two passes (3/8 in. deep, then 3/4 in.), and be patient. Trying to remove too much material too quickly may cause the router to kick back.

After the 2x3 pieces are done, reset the guide and cut the 2-1/2-in.-wide x 3/4-in.-half-laps on the front and rear legs (C and D) as shown in Figure C.

Shape the handles and construct the frame

To make comfortable hand grips, trim and round the end of each handle (Photos 2 and 3, p. 171). After rounding over the edges, clean up any saw kerfs and burn marks and soften any sharp edges with sandpaper.

Dry-fit all the side parts first to make sure everything fits properly, and use the jig to keep the framework square as it's assembled (Photo 4). Resist the temptation to drive screws without predrilling. The ash will split. Use a No. 7 size countersink bit for the No. 7 screws. Make the final few turns with a screwdriver if necessary to avoid driving them in too far. If the wood does accidentally split, squirt glue into the crack, back the screw out until the crack closes up, and clamp it tightly shut. When the glue dries, redrill the hole with a slightly larger bit so the screw won't force the wood apart.

Attach the bottom ledges (G) with glue and 2-in. screws, lining up the ledge with the bottom of the base (Photo 5). Be sure to leave a 13/16-in. gap between the ledge and the leg (C) to accommodate the rear cross brace (E). Cut out a 3/4-in. x 1-1/2-in. notch at each end of the rear cross brace (E) to fit around the bases (B) so its top edge is flush with the top of the bottom ledges. Then set the two cart sides upright on the table and screw on the cross supports (H; see Photo 6, p. 172) and the rear cross brace (Photo 7, p. 172). Clamp the temporary supports on the top to help keep the whole assembly stable and square. Don't stop to let the glue dry; the screws will hold the joints rigid.

Position the bottom slats (J) that form the bed of the cart lengthwise and fasten them from underneath so that big loads can slide in and out smoothly. Space them evenly across the bottom cross supports, using 7/16-in. spacers (Photo 7). The spacing won't be exact; adjust it slightly for the last two slats to make up differences.

1 Cut all the cart parts to the exact dimensions and assemble the router jig as shown in Figure A. Align the jig guide for 1-1/2 in. half-laps, clamp the bases and handles in place and cut the half-laps. Reset the guide for the 2-1/2-in.-wide half-laps and rout the leg joints.

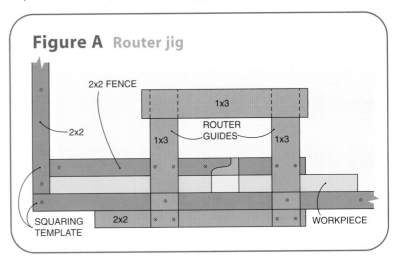

Figure A Router jig

Bracing strengthens the cart

The diagonal braces (F) help keep the cart square and rigid. Cut the braces to length, and glue and screw them to the frame and legs (Photo 8). Bevel the front edges slightly to soften them. And round over the bottom edges of the legs with the sander to eliminate sharp corners that might catch and splinter.

Mount the side rails (K) before cutting the front rail (L) to length to make sure it spaces the side rails perfectly flush with the outer edge of the front legs (Photo 9). Predrill the screw hole through the back leg accurately so that it catches the center of the side rail. Fasten it with a 2-1/2-in. screw (Photo 9). Fasten the front rail to each front leg with a single screw. Then screw the side rails to the front rail. Predrill with a larger (No. 9) countersink bit so the fragile end grain won't split. Use glue and 1-1/4-in. screws. Hand-tighten the screws to avoid overdriving them.

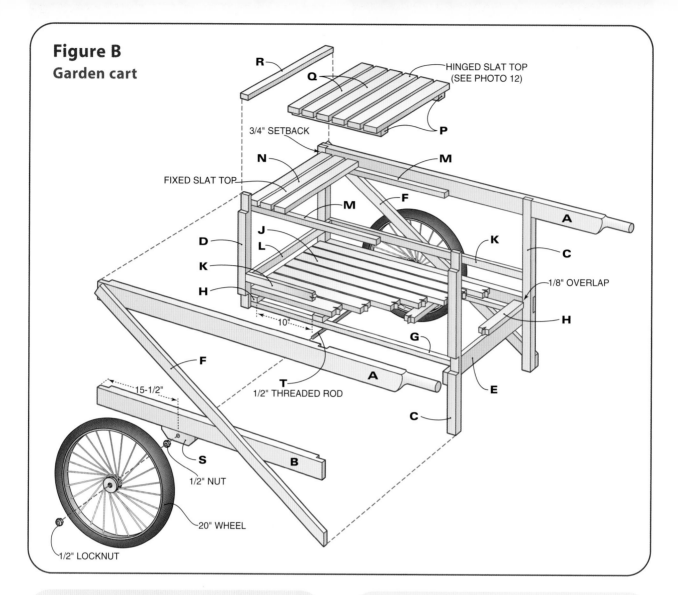

Figure B
Garden cart

R

Q

HINGED SLAT TOP
(SEE PHOTO 12)

P

3/4" SETBACK

FIXED SLAT TOP

N

M

M

F

A

D

J

K

K

C

L

H

1/8" OVERLAP

H

15-1/2"

10"

G

A

F

T
1/2" THREADED ROD

E

C

S

B

1/2" NUT

20" WHEEL

1/2" LOCKNUT

Shopping list

Item	Qty.
3/4" x 1" x 5' white ash (or 3/4" x 1-1/2" if 1" is unavailable)	1
3/4" x 1" x 7' white ash (or 3/4" x 1-1/2" if 1" is unavailable)	1
3/4" x 1-1/2" x 7' white ash	2
3/4" x 1-1/2" x 10' white ash	1
3/4" x 2-1/2" x 7' white ash	4
3/4" x 2-1/2" x 8' white ash	3
3/4" x 3-1/2" x 3' white ash	1
1-1/2" x 1-1/2" x 10' white ash	1
1-1/2" x 2-1/2" x 6' white ash	2
1-1/2" x 2-1/2" x 8' white ash	1
1/2" x 36" threaded rod	1
1/2" nuts (for threaded rod)	2
1/2" locknuts	2
20" solid rubber wheels	2
1 lb. each of 1-1/4", 1-5/8", 2" and 2-1/2" deck screws or galv. screws	
1-1/2" x 3" hinges	2

Cutting list

Key	Qty.	Size & description
A	2	1-1/2" x 2-1/2" x 60" (handles)
B	2	1-1/2" x 2-1/2" x 42" (bases)
C	2	1-1/2" x 1-1/2" x 27" (rear legs)
D	2	1-1/2" x 1-1/2" x 17" (front legs)
E	1	3/4" x 3-1/2" x 24" (rear cross brace)
F	2	3/4" x 1-1/2" x 50" (diagonal braces); cut to fit
G	2	3/4" x 1" x 39" (bottom ledges)
H	4	3/4" x 2-1/2" x 21" (cross supports)
J	7	3/4" x 2-1/2" x 40-1/8" (bottom slats)
K	2	3/4" x 1-1/2" x 39" (side rails)
L	1	3/4" x 1-1/2" x 22-1/2" (front rail)
M	2	3/4" x 1" x 26" (top ledges)
N	3	3/4" x 2-1/2" x 21" (fixed top slats)
P	2	3/4" x 1-1/2" x 17" (base for hinged slats)
Q	6	3/4" x 2-1/2" x 20-3/4" (hinged top slats)
R	1	3/4" x 1-1/2" x 24" (top rail)
S	2	1-1/2" x 1-1/2" x 6" (axle supports)
T	1	1/2" x 36" (threaded metal rod); cut to fit

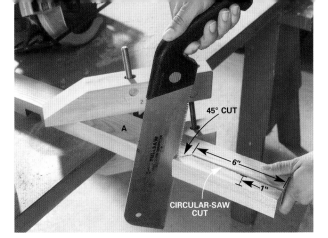

2 Cut the grips on the bottom edge of each handle with a circular saw (half-laps on the handles face inside). Then finish the cuts with a handsaw.

45° CUT
A
6"
1"
CIRCULAR-SAW CUT

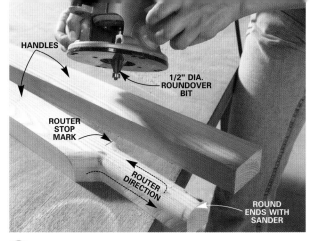

3 Round over the grip edges with a 1/2-in.-diameter round-over bit. Support the router base on the other handle while cutting.

HANDLES
1/2" DIA. ROUNDOVER BIT
ROUTER STOP MARK
ROUTER DIRECTION
ROUND ENDS WITH SANDER

4 Spread glue on the half-lap joints and clamp the cart side parts into the 90-degree corner of the jig. Predrill and drive a pair of screws into each joint.

REAR LEG
HANDLE
BASE
FRONT LEG
1-1/4" SCREW
COUNTERSINK BIT WITH DEPTH STOP

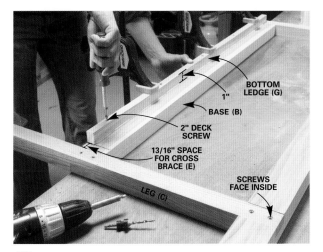

5 Attach a bottom ledge (G) to the inside of each base (B) with glue and screws. Tighten the screws at the ends by hand to avoid splitting the end of the ledge.

BOTTOM LEDGE (G)
1"
BASE (B)
2" DECK SCREW
13/16" SPACE FOR CROSS BRACE (E)
LEG (C)
SCREWS FACE INSIDE

Install the hinged top

Attach the two ledges (M) with glue and five 2-in. screws each, then attach the three fixed slats (Photo 10, p. 173). Assemble the hinged top against the square jig on the worktable, again driving the screws in from underneath to keep them hidden (Photo 11). Let the glue set for an hour before installing this top, to keep it perfectly square. Then fasten it to the top slat with hinges (Photo 12). Leave clearance on both sides so it won't rub against the handles when opened.

Finally, screw the top rail (R) across the tops of the front legs. Predrill the holes to avoid hitting the screws that hold the half-lap joint together.

Install the axle and wheels

To mount the wheels, turn the cart upside down on the worktable and mount the axle supports (S; see Photo 13). Use a drill press to first drill 9/16-in. holes in each axle support for the threaded rod axle. Or if using a hand drill, it's easier to line up the hole with the

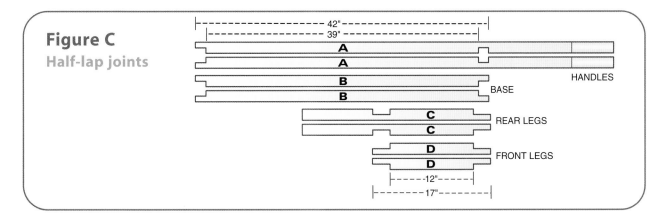

Figure C
Half-lap joints

42"
39"
A
A
B
B
HANDLES
BASE
C
C
REAR LEGS
D
D
FRONT LEGS
12"
17"

6 Set the two sides upright on a workbench and space them with cross supports at the base and temporary spacers. Then square and clamp them. Predrill, glue and screw on the cross supports (H).

7 Turn the cart on its side and screw the rear cross brace (E) to the legs. Then predrill, glue and screw on the bottom slats (J) from the bottom side. Use spacers and clamps to hold the slats in place.

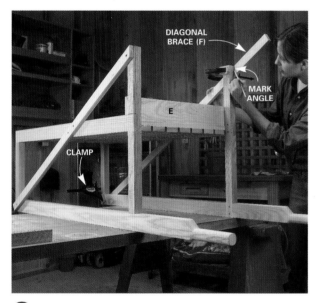

8 Flip the cart upside down, clamp the diagonal braces (F) into position at the front of the cart, and mark the angle cut at the leg. Cut, then glue and screw them to the top, base and leg with 1-5/8-in. screws.

9 Position the side rails (K) and screw them to the rear legs (C) and diagonal braces (F). Cut the front rail (L) to fit between the side rails and screw it to the front legs. Then screw the side rails to the front rail.

axle supports in place (Photo 13). Use a 9/16-in. bit for a little wiggle room when inserting the 1/2-in. threaded rod axle.

Now is the best time to apply an exterior finish. Brush on a couple of coats of an exterior penetrating oil, like would be used on a deck. Renew the finish after a few years.

Push the axle through the holes; ream out the holes a bit with a drill if the fit is too tight. To figure the exact axle length, first mount one complete wheel assembly, then mount the other with the exception of the final locknut (Photo 14). Then cut the axle to fit (Photo 15). Dab a little varnish on the cut end of the axle to prevent rusting, then put the wheel on. The wheels should spin freely; if not, back off the locknut a quarter turn.

Buyer's Guide

ASH:
Ash is available from hardwood suppliers and woodworking stores, and through online suppliers. Many lumberyards and home centers also carry or can special-order hardwoods, or can recommend local dealers. The following companies will cut wood to the widths for this project and ship it:

▪ Homestead Hardwoods; (419) 271-0030; homesteadhardwoods.com

▪ Eagle Bay Wood Products; (800) 229-1769; eaglebaywood.com

WHEELS:
20-in. solid rubber wheels (item No. 145121; $23 each).
Northern Tool and Equipment; (800) 221-0516; northerntool.com

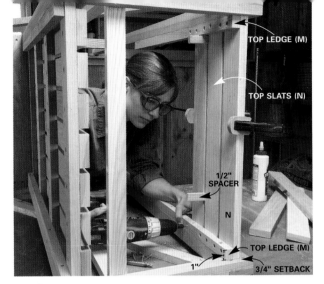

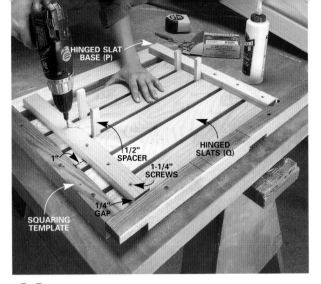

10 Glue and screw the top ledges (M) to the handles with 2-in. screws. Attach the three fixed top slats (N) from underneath with 1-1/4-in. screws.

11 Assemble the hinged top slat section in the squaring template to keep it square. Space the slats (Q) 1/2 in. apart and drive 1-1/4-in. screws.

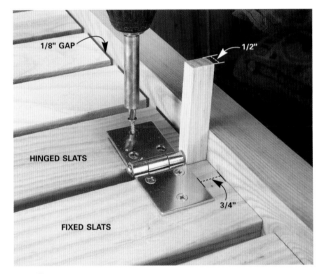

12 Set the hinged section on the top ledge, space it 1/2 in. from the fixed slats, and attach the hinges with 3/4-in. screws. Leave a 1/8-in. gap on each side.

13 Attach the axle supports (S) with glue and four 2-1/2-in. screws. Drill 9/16-in. axle holes at the center point on both sides.

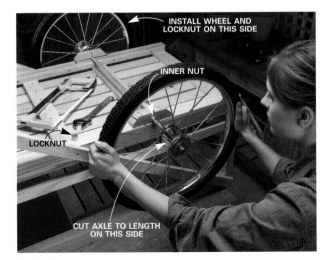

14 Push the rod through the axle supports and bolt one wheel on, keeping the locknut flush with the axle end. Slide the other wheel on, hold its locknut in place and mark the threaded rod at the locknut.

15 Cut the threaded axle with a hacksaw. Then unscrew the 1/2-in. inner nut to clean up the cut threads. Retighten the inner nut, install the second wheel and tighten down the outer locknut.

Compact
storage shed

Looking for a home for garden tools and supplies but have limited yard space? This small shed is a perfect storage solution. With its 6 x 6-ft. footprint and classic Georgian styling, it fits into tight spots and adds charm to any backyard. The "front room" (53 x 65 in.) provides plenty of space for shelves and even a small potting bench, while the double door on the back of the shed creates a spacious easy-access tool locker. For easy care, this project uses low-maintenance siding and trim materials that hold paint and resist rot better than wood.

Tools, time and money

This shed is engineered for easy, modular construction; build the major parts in the driveway and assemble them on site. While this isn't a complex project, it does require basic building skills. Here you'll learn how to assemble the frame, but not all the finish details like how to hang doors or shingle the roof.

A drill, a circular saw, a miter saw and a router are needed to complete the job. Although not absolutely essential, a table saw will make the project go much easier and faster. A compressor and an air-powered brad nailer are recommended for faster, better trim installation. Plan to spend two weekends building the shed and another day or two painting. The total materials bill for the shed is about $1,300. Opting for a blank wall on the back of the shed rather than a double door and a tool locker will save about $200.

Preconstruction planning

Call the local city building department to find out whether a permit is needed to build this 36-sq.-ft. shed. Also ask about any restrictions on placing the shed. If planning to build near the edge of the lot, for example, consider hiring a surveyor to locate the property lines. This shed can be built on a site that slopes as much as 6 in. over 6 ft. But if the site is steeper, consider building a low retaining wall to create a level site. To find some of the shed

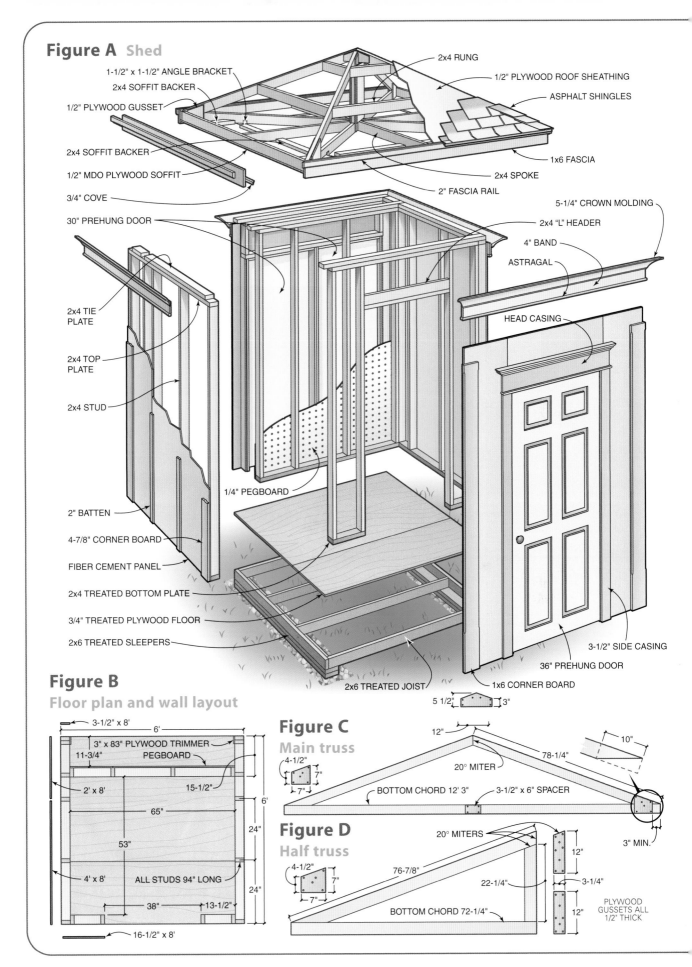

Figure A Shed

1-1/2" x 1-1/2" ANGLE BRACKET
2x4 SOFFIT BACKER
1/2" PLYWOOD GUSSET
2x4 SOFFIT BACKER
1/2" MDO PLYWOOD SOFFIT
3/4" COVE
30" PREHUNG DOOR
2x4 TIE PLATE
2x4 TOP PLATE
2x4 STUD
2" BATTEN
4-7/8" CORNER BOARD
FIBER CEMENT PANEL
2x4 TREATED BOTTOM PLATE
3/4" TREATED PLYWOOD FLOOR
2x6 TREATED SLEEPERS
1/4" PEGBOARD

2x4 RUNG
1/2" PLYWOOD ROOF SHEATHING
ASPHALT SHINGLES
1x6 FASCIA
2x4 SPOKE
2" FASCIA RAIL
5-1/4" CROWN MOLDING
2x4 "L" HEADER
4" BAND
ASTRAGAL
HEAD CASING
3-1/2" SIDE CASING
36" PREHUNG DOOR
1x6 CORNER BOARD
5 1/2"   3"

2x6 TREATED JOIST

Figure B
Floor plan and wall layout

3-1/2" x 8'
6'
3" x 83" PLYWOOD TRIMMER
11-3/4"   PEGBOARD
2' x 8'
15-1/2"
65"
53"
4' x 8'   ALL STUDS 94" LONG
38"   13-1/2"
16-1/2" x 8'
6'
24"
24"

Figure C
Main truss

12"
4-1/2"
7"
7"
78-1/4"
20° MITER
BOTTOM CHORD 12' 3"   3-1/2" x 6" SPACER
10"
3" MIN.

Figure D
Half truss

20° MITERS
4-1/2"
7"
7"
76-7/8"
22-1/4"
BOTTOM CHORD 72-1/4"
12"
3-1/4"
12"
PLYWOOD GUSSETS ALL 1/2" THICK

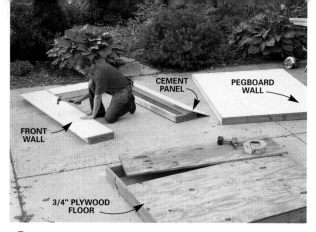

FRONT WALL

CEMENT PANEL

PEGBOARD WALL

3/4" PLYWOOD FLOOR

1 Frame the walls and floor following Figures A and B. Cover the floor with 3/4-in. plywood, the walls with cement panels and the divider wall with pegboard.

MAIN TRUSS

HALF TRUSS

SPACER

GUSSET

2 Cut the truss parts and assemble them with 1/2-in. plywood gussets and 1-1/4-in. screws. Screw 1/2-in. spacers to the bottom chord on the main truss.

HUB GUSSET

MAIN TRUSS

GUSSET

HALF TRUSS

3 Screw half trusses to the main truss and tie them together with 9 x 21-in. hub gussets and 2-1/2-in. screws. Trim the main truss to form a pyramid.

Materials list

Item	Qty.	Item	Qty.
2x6 x 12' treated	4	Doorknobs	3
2x4 x 8' (2 treated, 28 untreated)	30	1 square of shingles	
		30' of ridge shingles	
2x4 x 10'	6	Construction	
2x4 x 12'	4	adhesive	4 tubes
2x4 x 14'	1	Acrylic caulk	2 tubes
2x4 x 16'	2	L-brackets	8
3/4" treated plywood	2	3" exterior screws	1 lb.
1/2" CDX plywood	5	2-1/2" exterior screws	1 lb.
MDO plywood	2	1-5/8" exterior screws	1 lb.
1x6 x 16' composite trim	14	1-1/4" exterior screws	1 lb.
4 x 8' fiber cement panels	5	8d galvanized nails	5 lbs.
		16d galvanized nails	5 lbs.
10' metal drip edge	4	1" roofing nails	5 lbs.
30" doors	2	1-1/4" brads	
36" door	1	1-3/4" brads	
		Pea gravel (50-lb. bags)	10

The 22-in.-tall copper roof finial is available from Weather Vanes of Maine, (207) 548-0050, weathervanesofmaine.com. Item No. 702, $125 plus shipping.

materials—especially the fiber cement panels and composite trim boards—call local lumberyards or special-order through a home center. Special orders can take six weeks to arrive, so choose the materials long before the building starts.

Frame the whole shed on the driveway

Framing the floor and walls is the fastest part of this project. Before getting started, select the prehung front door to get the dimensions of the rough opening needed in the front wall. This project shows a 36-in. door that required a 38 x 82-1/2-in. rough opening. A different door may require slightly different dimensions. The big opening at the back of the shed will easily accept two 30-in.-wide prehung doors.

Frame the 6 x 6-ft. floor from pressure-treated 2x6s as shown in Figure A. Whenever fastening treated lumber, be sure to use nails or screws that are rated to withstand the corrosive chemicals in the lumber (check the fastener packaging). Use pressure-treated 2x4s for the bottom plates of the walls. Cut the plates to the dimensions shown in Figure B, p. 175. Then cut 20 wall studs to 94 in. and assemble the four walls. Also frame the small header wall (14 x 65 in.) that fits above the back doors.

Before sheathing the floor and wall frames, take corner-to-corner diagonal measurements to make sure each frame is square. Fasten 3/4-in. treated plywood to the floor frame with 1-5/8-in. screws. Also screw pegboard to the interior pegboard wall. Nail cement panels to the front and sidewalls (Photo 1). Position the cement panels flush with the bottom plate, not the top plate (the wall frames are 1 in. taller than the cement panels). The two sidewalls have identical framing, but be sure to attach the sheathing so the right and left sides mirror each other. The cement panels on the front wall overhang the framing by 3 in.

A complex roof made simple

A typical pyramid roof requires lots of compound angle cuts and endless trips up a ladder to test-fit all the tricky parts. Not this one. There are no compound angles or complex calculations at all. And ground-level construction means faster progress with less strain.

Build the main truss and two half trusses first (Photo 2).

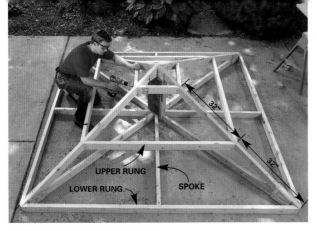

UPPER RUNG
LOWER RUNG   SPOKE

4 Fasten the upper rungs between the trusses with 2-1/2-in. screws. Position the outer edge of the rungs flush with the tops of the trusses.

FLOOR
PEA GRAVEL
SLEEPER

5 Dig two trenches 6 in. deep and fill them with pea gravel. Then level treated 2x6 sleepers over the gravel and set the floor on the sleepers.

6 Anchor the walls to the floor with 3-in. screws. Start with a sidewall, then add the front wall, followed by the pegboard wall and the other sidewall.

TIE PLATE
REAR HEADER
PLYWOOD TRIMMER

7 Set the rear header on 1/2-in. plywood trimmers and screw it into place from inside. Nail on overlapping tie plates to lock the walls together.

Choose the straightest 2x4s for these parts. Figures C and D, p. 175, show the dimensions and angles. The angle cuts don't have to be perfect; the gussets will make the trusses plenty strong even if the parts don't fit tightly.

Join the three trusses with two hub gussets (Photo 3) made from plywood left over from the floor. The "rungs" that fit between the trusses have 45-degree bevel cuts on both ends. Tilt the shoe of the circular saw to cut bevels or use a miter saw. In order to create a square roof frame, all four lower rungs must be the same length. Cut them to 103-1/8 in., set them all in place to check the fit and then trim them all by the same amount until they fit identically between the trusses.

With the lower rungs in place, insert the spokes (Photo 4). One end of each spoke has a double bevel cut; make a 45-degree bevel from one side, then flip the 2x4 over and cut from the other side. This forms a 90-degree point that fits into the corner where the main truss and half truss meet. To complete the roof frame, install the upper rungs (Photo 4).

Assemble the shed on site

The shed floor rests on a simple foundation: 2x6 pressure-treated "sleepers" laid on a bed of pea gravel. Dig two parallel trenches about 10 in. wide, 6 in. deep and centered 6 ft. apart. The trenches can run parallel to the sidewalls or the front and back walls of the

shed. Fill the trenches with pea gravel. Lay the 6-ft.-long sleepers on the gravel. Using a level, determine which sleeper is higher (Photo 5). Level the higher sleeper along its length by adding or removing small amounts of gravel. Then add a little gravel under the other sleeper to make it level with the first. On a sloped site, one end of a sleeper may sit below grade while the other rests above the surrounding soil. Screw extra layers of 2x6 over the sleepers to compensate for a sloped site if needed. Set the floor on the sleepers so that the joists span the space between the sleepers. At each corner, drive a 3-in. screw at an angle through the floor frame into the sleepers.

Stand the walls and set the roof

Have a helper assist with carrying and standing up the walls. Set one of the sidewalls in place and screw it to the floor every 2 ft. Position the bottom plate (not the cement sheathing) flush with the outer edge of the floor. Use a level to make sure the rear end of the wall is plumb and brace it with a 2x4 (Photo 6). Position the front wall and screw it to the floor. Then drive 1-5/8-in. screws through the overhanging front sheathing to tie the front and sidewalls together. Add the pegboard wall next, followed by the other sidewall and finally the rear header wall. Make sure all the walls are plumb, and nail tie plates over the walls (Photo 7).

To safely set the 160-lb. roof frame into place, get a helper, two

SOFFIT BACKERS

8 Screw 16-ft. 2x4s to the shed to form a ramp. Position the stepladders before sliding the roof frame up the ramp and onto the shed. Center the roof frame and fasten the trusses at each corner with a pair of angle brackets. Install 2x4s to provide nailing backers for the soffit.

stepladders and a ramp made from a pair of 16-ft.-long 2x4s. Secure each 2x4 with three 3-in. screws and brace them near the middle with a horizontal 2x4. Then simply slide the roof frame up the ramp and onto the shed (Photo 8). Center the roof frame so that all four lower rungs are the same distance (16-1/2 in.) from and parallel to the walls. Fasten the roof frame with metal angle brackets and install soffit backers (Photo 8) before you sheathe the roof with 1/2-in. plywood (Photo 9).

Elegant trim from plain boards

Most of the trim on this shed is made from a "composite" material that stands up to Mother Nature better than wood. The composite boards are 5/8 in. thick and come in the same widths as standard wood boards. In a few cases, these boards are used "as is." But most of the trim parts are dressed up with a router. The router work adds only a couple of hours to the project and creates a much more elegant look. Three router bits are needed to shape the trim boards: a 1/4-in. round-over, a 3/8-in. round-over and a 3/8-in. cove bit. Figures E and F provide the specifics. Here are some other details:

- Install the fascia and fascia rails first (Figure E). Then shingle the roof. This shed used asphalt shingles. Be sure to install metal drip edge over the fascia.
- Composite trim must be butted at corners, not mitered, since miter joints often open over time.
- For soffit material, the project used 1/2-in. MDO (medium density overlay), which is plywood with a tough resin coating. MDO is available at some home centers and lumberyards ($45 per 4 x 8-ft. sheet). If desired, use plywood or fiber cement soffit board.
- For the crown molding under the soffits, the project used a large (5-1/4-in.) cove profile

(Figure E). To get molding that wide, visit a lumberyard or special-order from a home center.

- Corner boards hide nail heads and the edges of the cement panels (Photo 10). To hide the cement panel joints and other nails, nail and glue two 2-in.-wide battens over the studs on each sidewall.

Doors and casing

The shed uses a classic six-panel door for the front, trimmed with elaborate casing. To make the side casings, just rip the trim material to 3-1/2 in. wide and rout both edges with a round-over bit. Install the side casings so they project 1/4 in. above the door-jamb opening. The side casings may be slightly longer or shorter than the length listed in Figure G.

Photo 11 shows how to assemble the head casing that fits over the side casings. The five parts that make up the head casing may also be longer or shorter than the lengths listed in Figure G. To determine the correct lengths, measure across the side

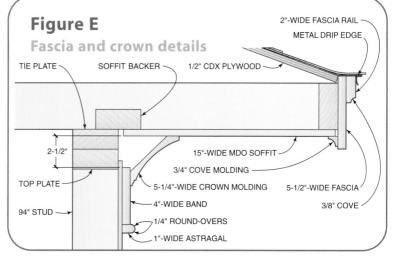

Figure E
Fascia and crown details

- 2"-WIDE FASCIA RAIL
- METAL DRIP EDGE
- TIE PLATE
- SOFFIT BACKER
- 1/2" CDX PLYWOOD
- 2-1/2"
- TOP PLATE
- 94" STUD
- 15"-WIDE MDO SOFFIT
- 3/4" COVE MOLDING
- 5-1/4"-WIDE CROWN MOLDING
- 4"-WIDE BAND
- 1/4" ROUND-OVERS
- 1"-WIDE ASTRAGAL
- 5-1/2"-WIDE FASCIA
- 3/8" COVE

9 Sheathe the roof with 1/2-in. plywood. Cut each piece 3 in. extra long, nail it in place and cut off the excess. Temporary support blocks help position the plywood as it's being nailed.

SUPPORT BLOCK

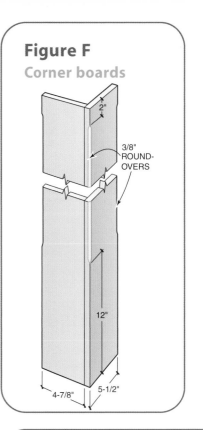

Figure F
Corner boards

2"

3/8" ROUND-OVERS

12"

4-7/8" 5-1/2"

CORNER BOARD

10 Nail and glue the corner boards in place. Install the narrower side first, making sure it's flush with the corner. Then add the full-width piece.

FRIEZE

5-1/4" CROWN

11 Nail and glue the moldings to the frieze board one at a time. Then fasten the head casing above the door with construction adhesive and brad nails.

Figure G Door trim

2-3/8" x 46" 3/8" COVE
1-3/4" x 44-3/4" 3/8" ROUND-OVER
3/8" COVE
1-1/4" x 43-3/4" 1/4" ROUND-OVER
FRIEZE 5-1/2" x 42-1/2"

1/4" DOORJAMB REVEAL
3/8" ROUND-OVER 1" x 43-3/4"
SIDE CASING 3-1/2" x 81"

(THE LENGTHS OF THE TRIM COMPONENTS MAY DIFFER)

casings from the outer edge on one to the outer edge of the other. The measurement for this shed was 42-1/2 in. If the measurement is more or less, just add or subtract from the length measurements given in Figure G.

For the tool locker on the back of the shed, this project uses two simple prehung 30-in. steel doors: a left-hand swing and a right (about $100 each). Pull the factory-installed trim off the doors and screw the jambs together to form a double door. To stiffen the assembly, screw a 4-in.-wide strip of 1/2-in. plywood across the top of the jambs. Then install the double door backward, so it swings out rather than inward (see p. 174).

The corner boards on the back side of the shed act as the door casing, so they can't be installed until the doors are in place. Don't round over the edges of these back corner boards. To complete the back-door casing, install a composite 1x6 above the doors.

Primer and caulk for a lasting paint job

Prime the wood and fiber cement with high-quality acrylic primer. The composite trim is factory-primed, but prime any exposed cut ends and all the routed profiles. Be sure to prime the bottom ends of the corner boards and battens so they don't absorb moisture. The primer will raise wood fibers in the exposed composite, leaving a rough surface. Remove these "whiskers" by lightly sanding with 100-grit sandpaper.

Careful, thorough caulking is essential for a lasting paint job because it prevents moisture from penetrating the cement panels and trim. Fill all the nail holes and seal any gaps between and along the trim parts with acrylic caulk. Also caulk the two short cement panel joints above the door. After the caulk cures, apply two coats of high-quality acrylic paint.

Pine garden hutch

Wouldn't it be nice to have all your gardening tools and supplies in one handy location? This pine hutch holds long-handled tools like shovels, rakes and hoes on one side, and smaller tools and supplies on shelves on the other side. The lumber and copper sheet cost about $300.

Start by building the face frame

Build the face frame (Photo 3) first and use it as a guide for assembling the doors and cutting the curve on the back panel.

A full sheet of 3/4-in. MDF or particleboard set on sawhorses makes a good workbench for this project. Set up for marking the arcs (for the curved pieces) by drawing a center line parallel to the long edge of the sheet. Center a 4-ft. length of 1x12 on the line. Line up the top edge with the edge of the workbench and clamp it. Screw the point of the homemade compass in the center line 21-5/8 in. below the bottom edge of the 1x12 (Photo 1).

1 Build a large compass by drilling holes in a 36-in. long stick using Figure B as a guide. Draw arcs for the face frame top (A1) and door frame tops (D) on a 4-ft. 1x12. On a second 4-ft. 1x12, draw arcs for the curved molding (A2) under the front roof (Figure B, p. 182).

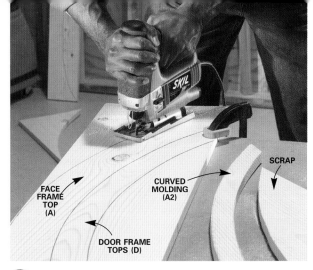

2 Saw out the curved pieces with a jigsaw. Use the pattern on p. 172 to draw the curve on the face frame bottom (C1) and saw it out.

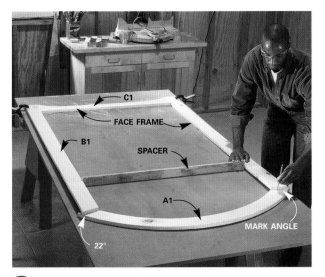

3 Cut the side pieces (B1) to length with 22-degree angles on the tops. Snug the face frame sides to the bottom (C1) and to a 39-in.-long spacer and clamp them to the table. Scribe lines on the curved top (A1) and cut off the ends.

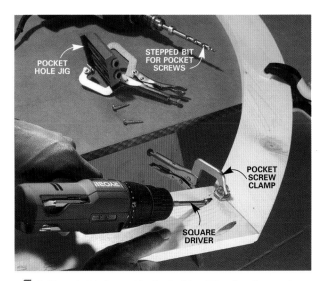

4 Drill pocket holes on the back side of the face frame pieces with a pocket hole jig. Glue the joints and connect them with pocket screws.

Draw three arcs for the face frame top and door top pieces (Figure B, p. 182). Then replace the 1x12 with another 48-in. 1x12 and relocate the screw point (see Figure B). Draw two arcs to outline the 1-1/2 in. wide curved roof trim molding. Cut out the curves (Photo 2).

Even with careful jigsaw work, sand the curves for a smooth arch. Use 80-grit sandpaper on a sanding block to even out the curve and remove saw marks. Then sand again with 100- and 120-grit paper. For the best-looking finish, sand all the boards before assembly. Use a random orbital sander or hand-sand with the grain of the wood.

After cutting and sanding the curved pieces, rip the remaining face frame and door trim pieces to width and cut them to length according to Figure A and the Cutting list, both on p. 182. Use the pattern on p. 182 to cut the curve on the 39-in.-long 1x6 bottom frame piece (C1). Cut the same curve on the 44-in.-long x 5-in.-wide piece (C2). Use this for the bottom cleat (Photo 5, p. 183). Assemble the face frames and door frames and the back frame with pocket screws. Photos 3 and 6 show how to mark for the angle cuts where the curved pieces join the straight ones.

Use a miter box to cut angles on the ends of the curved pieces, and steady them by supporting them with one of the scrap concave corners cut from the 1x12. Place the straight edge of the concave scrap against the fence and nestle the curves. Then sight along the blade and adjust the angle to cut along the line. Use this same technique for cutting the angles on the ends of the curved door frame tops (D) as shown in Photo 6.

After assembling the face frame, flip it over and screw on the cleats (B2 and C2; Photo 5). The cleats overlap the joints to add strength and serve as a nailing surface for the floorboards and side panels.

Figure A Garden hutch

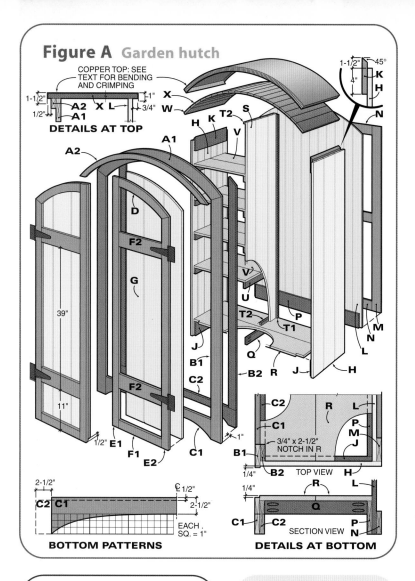

DETAILS AT TOP

COPPER TOP: SEE TEXT FOR BENDING AND CRIMPING

1-1/2" 45°
4"

DETAILS AT TOP

BOTTOM PATTERNS

EACH SQ. = 1"

TOP VIEW

3/4" x 2-1/2" NOTCH IN R

SECTION VIEW

DETAILS AT BOTTOM

Figure B
Arc patterns

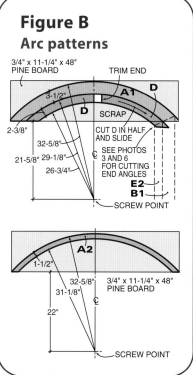

3/4" x 11-1/4" x 48" PINE BOARD

TRIM END

CUT D IN HALF AND SLIDE

SEE PHOTOS 3 AND 6 FOR CUTTING END ANGLES

SCREW POINT

3/4" x 11-1/4" x 48" PINE BOARD

SCREW POINT

Shopping list

Description	Qty.
1x2 x 8' pine	3
1x3 x 8' pine	9
1x4 x 6' pine	4
1x4 x 8' pine	3
1x6 x 6' pine	4
1x10 x 8' pine	3
1x12 x 8' pine	1
1x8 x 6' t&g pine	15
1x8 x 8' t&g pine	7
8" gate hinges	4
Latch	1
Tubes of construction adhesive	2
Magnetic catches	4
Water-resistant wood glue	
1-1/4" finish nails	
Copper or brass weather-strip nails	
Pocket screws and jig	
2' x 5' 16-oz. copper sheet	

Cutting list

Key	Pcs.	Size & description
FACE FRAME		
A1, D	1	48" x 3/4" x 11-1/4" (curved frame and door tops)
A2	1	48" x 3/4" x 11-1/4" (curved molding; cut curve and ends)
B1	2	68" x 3/4" x 3-1/2" (sides)*
B2	2	66" x 3/4" x 2-1/2" (side cleats)*
C1	1	39" x 3/4" x 5-1/2" (bottom; cut curve to pattern)
C2	1	44" x 3/4" x 5" (bottom cleat; cut curve to pattern)
DOORS		
D	2	Curved tops (cut from "door top" above)
E1	2	68-5/8" x 3/4" x 2-1/4" (door sides)*
E2	2	61" x 3/4" x 2-1/4" (door sides)*
F1	2	14-13/16" x 3/4" x 2-1/4" (door bottom rail); see Figure B
F2	4	14-13/16" x 3/4" x 4" (intermediate rails)
G	6	72" t&g 1x8 (door panels); cut to fit
SIDES		
H	6	68-1/4" t&g 1x8 (19-1/2" x 68-1/4" side panels)
J	2	5" x 3/4" x 17-1/4" (bottom cleats)
K	2	5-1/2" x 3/4" x 17-1/4" (top cleats; bevel top to 45 degrees)
BACK		
L	7	78" t&g 1x8 (44" x 78" back panel; cut top curve)
M	2	3-1/2" x 3/4" x 68" (frame sides)
N	3	3-1/2" x 3/4" x 37" (frame crosspiece)
P	1	5" x 3/4" x 42-1/2" (bottom cleat)
INTERIOR PARTS		
Q	1	2" x 3/4" x 16-1/2" (floor crosspiece)
R	2	9" x 3/4" x 44" (floorboards)
S	3	72" t&g 1x8 (17-1/4" x 72" center panel)
T1	1	3/4" x 3/4" x 72" (center panel cleats)
T2	2	3/4" x 3/4" x 17-1/4" (center panel cleats)
U	8	1-1/2" x 3/4" x 17-1/4" (shelf cleats)
V	8	8-5/8" x 3/4" x 21-5/8" (shelf boards)
W	3	3-1/2" x 3/4" x 21-1/2" (roof boards)
X	18	2-1/2" x 3/4" x 21-1/2" (roof boards)

* Cut top angles at 22 degrees

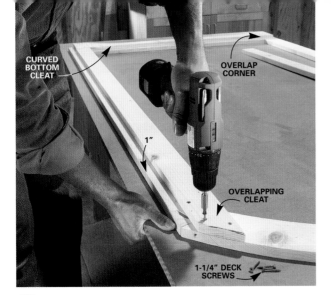

5 Cut backing cleats (B2 and C2) that overlap the face frame joints (Figure A, parts A1, B1 and C1). Predrill and screw them to the back of the face frame.

Labels in image: CURVED BOTTOM CLEAT, OVERLAP CORNER, 1", OVERLAPPING CLEAT, 1-1/4" DECK SCREWS

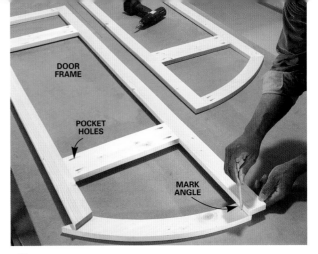

6 Assemble the door frame with pocket screws as shown. Then cut the curved top (D) in half and cut angles on the ends to fit. Attach them with pocket screws as well. Place the assembled door frames in the face frame to check the fit. Plane and sand as needed to allow a 1/8-in. space around and between the door frames.

Labels in image: DOOR FRAME, POCKET HOLES, MARK ANGLE

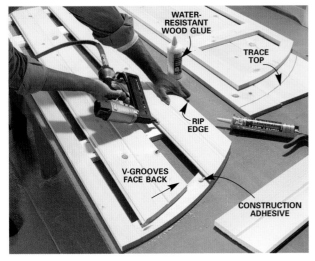

7 Temporarily assemble the door panels and center the frames over them. Mark the bottom, sides and top. Rip the sides and cut the top curve. Cut the bottoms 1/4 in. shorter than marked. Then glue and nail the boards together with wood glue and fasten them to the frame with construction adhesive.

Labels in image: WATER-RESISTANT WOOD GLUE, TRACE TOP, RIP EDGE, V-GROOVES FACE BACK, CONSTRUCTION ADHESIVE

8 Assemble the back frame (M and N) with pocket screws. Glue and nail tongue-and-groove boards to it to form the cabinet back. Rip the first and last boards to fit.

Labels in image: BACK PANEL, BACK FRAME, M, N

Take time building the doors

Use the completed face frame as a guide to check the fit of the doors as they're built. The goal is to end up with a 1/8-in. space between the doors and the face frame and between the two doors. Sand or plane them as needed to create an even gap. Build and fit the door frames first. Then use them as a guide to cut out the tongue-and-groove boards that make up the door panels (Photo 7). Rip the groove off the first board in each door panel and then rip the last board to fit. Glue and nail the boards to the frames and then sand the edges flush. A belt sander works great for this task.

Build the side and back panels

The panels for the sides and back are constructed just like the door panels. Rip the tongues and grooves from the outermost boards after figuring out how wide they should be (Photo 8). The exact ripping widths will probably vary between projects, based on the boards that are used. The easiest approach is to temporarily assemble the tongue-and-groove boards, using clamps if needed to draw them tight together. Then mark the panel widths on them, making sure to measure over the panel to remove an equal amount from the outside boards. Rip the outside boards to width. Then assemble the panels. Run a small bead of water-resistant wood glue along the tongue of each board before sliding it into the groove. Clean up any squeezed-out glue right away with a damp cloth. When the glue hardens, the panels will be rigid and strengthen the cabinet. Use construction adhesive to glue the panels to the frames and/or cleats.

Here are a few special considerations for building the panels. First, use a framing square to make sure the panels are perfectly square before the glue dries. Cut the curve on the back panel after it's constructed (Photo 9, p. 184). The beveled top cleat on the side panels (K) is a little tricky. Study Photos 10 and 13 and Figure A to see its location and orientation.

9 Center the face frame over the back panel and line up the bottoms. Mark the top curve. Saw it out with a jigsaw.

10 Assemble the side panels (Figure A). Then glue and nail the side panels to the back panel and the face frame.

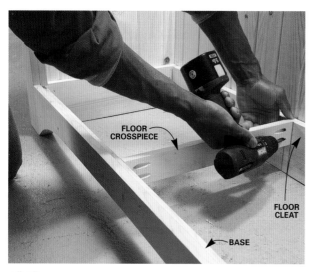

11 Screw in the crosspiece (Q) with pocket screws to support the floorboards. Notch the first floorboard (R) to fit around the face frame and glue and nail it down. Cut the back floorboard to fit and nail it in.

12 Glue and nail together the center divider and attach it to the bottom and back with cleats (T1 and T2) and screws. Attach the top to the ceiling boards after they're installed (Photo 13).

Assemble the cabinet, then mount the doors

Glue and nail the completed panels and face frame together (Photo 10). Then add the floorboards and center panel (Photo 12). Center the curved molding (A2) and nail it to the top of the face frame. Finally, glue and nail the roof boards along the curve (Photo 13). Start with 1x4s aligned with the ends of the curved molding. Then complete the roof with 1x3s, working from both sides to the center. To make sure everything is square, temporarily tack the 1x4 in place. Then set four of the 1x3s on the roof with their ends perfectly aligned and measure the front overhang to make sure it's consistent. If the overhang is getting larger or smaller, move the back end of the 1x4 down or up, respectively, to correct the problem.

When the cabinet is complete, tip it on its back to install the doors (Photo 14). Use any strong, gate-type hinge. Just make sure to leave an even space around the perimeter of the doors and between them. Use a belt sander to trim tight spots.

Crimping tool simplifies curve of the metal roof

Start with a 24-in. x 60-in. piece of 16-oz. copper sheeting. Screw down a 2x4 frame on the bench top to provide clearance for bending down the edges. Start by snipping the corners of the copper with tin snips (Photo 15). Then hand-bend the edges of the sheet down over the 2x4s. The last step is to crimp the edges with the crimping tool (see Buyer's Guide, at right) to curve the sheet (Photo 16). Keep the crimps parallel by aligning one of the crimping blades in the previously made crimp before squeezing it. Crimp about 12 in. on the front. Then crimp 24 in. on the back to even up the curve. Continue alternating until the end. Adjust the arch for an exact fit once the copper is back on top of the cabinet. Hold off, however, on nailing the copper in place (Photo 17) until after applying a finish to the hutch.

Since the hutch is pine and will rot quickly if left unprotected outdoors, apply a durable finish. This hutch has an oil stain and

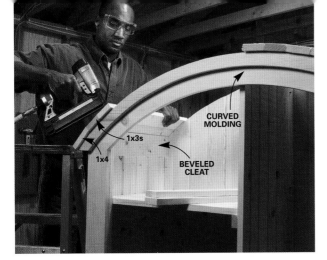

13 Nail the curved molding (A2) to the face frame. Then glue and nail the ceiling boards to the top of the cabinet. Start by overhanging the 1x4s as shown and work from both sides to the center with the 1x3 boards. Cut the last piece to fit.

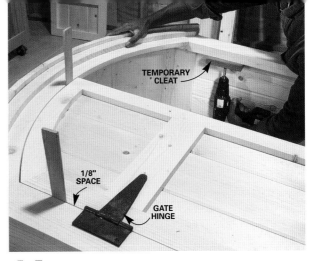

14 Screw temporary cleats to the back of the face frame to support the doors. Set the doors in place and trim them if necessary to allow 1/8-in. clearance all around. Predrill for hinge screws and screw on the door hinges and hardware.

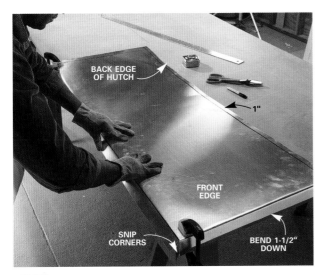

15 Center the 24-in.-wide copper sheet over the cabinet top with a 1-1/2-in. overhang in front. Mark along the back, front and ends with a permanent marker. Add 1-1/2 in. to the ends and cut the copper sheet to length with tin snips. Snip the corners as shown. Bend the front, back and ends down over the 2x4 frame.

three coats of spar varnish. Be sure to seal the bottom edges thoroughly. If putting the hutch in a wet location, install metal or plastic feet on all four corners to elevate it slightly. Setting the hutch on an uneven surface can cause the doors to bind or fit poorly. Shim under the cabinet to level it, if needed.

Buyer's Guide

Malco C4 5 blade downspout crimper is available online from amazon.com ($26 plus shipping), or Seven Corners Hardware, (800) 328-0457, 7corners.com.

The #R3 Kreg Jig Jr. ($22) and the #KHC Premium Face Clamp 3-in. reach ($45) are available online at kregtool.com, or call (800) 447-8638 to find a local retailer.

The hinges (CK-02010642; $6.99) and primitive latch (CK-02006027; $5.60) are available from Van Dyke's Restorers, (800) 787-3355, vandykes.com.

The 16-oz. copper sheet is available from Sheridan Sheet Metal Co., (763) 537-3686. Call for the current price and shipping cost.

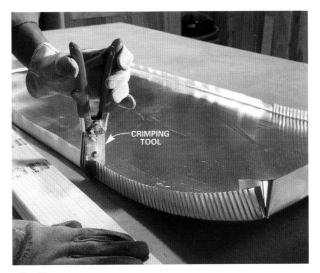

16 Crimp the front and back edges to form the curved top using a special sheet metal crimping tool. Alternate between the front and back until you reach the end.

17 Drill 1/16-in. pilot holes (through the copper only) about every 12 in. along the edges. Drive small copper or brass weatherstrip nails through the copper into the wood slats to hold the copper roofing in place.

Out-of-the-way storage

I s that stack of cardboard boxes in the corner of the garage about ready to tumble? Holiday decorations, camping gear, seasonal clothing and extra bedding take up valuable space. And who can tell one brown box from another?

This system is designed to get all that stuff up and out of the way and into unclaimed space near the garage ceiling. This handy system is built around special reinforced plastic totes that hang from carriages made from 2x4s and plywood strips. This article shows how to assemble these simple carriages, align them perpen-dicular to the ceiling joists, then anchor them into place with lag screws. It's that easy. Add labels to the sides of the totes to tell at a glance where to find that long-term storage item. Build and install the carriages in an afternoon and start organizing right away!

This system can be installed just about anywhere. However, keep the totes at least 2 ft. from light fixtures, door springs and garage door openers.

The special reinforced totes (see Buyer's Guide, p. 188) shown here are a bit stronger than those found at home centers or

1 Measure the top of the tote to determine the width of the tote rims (3/4 in.) and the size of the bottom flanges of the carriages (in this case, 3 in.).

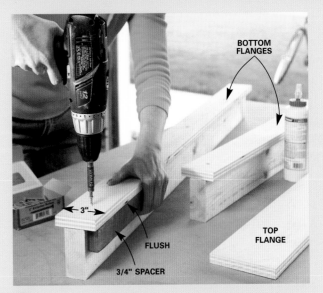

2 Cut 3-in.-wide strips of 3/4-in. plywood for the bottom flange. Center them on 4-ft.-long 2x4s, then glue and screw them. Use 2-in. screws every 10 in.

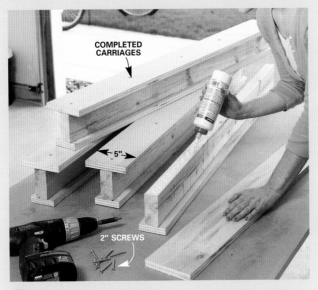

3 Flip the carriage assemblies over. Center the 5-in.-wide plywood top flanges and glue and screw them to complete the carriage assemblies.

4 Locate the ceiling joists with a stud finder and snap chalk lines to mark them. Probe with a finish nail to make sure the lines fall on joist centers.

✳ Materials list

Item	Qty.
2x4 x 8"	2
4' x 8' sheet of 3/4" plywood	1/2
1x2 x 8' pine stop strip	1
Carpenter's glue	1 pint
1/4" x 3-1/2" lag screws and washers	16
2" wood screws	1 box
3" wood screws	1 box
23-1/2" x 19-1/2" x 13" plastic totes	6

✳ Cutting list

Qty.	Size & description
4	3/4" x 3" x 48" plywood bottom carriage flanges
4	3/4" x 5" x 48" plywood top carriage flanges
4	1-1/2" x 3-1/2" pine carriage stringers
1	3/4" x 1-1/2" x 8' pine stop strip*

*Based on the tote sizes shown here

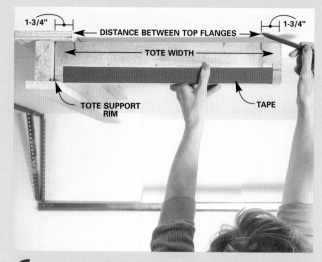

5 Mark each carriage 12 in. from the end and align the mark with the joist location. Screw the carriage temporarily to each joist on one side of the flange with 3-in. screws.

6 Cut a 2x4 template from the tote dimensions and mark the location of the top edge of the next carriage. Mark the rear side as well, then screw it and the other carriages in place on one side only.

7 Check the fit of the totes and make sure the rims have maximum bearing on the lower flanges. Make any necessary adjustments.

8 Drill 3/16-in. pilot holes in the top flanges. Then drive pairs of 3-1/2-in. lag screws into each joist, removing the temporary screws. Use a minimum of four lag screws per carriage.

9 Mark the centers of the carriages and screw a 1x2 stop along the marks. The stop will keep the totes from sliding too far into the carriages.

discount stores. The reinforced rims on these containers will support weights of 35 lbs. or more, which is perfect for lightweight storage. And the totes will be easy enough to lift into place while standing on a ladder. To be on the safe side, the total weight of all the totes shouldn't exceed 210 lbs., so find a different place to store books and heavy hardware. Custom plastic lids are also available for dust-free storage (see Buyer's Guide).

This storage system is relatively inexpensive. The special totes cost about $16 each, and the carriages, made from 2x4s and 3/4-in. plywood strips, cost about $26. With hardware, this six-bin project cost about $125. Just follow the step-by-step photos and get organized!

If using other types of containers, measure the rims carefully and adjust the bottom flange width to assure full support. And no matter what the joist spacing (24 in. or 16 in.), be sure to fasten the carriages with at least four lag screws.

Before ordering the totes, measure the height above the garage door and find totes that'll work. These 13-in.-deep totes required 18 in. of clearance, including the carriages. For lower clearances, buy totes that are 8 and 10 in. deep but with the same top size.

Buyer's Guide

Storage totes are available from Simplastics at www.simplastics.com or (800) 966-9090. This project used No. snt-230-BL sold in quantities of three. Lids and shallower totes are also available.

Also find totes at United States Plastic Corp., usplastic.com. The size equivalent SKU is 52005.

Garage storage ideas

Painting gear hangout

Organize paint brushes, scrapers, roller frames, rags and paint cans with this shelf made from two 1x8 boards screwed together and reinforced with metal shelf brackets ($1). This one is 38 in. long to fit three brackets of sliding spring grips ($4 each at home centers) mounted under the shelf for tool storage. Build and attach this shelf to a shop or basement wall.

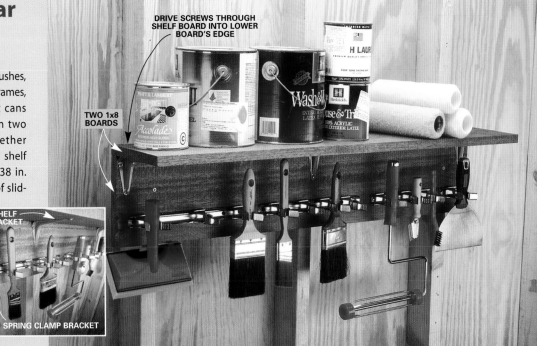

DRIVE SCREWS THROUGH SHELF BOARD INTO LOWER BOARD'S EDGE

TWO 1x8 BOARDS

SHELF BRACKET

SPRING CLAMP BRACKET

Hang it up

Organize the garage with these GearWall multiuse grooved panels from Gladiator. The built-in continuous horizontal grooves spaced every 6 in. handle various hanging accessories, such as bike hooks, baskets for loose stuff, shelving and various styles of racks to hang just about anything. It's simple. Buy individual 1x8-ft. tongue-and-groove panels ($70 per two-pack) and screw them directly to the garage studs (or through drywall into the studs). Cut the panels to any length and add as many rows as needed to fit any wall.

Prices for accessories range from $10 to $45. It's not the cheapest storage system in the world, but it makes even the worst garage look great. Panels and accessories are available at Lowe's and by ordering directly from Gladiator.

Gladiator Garageworks
(866) 342-4089. gladiatorgw.com

Workshop smarts

Knock-down utility table

When cramped for workbench space, this super-stable plywood table can't be beat. Assemble it in about two minutes, knock it apart just as fast and store it flat against a wall in a stack less than 6 in. thick. It's easy to make from 3/4-in. plywood and four short 2x4 blocks (Figure A).

Cut the slots for the interlocking legs with a circular saw or jigsaw. Cut them slightly wider than 3/4 in. so they don't interlock too tightly. Notch the bottom edges, leaving 6-in.-long feet to reduce rocking on uneven floors.

Screw the 2x4 blocks to the top corners of each base piece. Then predrill the blocks and drive screws into the top to make it extra secure. Screwing the top down is optional.

✳ Cutting list

Base: 3/4" x 36" x 48" (2 pieces)
Top: 3/4" x 48" x 48"
Blocks: 2x4 x 4" (4 pieces)

Figure A Table details

36"

3/4" x 17" SLOT

48"

3/4" x 18" SLOT

2x4 x 4"

2"

6" 1"

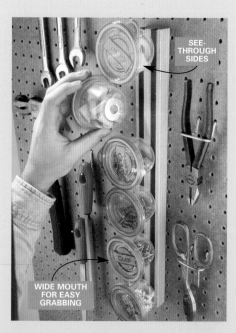

SEE-THROUGH SIDES

WIDE MOUTH FOR EASY GRABBING

Magnetic mini storage

Want to build this handy storage roost for all the little screws, earplugs, nuts and washers in the shop? Pick up a pack of Glad 4-oz. cups, a magnetic strip, several 7/16-in. washers and a tube of E6000 glue ($4 at craft and hobby stores). Apply glue to the cup's concave bottom, press in a washer flush with the bottom rim and let the glue set for 24 hours. That's it. Mount the mag-net, load the cups, snap on the lids and all the itty-bitties are easy to spot, nab and put away. Magnetic strips are available from Rockler (800-279-4441, rockler.com) and Magna-products (800-338-0527).

The magnetic strip provides more than enough magnet power to hold a cup crammed with screws.

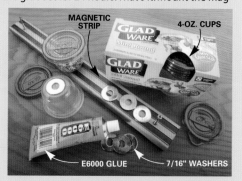

MAGNETIC STRIP

4-OZ. CUPS

GLAD WARE

GLAD WARE

E6000 GLUE

7/16" WASHERS

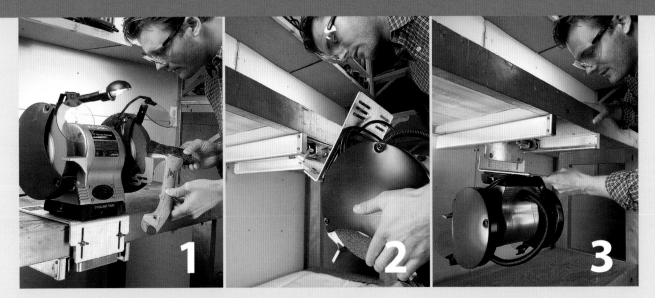

Under-the-bench tool storage

Some tools just don't get used that often, but there they sit, monopolizing precious bench space. The Bench Slide Mount ($130) can free up bench space in no time by pivoting and sliding tools out of the way under the bench when not in use. It looks like a cross between a garage door and a drawer slide.

The Bench Slide Mount has a 75-lb. capacity and is easy to install. Screw the track to the bottom of the workbench and bolt the tool to the mounting plate. The mounting plate is adjustable for workbenches of different thicknesses, from 1-3/4 in. to 4-1/2 in.

The mounting plate that comes with the Bench Slide Mount measures 9 x 9-1/2 in. A 12 x 18-1/2-in. plate ($20) for larger tools is also available. Stops on the end of the track prevent the tool from tumbling to the floor as it slides out from under the bench.

The Bench Slide Mount is available at benchslidemount.com.

Table saw worktable

Turn a table saw into extra workbench space with a piece of 3/4-in. plywood. Size the plywood to fit the table saw table, and nail and glue on just enough 1x2 edge strips for a snug, no-slide fit. Use this table for lightweight and low-impact jobs. For heavy pounding, use a proper workbench or the floor.

> **CAUTION:**
> Unplug the saw and crank the saw blade below the table surface before using this top.

1x2 EDGE STRIP

Also Available from Reader's Digest

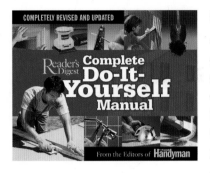

Complete Do-It-Yourself Manual

This definitive do-it-yourself guide to home repair, maintenance, and improvements is guaranteed to save you time and money. Completely revised and redesigned with over 3,000 color photos and illustrations, this must-have home reference contains the latest techniques and updated user-friendly instructions for a wide range of projects.

ISBN 13: 978-0-7621-0579-3
$35.00 USA

Best Weekend Projects

Whether you have two hours or two days, it's easy to make improvements with the 80 innovative ideas in this handy guide. Each project is presented with illustrated, step-by-step instructions as well as concise plans, complete cutting lists, and hundreds of beautiful color photographs of the finished product.

ISBN 13: 978-0-7621-0927-2
$17.95 USA

Save Energy, Save Money!

This essential guide—based on the latest ideas and newest technology in energy-efficient home-management—from the experts at The Family Handyman—will show you how to save money based on the condition and location of your home, your budget, and your skill level.

ISBN 13: 978-0-7621-0902-9
$17.95 USA

Reader's Digest books can be purchased through retail and online bookstores.

In the United States books are distributed by Penguin Group (USA), Inc.
For more information or to order books, call 1-800-788-6262.